SUPER HOROSCOPE
TAURUS

2006
APRIL 21 – MAY 20

BERKLEY BOOKS, NEW YORK

THE BERKLEY PUBLISHING GROUP
Published by the Penguin Group
Penguin Group (USA) Inc.
375 Hudson Street, New York, New York 10014, USA
Penguin Group (Canada), 10 Alcorn Avenue, Toronto, Ontario M4V 3B2, Canada
(a division of Pearson Penguin Canada Inc.)
Penguin Books Ltd., 80 Strand, London WC2R 0RL, England
Penguin Group Ireland, 25 St. Stephen's Green, Dublin 2, Ireland (a division of Penguin Books Ltd.)
Penguin Group (Australia), 250 Camberwell Road, Camberwell, Victoria 3124, Australia
(a division of Pearson Australia Group Pty. Ltd.)
Penguin Books India Pvt. Ltd., 11 Community Centre, Panchsheel Park, New Delhi—110 017, India
Penguin Group (NZ), Cnr. Airborne and Rosedale Roads, Albany, Auckland 1310, New Zealand
(a division of Pearson New Zealand Ltd.)
Penguin Books (South Africa) (Pty.) Ltd., 24 Sturdee Avenue, Rosebank, Johannesburg 2196,
South Africa

Penguin Books Ltd., Registered Offices: 80 Strand, London WC2R 0RL, England

2006 SUPER HOROSCOPE TAURUS

The publishers regret that they cannot answer individual letters requesting personal horoscope information.

PRINTING HISTORY
Berkley trade paperback edition / July 2005

Berkley trade paperback ISBN: 0-425-20217-8

Library of Congress Cataloging-in-Publication Data

ISSN: 1535-0509

PRINTED IN THE UNITED STATES OF AMERICA

10 9 8 7 6 5 4 3 2 1

CONTENTS

THE CUSP-BORN TAURUS

Are you *really* a Taurus? If your birthday falls during the fourth week of April, at the beginning of Taurus, will you still retain the traits of Aries, the sign of the Zodiac before Taurus? And what if you were born late in May—are you more Gemini than Taurus? Many people born at the edge, or cusp, of a sign have difficulty determining exactly what sign they are. If you are one of these people, here's how you can figure it out, once and for all.

Consult the cusp table on the facing page, then locate the year of your birth. The table will tell you the precise days on which the Sun entered and left your sign for the year of your birth. In that way you can determine if you are a true Taurus—or whether you are an Aries or a Gemini—according to the variations in cusp dates from year to year (see also page 17).

If you were born at the beginning or end of Taurus, yours is a lifetime reflecting a process of subtle transformation. Your life on Earth will symbolize a significant change in consciousness, for you are either about to enter a whole new way of living or are leaving one behind.

If you were born toward the end of April, you may want to read the horoscope book for Aries as well as for Taurus. The investment might be strangely revealing, for Aries contains the secret to many of your complexities and unexpressed assets and liabilities.

But this is the very irony of an Aries-Taurus cusp. The more fixed you become, the less able you are to seek out adventure, take chances, gamble—and win. Your natural tendency is to acquire, build, and collect. The more you possess, the more permanent your status in life; thus, the less able you are to simply pick up and go back to zero. Fulfillment comes through loyalty, constancy, and success in the material world.

If you were born during the third week of May, you may want to see the Gemini horoscope book as well as Taurus, for without Gemini your assets are often too stable, too fixed. Gemini provides you with fluidity and gets you moving.

You are a blend of stability and mobility—rich, raw material—with a dexterity of mind and body. Even around a fixed and constant center, change is always taking place. No matter how you

4

hang on, there will be a series of changes, experiences, new people, new faces, places, facts, and events.

You are conservative with the very definite hint of an open mind, the blend of hardheaded realism and freewheeling experimentalism, earthy, tactile sensuality, and bold participation in life's joys.

THE CUSPS OF TAURUS

DATES SUN ENTERS TAURUS (LEAVES ARIES)

April 20 every year from 1900 to 2010, except for the following:

	April 19			April 21
1948	1972	1988	2000	1903
52	76	89	2001	07
56	80	92	2004	11
60	81	93	2005	19
64	84	96	2008	
68	85	97	2009	

DATES SUN LEAVES TAURUS (ENTERS GEMINI)

May 21 every year from 1900 to 2010, except for the following:

	May 20			May 22
1948	1972	1988	2000	1903
52	76	89	2001	07
56	80	92	2004	11
60	81	93	2005	19
64	84	96	2008	
68	85	97	2009	

THE ASCENDANT: TAURUS RISING

Could you be a "double" Taurus? That is, could you have Taurus as your Rising sign as well as your Sun sign? The tables on pages 8–9 will tell you Taurus what your Rising sign happens to be. Just find the hour of your birth, then find the day of your birth, and you will see which sign of the Zodiac is your Ascendant, as the Rising sign is called. The Ascendant is called that because it is the sign rising on the eastern horizon at the time of your birth. For a more detailed discussion of the Rising sign and the twelve houses of the Zodiac, see pages 17–20.

The Ascendant, or Rising sign, is placed on the 1st house in a horoscope, of which there are twelve houses. The 1st house represents your response to the environment—your unique response. Call it identity, personality, ego, self-image, facade, come-on, body-mind-spirit—whatever term best conveys to you the meaning of the you that acts and reacts in the world. It is a you that is always changing, discovering a new you. Your identity started with birth and early environment, over which you had little conscious control, and continues to experience, to adjust, to express itself. The 1st house also represents how others see you. Has anyone ever guessed your sign to be your Rising sign? People may respond to that personality, that facade, that body type governed by your Rising sign.

Your Ascendant, or Rising sign, modifies your basic Sun sign personality, and it affects the way you act out the daily predictions for your Sun sign. If your Rising sign is indeed Taurus, what follows is a description of its effects on your horoscope. If your Rising sign is not Taurus, but some other sign of the Zodiac, you may wish to read the horoscope book for that sign as well.

With Taurus on the Ascendant, that is, in your 1st house, the planet rising in the 1st house is Venus, ruler of Taurus. Venus confers an intuitive, creative mind, and a liking for ease and luxury. Venus here gives you a sociable nature—loyal, lovable, and loving. But there are contradictions! Like the Bull, the zodiacal symbol of Taurus, you strike contrasting poses. In repose, you can be seen sweetly, peaceably smelling the flowers. Enraged, you trample the very turf that supports you. A passionate, selfish, demanding streak overcomes the mild, gentle, docile mood.

You have a well-developed need for people. Personal relationships are important to you, often centering around your love life. Bestowed with ample good looks and sensual appeal, you do not lack for admirers. In fact, you are sought after, often chased. Though generally loyal and steadfast, and capable of success in marriage, you may, however, have an irresistible urge for secret affairs, which arouse other people's jealousy and antagonism. There is also the danger that you can be caught between a fierce possessiveness and a thoughtless desire to acquire popularity in an indiscriminating way.

You have an even greater need for money. For you with Taurus Rising, money symbolizes the successful self. You intend to earn money in a steady, practical way, especially one that is time-honored and contains few risks. But you tend to spend money lavishly, when your comfort and edification demand it. You like sparkle and glitter, ornamentation, and nourishment. Food, clothes, "things" can become extravagances you cannot afford. Only when threats to your personal security loom do you jealously guard your money. You may also confuse money and love, using the one to get the other and vice versa.

You have a strong creative drive, tending toward the arts and crafts. Your self-expression is best achieved by creating sensations that are pleasing to the eye and to the body in general. You are, however, capable of sustained efforts of the mind, for you are both patient and intuitive. For you, the creator, one problem lies in being too fixed in your vision, too proud to ask for help, and too self-centered to think you need it. If you get bogged down, you abandon your undertakings for a lazy, self-indulgent spell. You also keep a too tenacious hold on your creations.

Because you are basically cautious, what you create or build is usually very sound. Success through stability is your motto. Your efforts, focused in a relationship or in a product, have a tempering, personalizing influence. Sometimes you shy away from group efforts if they stress generalities or nonpersonal goals. In a setting where intimacy is discouraged, your drive is inhibited. On the other hand, you have deep compassion and an unselfish need to serve others. When an activity or cause sponsors both personal satisfaction and kindly justice, you will work for it laboriously. Otherwise, you prefer the pursuit of heady living, sometimes alone, sometimes with a partner.

For Taurus Rising, two key words are sense and sensibility. Weave them together into a rich, thick tapestry, rather than raveling them in bits and pieces of pleasure.

RISING SIGNS FOR TAURUS
Day of Birth

Hour of Birth*	April 20–25	April 26–29	April 30–May 4
Midnight	Capricorn	Capricorn	Capricorn
1 AM	Capricorn	Aquarius	Aquarius
2 AM	Aquarius	Aquarius	Aquarius; Pisces 5/4
3 AM	Pisces	Pisces	Pisces
4 AM	Pisces; Aries 4/22	Aries	Aries
5 AM	Aries	Taurus	Taurus
6 AM	Taurus	Taurus	Taurus; Gemini 5/4
7 AM	Gemini	Gemini	Gemini
8 AM	Gemini	Gemini	Gemini; Cancer 5/2
9 AM	Cancer	Cancer	Cancer
10 AM	Cancer	Cancer	Cancer
11 AM	Cancer; Leo 4/22	Leo	Leo
Noon	Leo	Leo	Leo
1 PM	Leo	Leo	Virgo
2 PM	Virgo	Virgo	Virgo
3 PM	Virgo	Virgo	Virgo
4 PM	Virgo; Libra 4/23	Libra	Libra
5 PM	Libra	Libra	Libra
6 PM	Libra	Libra; Scorpio 4/29	Scorpio
7 PM	Scorpio	Scorpio	Scorpio
8 PM	Scorpio	Scorpio	Scorpio
9 PM	Scorpio; Sagittarius 4/23	Sagittarius	Sagittarius
10 PM	Sagittarius	Sagittarius	Sagittarius
11 PM	Sagittarius	Sagittarius; Capricorn 4/27	Capricorn

*Hour of birth given here is for Standard Time in any time zone. If your hour of birth was recorded in Daylight Saving Time, subtract one hour from it and consult that hour in the table above. For example, if you were born at 6 AM D.S.T., see 5 AM above.

Hour of Birth*	Day of Birth		
	May 5–10	May 11–15	May 16–21
Midnight	Capricorn	Aquarius	Aquarius
1 AM	Aquarius	Aquarius	Aquarius; Pisces 5/18
2 AM	Pisces	Pisces	Pisces
3 AM	Pisces; Aries 5/6	Aries	Aries
4 AM	Aries	Taurus	Taurus
5 AM	Taurus	Taurus	Taurus; Gemini 5/19
6 AM	Gemini	Gemini	Gemini
7 AM	Gemini	Gemini	Gemini; Cancer 5/18
8 AM	Cancer	Cancer	Cancer
9 AM	Cancer	Cancer	Cancer
10 AM	Cancer; Leo 5/8	Leo	Leo
11 AM	Leo	Leo	Leo
Noon	Leo	Leo	Virgo
1 PM	Virgo	Virgo	Virgo
2 PM	Virgo	Virgo	Virgo
3 PM	Virgo; Libra 5/8	Libra	Libra
4 PM	Libra	Libra	Libra
5 PM	Libra	Scorpio	Scorpio
6 PM	Scorpio	Scorpio	Scorpio
7 PM	Scorpio	Scorpio	Scorpio
8 PM	Scorpio; Sagittarius 5/8	Sagittarius	Sagittarius
9 PM	Sagittarius	Sagittarius	Sagittarius
10 PM	Sagittarius	Sagittarius; Capricorn 5/12	Capricorn
11 PM	Capricorn	Capricorn	Capricorn

*See note on facing page.

THE PLACE OF ASTROLOGY
IN TODAY'S WORLD

Does astrology have a place in the fast-moving, ultra-scientific world we live in today? Can it be justified in a sophisticated society whose outriders are already preparing to step off the moon into the deep space of the planets themselves? Or is it just a hangover of ancient superstition, a psychological dummy for neurotics and dreamers of every historical age?

These are the kind of questions that any inquiring person can be expected to ask when they approach a subject like astrology which goes beyond, but never excludes, the materialistic side of life.

The simple, single answer is that astrology works. It works for many millions of people in the western world alone. In the United States there are 10 million followers and in Europe, an estimated 25 million. America has more than 4000 practicing astrologers, Europe nearly three times as many. Even down-under Australia has its hundreds of thousands of adherents. In the eastern countries, astrology has enormous followings, again, because it has been proved to work. In India, for example, brides and grooms for centuries have been chosen on the basis of their astrological compatibility.

Astrology today is more vital than ever before, more practicable because all over the world the media devotes much space and time to it, more valid because science itself is confirming the precepts of astrological knowledge with every new exciting step. The ordinary person who daily applies astrology intelligently does not have to wonder whether it is true nor believe in it blindly. He can see it working for himself. And, if he can use it—and this book is designed to help the reader to do just that—he can make living a far richer experience, and become a more developed personality and a better person.

Astrology and Relationships

Astrology is the science of relationships. It is not just a study of planetary influences on man and his environment. It is the study of man himself.

We are at the center of our personal universe, of all our relationships. And our happiness or sadness depends on how we act, how we relate to the people and things that surround us. The emotions that we generate have a distinct effect—for better or worse—on the world around us. Our friends and our enemies will confirm this. Just look in the mirror the next time you are angry. In other words, each of us is a kind of sun or planet or star radiating our feelings on the environment around us. Our influence on our personal universe, whether loving, helpful, or destructive, varies with our changing moods, expressed through our individual character.

Our personal "radiations" are potent in the way they affect our moods and our ability to control them. But we usually are able to throw off our emotion in some sort of action—we have a good cry, walk it off, or tell someone our troubles—before it can build up too far and make us physically ill. Astrology helps us to understand the universal forces working on us, and through this understanding, we can become more properly adjusted to our surroundings so that we find ourselves coping where others may flounder.

The Challenge of Love

The challenge of love lies in recognizing the difference between infatuation, emotion, sex, and, sometimes, the intentional deceit of the other person. Mankind, with its record of broken marriages, despair, and disillusionment, is obviously not very good at making these distinctions.

Can astrology help?

Yes. In the same way that advance knowledge can usually help in any human situation. And there is probably no situation as human, as poignant, as pathetic and universal, as the failure of man's love.

Love, of course, is not just between man and woman. It involves love of children, parents, home, and friends. But the big problems usually involve the choice of partner.

Astrology has established degrees of compatibility that exist between people born under the various signs of the Zodiac. Because people are individuals, there are numerous variations and modifications. So the astrologer, when approached on mate and marriage matters, makes allowances for them. But the fact remains that some groups of people are suited for each other and some are not, and astrology has expressed this in terms of characteristics we all can study and use as a personal guide.

No matter how much enjoyment and pleasure we find in the different aspects of each other's character, if it is not an overall compatibility, the chances of our finding fulfillment or enduring happiness in each other are pretty hopeless. And astrology can help us to find someone compatible.

Astrology and Science

Closely related to our emotions is the "other side" of our personal universe, our physical welfare. Our body, of course, is largely influenced by things around us over which we have very little control. The phone rings, we hear it. The train runs late. We snag our stocking or cut our face shaving. Our body is under a constant bombardment of events that influence our daily lives to varying degrees.

The question that arises from all this is, what makes each of us act so that we have to involve other people and keep the ball of activity and evolution rolling? This is the question that both science and astrology are involved with. The scientists have attacked it from different angles: anthropology, the study of human evolution as body, mind and response to environment; anatomy, the study of bodily structure; psychology, the science of the human mind; and so on. These studies have produced very impressive classifications and valuable information, but because the approach to the problem is fragmented, so is the result. They remain "branches" of science. Science generally studies effects. It keeps turning up wonderful answers but no lasting solutions. Astrology, on the other hand, approaches the question from the broader viewpoint. Astrology began its inquiry with the totality of human experience and saw it as an effect. It then looked to find the cause, or at least the prime movers, and during thousands of years of observation of man and his *universal* environment came up with the extraordinary principle of planetary influence—or astrology, which, from the Greek, means the science of the stars.

Modern science, as we shall see, has confirmed much of astrology's foundations—most of it unintentionally, some of it reluctantly, but still, indisputably.

It is not difficult to imagine that there must be a connection between outer space and Earth. Even today, scientists are not too sure how our Earth was created, but it is generally agreed that it is only a tiny part of the universe. And as a part of the universe, people on Earth see and feel the influence of heavenly bodies in almost every aspect of our existence. There is no doubt that the Sun has the greatest influence on life on this planet. Without it there would be no life, for without it there would be no warmth, no division into day and night, no cycles of time or season at all. This is clear and easy to see. The influence of the Moon, on the other hand, is more subtle, though no less definite.

There are many ways in which the influence of the Moon manifests itself here on Earth, both on human and animal life. It is a well-known fact, for instance, that the large movements of water on our planet—that is the ebb and flow of the tides—are caused by the Moon's gravitational pull. Since this is so, it follows that these water movements do not occur only in the oceans, but that all bodies of water are affected, even down to the tiniest puddle.

The human body, too, which consists of about 70 percent water, falls within the scope of this lunar influence. For example the menstrual cycle of most women corresponds to the 28-day lunar month; the period of pregnancy in humans is 273 days, or equal to nine lunar months. Similarly, many illnesses reach a crisis at the change of the Moon, and statistics in many countries have shown that the crime rate is highest at the time of the Full Moon. Even human sexual desire has been associated with the phases of the Moon. But it is in the movement of the tides that we get the clearest demonstration of planetary influence, which leads to the irresistible correspondence between the so-called metaphysical and the physical.

Tide tables are prepared years in advance by calculating the future positions of the Moon. Science has known for a long time that the Moon is the main cause of tidal action. But only in the last few years has it begun to realize the possible extent of this influence on mankind. To begin with, the ocean tides do not rise and fall as we might imagine from our personal observations of them. The Moon as it orbits around Earth sets up a circular wave of attraction which pulls the oceans of the world after it, broadly in an east to west direction. This influence is like a phantom wave crest, a loop of power stretching from pole to pole which passes over and around the Earth like an invisible shadow. It travels with equal effect across the land masses and, as scientists were recently amazed to observe, caused oysters placed in the dark in the middle of the United States where there is no sea to open their shells to receive the nonexistent tide. If the land-locked oysters react to this invisible signal, what effect does it have on us who not so long ago in evolutionary time came out of the sea and still have its salt in our blood and sweat?

Less well known is the fact that the Moon is also the primary force behind the circulation of blood in human beings and animals, and the movement of sap in trees and plants. Agriculturists have established that the Moon has a distinct influence on crops, which explains why for centuries people have planted according to Moon cycles. The habits of many animals, too, are directed by the movement of the Moon. Migratory birds, for instance, depart only at or near the time of the Full Moon. And certain sea creatures, eels in particular, move only in accordance with certain phases of the Moon.

Know Thyself—Why?

In today's fast-changing world, everyone still longs to know what the future holds. It is the one thing that everyone has in common:
rich and poor, famous and infamous, all are deeply concerned about tomorrow.

But the key to the future, as every historian knows, lies in the past. This is as true of individual people as it is of nations. You cannot understand your future without first understanding your past, which is simply another way of saying that you must first of all know yourself.

The motto "know thyself" seems obvious enough nowadays, but it was originally put forward as the foundation of wisdom by the ancient Greek philosophers. It was then adopted by the "mystery religions" of the ancient Middle East, Greece, Rome, and is still used in all genuine schools of mind training or mystical discipline, both in those of the East, based on yoga, and those of the West. So it is universally accepted now, and has been through the ages.

But how do you go about discovering what sort of person you are? The first step is usually classification into some sort of system of types. Astrology did this long before the birth of Christ. Psychology has also done it. So has modern medicine, in its way.

One system classifies people according to the source of the impulses they respond to most readily: the muscles, leading to direct bodily action; the digestive organs, resulting in emotion; or the brain and nerves, giving rise to thinking. Another such system says that character is determined by the endocrine glands, and gives us such labels as "pituitary," "thyroid," and "hyperthyroid" types. These different systems are neither contradictory nor mutually exclusive. In fact, they are very often different ways of saying the same thing.

Very popular, useful classifications were devised by Carl Jung, the eminent disciple of Freud. Jung observed among the different faculties of the mind, four which have a predominant influence on character. These four faculties exist in all of us without exception, but not in perfect balance. So when we say, for instance, that someone is a "thinking type," it means that in any situation he or she tries to be rational. Emotion, which may be the opposite of thinking, will be his or her weakest function. This thinking type can be sensible and reasonable, or calculating and unsympathetic. The emotional type, on the other hand, can often be recognized by exaggerated language—everything is either marvelous or terrible—and in extreme cases they even invent dramas and quarrels out of nothing just to make life more interesting.

The other two faculties are intuition and physical sensation. The sensation type does not only care for food and drink, nice clothes and furniture; he or she is also interested in all forms of physical experience. Many scientists are sensation types as are athletes and nature-lovers. Like sensation, intuition is a form of perception and we all possess it. But it works through that part of the mind which is not under conscious control—consequently it sees meanings and connections which are not obvious to thought or emotion. Inventors and original thinkers are always intuitive, but so, too, are superstitious people who see meanings where none exist.

Thus, sensation tells us what is going on in the world, feeling (that is, emotion) tells us how important it is to ourselves, thinking enables us to interpret it and work out what we should do about it, and intuition tells us what it means to ourselves and others. All four faculties are essential, and all are present in every one of us. But some people are guided chiefly by one, others by another. In addition, Jung also observed a division of the human personality into the extrovert and the introvert, which cuts across these four types.

A disadvantage of all these systems of classification is that one cannot tell very easily where to place oneself. Some people are reluctant to admit that they act to please their emotions. So they deceive themselves for years by trying to belong to whichever type they think is the "best." Of course, there is no best; each has its faults and each has its good points.

The advantage of the signs of the Zodiac is that they simplify classification. Not only that, but your date of birth is personal—

it is unarguably yours. What better way to know yourself than by going back as far as possible to the very moment of your birth? And this is precisely what your horoscope is all about, as we shall see in the next section.

WHAT IS A HOROSCOPE?

If you had been able to take a picture of the skies at the moment of your birth, that photograph would be your horoscope. Lacking such a snapshot, it is still possible to recreate the picture—and this is at the basis of the astrologer's art. In other words, your horoscope is a representation of the skies with the planets in the exact positions they occupied at the time you were born.

The year of birth tells an astrologer the positions of the distant, slow-moving planets Jupiter, Saturn, Uranus, Neptune, and Pluto. The month of birth indicates the Sun sign, or birth sign as it is commonly called, as well as indicating the positions of the rapidly moving planets Venus, Mercury, and Mars. The day and time of birth will locate the position of our Moon. And the moment—the exact hour and minute—of birth determines the houses through what is called the Ascendant, or Rising sign.

With this information the astrologer consults various tables to calculate the specific positions of the Sun, Moon, and other planets relative to your birthplace at the moment you were born. Then he or she locates them by means of the Zodiac.

The Zodiac

The Zodiac is a band of stars (constellations) in the skies, centered on the Sun's apparent path around the Earth, and is divided into twelve equal segments, or signs. What we are actually dividing up is the Earth's path around the Sun. But from our point of view here on Earth, it seems as if the Sun is making a great circle around our planet in the sky, so we say it is the Sun's apparent path. This twelvefold division, the Zodiac, is a reference system for the astrologer. At any given moment the planets—and in astrology both the Sun and Moon are considered to be planets—can all be located at a specific point along this path.

Now where in all this are you, the subject of the horoscope? Your character is largely determined by the sign the Sun is in. So that is where the astrologer looks first in your horoscope, at your Sun sign.

The Sun Sign and the Cusp

There are twelve signs in the Zodiac, and the Sun spends approximately one month in each sign. But because of the motion of the Earth around the Sun—the Sun's apparent motion—the dates when the Sun enters and leaves each sign may change from year to year. Some people born near the cusp, or edge, of a sign have difficulty determining which is their Sun sign. But in this book a Table of Cusps is provided for the years 1900 to 2010 (page 5) so you can find out what your true Sun sign is.

Here are the twelve signs of the Zodiac, their ancient zodiacal symbol, and the dates when the Sun enters and leaves each sign for the year 2006. Remember, these dates may change from year to year.

ARIES	Ram	March 20–April 20
TAURUS	Bull	April 20–May 21
GEMINI	Twins	May 21–June 21
CANCER	Crab	June 21–July 22
LEO	Lion	July 22–August 23
VIRGO	Virgin	August 23–September 23
LIBRA	Scales	September 23–October 23
SCORPIO	Scorpion	October 23–November 22
SAGITTARIUS	Archer	November 22–December 21
CAPRICORN	Sea Goat	December 21–January 20
AQUARIUS	Water Bearer	January 20–February 18
PISCES	Fish	February 18–March 20

It is possible to draw significant conclusions and make meaningful predictions based simply on the Sun sign of a person. There are many people who have been amazed at the accuracy of the description of their own character based only on the Sun sign. But an astrologer needs more information than just your Sun sign to interpret the photograph that is your horoscope.

The Rising Sign and the Zodiacal Houses

An astrologer needs the exact time and place of your birth in order to construct and interpret your horoscope. The illustration on the next page shows the flat chart, or natural wheel, an astrologer uses. Note the inner circle of the wheel labeled 1 through 12. These 12 divisions are known as the houses of the Zodiac.

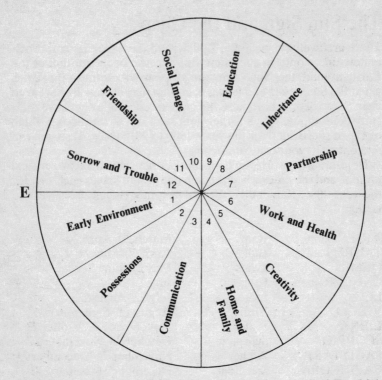

The 1st house always starts from the position marked E, which corresponds to the eastern horizon. The rest of the houses 2 through 12 follow around in a "counterclockwise" direction. The point where each house starts is known as a cusp, or edge.

The cusp, or edge, of the 1st house (point E) is where an astrologer would place your Rising sign, the Ascendant. And, as already noted, the exact time of your birth determines your Rising sign. Let's see how this works.

As the Earth rotates on its axis once every 24 hours, each one of the twelve signs of the Zodiac appears to be "rising" on the horizon, with a new one appearing about every 2 hours. Actually it is the turning of the Earth that exposes each sign to view, but in our astrological work we are discussing apparent motion. This Rising sign marks the Ascendant, and it colors the whole orientation of a horoscope. It indicates the sign governing the 1st house of the chart, and will thus determine which signs will govern all the other houses.

To visualize this idea, imagine two color wheels with twelve divisions superimposed upon each other. For just as the Zodiac is divided into twelve constellations that we identify as the signs, another twelvefold division is used to denote the houses. Now imagine one wheel (the signs) moving slowly while the other wheel (the houses) remains still. This analogy may help you see how the signs keep shifting the "color" of the houses as the Rising sign continues to change every two hours. To simplify things, a Table of Rising Signs has been provided (pages 8–9) for your specific Sun sign.

Once your Rising sign has been placed on the cusp of the 1st house, the signs that govern the rest of the 11 houses can be placed on the chart. In any individual's horoscope the signs do not necessarily correspond with the houses. For example, it could be that a sign covers part of two adjacent houses. It is the interpretation of such variations in an individual's horoscope that marks the professional astrologer.

But to gain a workable understanding of astrology, it is not necessary to go into great detail. In fact, we just need a description of the houses and their meanings, as is shown in the illustration above and in the table below.

THE 12 HOUSES OF THE ZODIAC

1st	Individuality, body appearance, general outlook on life	Personality house
2nd	Finance, possessions, ethical principles, gain or loss	Money house
3rd	Relatives, communication, short journeys, writing, education	Relatives house
4th	Family and home, parental ties, land and property, security	Home house
5th	Pleasure, children, creativity, entertainment, risk	Pleasure house
6th	Health, harvest, hygiene, work and service, employees	Health house
7th	Marriage and divorce, the law, partnerships and alliances	Marriage house
8th	Inheritance, secret deals, sex, death, regeneration	Inheritance house
9th	Travel, sports, study, philosophy Ω house	Travel house
10th	Career, social standing, success and honor	Business house
11th	Friendship, social life, hopes and wishes	Friends house
12th	Troubles, illness, secret enemies, hidden agendas	Trouble house

The Planets in the Houses

An astrologer, knowing the exact time and place of your birth, will use tables of planetary motion in order to locate the planets in your horoscope chart. He or she will determine which planet or planets are in which sign and in which house. It is not uncommon, in an individual's horoscope, for there to be two or more planets in the same sign and in the same house.

The characteristics of the planets modify the influence of the Sun according to their natures and strengths.

Sun: Source of life. Basic temperament according to the Sun sign. The conscious will. Human potential.

Moon: Emotions. Moods. Customs. Habits. Changeable. Adaptive. Nurturing.

Mercury: Communication. Intellect. Reasoning power. Curiosity. Short travels.

Venus: Love. Delight. Charm. Harmony. Balance. Art. Beautiful possessions.

Mars: Energy. Initiative. War. Anger. Adventure. Courage. Daring. Impulse.

Jupiter: Luck. Optimism. Generous. Expansive. Opportunities. Protection.

Saturn: Pessimism. Privation. Obstacles. Delay. Hard work. Research. Lasting rewards after long struggle.

Uranus: Fashion. Electricity. Revolution. Independence. Freedom. Sudden changes. Modern science.

Neptune: Sensationalism. Theater. Dreams. Inspiration. Illusion. Deception.

Pluto: Creation and destruction. Total transformation. Lust for power. Strong obsessions.

Superimpose the characteristics of the planets on the functions of the house in which they appear. Express the result through the character of the Sun sign, and you will get the basic idea.

Of course, many other considerations have been taken into account in producing the carefully worked out predictions in this book: the aspects of the planets to each other; their strength according to position and sign; whether they are in a house of exaltation or decline; whether they are natural enemies or not; whether a planet occupies its own sign; the position of a planet in relation to its own house or sign; whether the sign is male or female; whether the sign is a fire, earth, water, or air sign. These are only a few of the colors on the astrologer's pallet which he or she must mix with the inspiration of the artist and the accuracy of the mathematician.

How To Use These Predictions

A person reading the predictions in this book should understand that they are produced from the daily position of the planets for a group of people and are not, of course, individually specialized. To get the full benefit of them our readers should relate the predictions to their own character and circumstances, coordinate them, and draw their own conclusions from them.

If you are a serious observer of your own life, you should find a definite pattern emerging that will be a helpful and reliable guide.

The point is that we always retain our free will. The stars indicate certain directional tendencies but we are not compelled to follow. We can do or not do, and wisdom must make the choice.

We all have our good and bad days. Sometimes they extend into cycles of weeks. It is therefore advisable to study daily predictions in a span ranging from the day before to several days ahead.

Daily predictions should be taken very generally. The word "difficult" does not necessarily indicate a whole day of obstruction or inconvenience. It is a warning to you to be cautious. Your caution will often see you around the difficulty before you are involved. This is the correct use of astrology.

In another section (pages 78–84), detailed information is given about the influence of the Moon as it passes through each of the twelve signs of the Zodiac. There are instructions on how to use the Moon Tables (pages 85–92), which provide Moon Sign Dates throughout the year as well as the Moon's role in health and daily affairs. This information should be used in conjunction with the daily forecasts to give a fuller picture of the astrological trends.

HISTORY OF ASTROLOGY

The origins of astrology have been lost far back in history, but we do know that reference is made to it as far back as the first written records of the human race. It is not hard to see why. Even in primitive times, people must have looked for an explanation for the various happenings in their lives. They must have wanted to know why people were different from one another. And in their search they turned to the regular movements of the Sun, Moon, and stars to see if they could provide an answer.

It is interesting to note that as soon as man learned to use his tools in any type of design, or his mind in any kind of calculation, he turned his attention to the heavens. Ancient cave dwellings reveal dim crescents and circles representative of the Sun and Moon, rulers of day and night. Mesopotamia and the civilization of Chaldea, in itself the foundation of those of Babylonia and Assyria, show a complete picture of astronomical observation and well-developed astrological interpretation.

Humanity has a natural instinct for order. The study of anthropology reveals that primitive people—even as far back as prehistoric times—were striving to achieve a certain order in their lives. They tried to organize the apparent chaos of the universe. They had the desire to attach meaning to things. This demand for order has persisted throughout the history of man. So that observing the regularity of the heavenly bodies made it logical that primitive peoples should turn heavenward in their search for an understanding of the world in which they found themselves so random and alone.

And they did find a significance in the movements of the stars. Shepherds tending their flocks, for instance, observed that when the cluster of stars now known as the constellation Aries was in sight, it was the time of fertility and they associated it with the Ram. And they noticed that the growth of plants and plant life corresponded with different phases of the Moon, so that certain times were favorable for the planting of crops, and other times were not. In this way, there grew up a tradition of seasons and causes connected with the passage of the Sun through the twelve signs of the Zodiac.

Astrology was valued so highly that the king was kept informed of the daily and monthly changes in the heavenly bodies, and the results of astrological studies regarding events of the future. Head astrologers were clearly men of great rank and position, and the office was said to be a hereditary one.

Omens were taken, not only from eclipses and conjunctions of the Moon or Sun with one of the planets, but also from storms and earthquakes. In the eastern civilizations, particularly, the reverence inspired by astrology appears to have remained unbroken since the very earliest days. In ancient China, astrology, astronomy, and religion went hand in hand. The astrologer, who was also an astronomer, was part of the official government service and had his own corner in the Imperial Palace. The duties of the Imperial astrologer, whose office was one of the most important in the land, were clearly defined, as this extract from early records shows:

This exalted gentleman must concern himself with the stars in the heavens, keeping a record of the changes and movements of the Planets, the Sun and the Moon, in order to examine the movements of the terrestrial world with the object of prognosticating good and bad fortune. He divides the territories of the nine regions of the empire in accordance with their dependence on particular celestial bodies. All the fiefs and principalities are connected with the stars and from this their prosperity or misfortune should be ascertained. He makes prognostications according to the twelve years of the Jupiter cycle of good and evil of the terrestrial world. From the colors of the five kinds of clouds, he determines the coming of floods or droughts, abundance or famine. From the twelve winds, he draws conclusions about the state of harmony of heaven and earth, and takes note of good and bad signs that result from their accord or disaccord. In general, he concerns himself with five kinds of phenomena so as to warn the Emperor to come to the aid of the government and to allow for variations in the ceremonies according to their circumstances.

The Chinese were also keen observers of the fixed stars, giving them such unusual names as Ghost Vehicle, Sun of Imperial Concubine, Imperial Prince, Pivot of Heaven, Twinkling Brilliance, Weaving Girl. But, great astrologers though they may have been, the Chinese lacked one aspect of mathematics that the Greeks applied to astrology—deductive geometry. Deductive geometry was the basis of much classical astrology in and after the time of the Greeks, and this explains the different methods of prognostication used in the East and West.

Down through the ages the astrologer's art has depended, not so much on the uncovering of new facts, though this is important, as on the interpretation of the facts already known. This is the essence of the astrologer's skill.

But why should the signs of the Zodiac have any effect at all on the formation of human character? It is easy to see why people thought they did, and even now we constantly use astrological expressions in our everyday speech. The thoughts of "lucky star," "ill-fated," "star-crossed," "mooning around," are interwoven into the very structure of our language.

Wherever the concept of the Zodiac is understood and used, it could well appear to have an influence on the human character. Does this mean, then, that the human race, in whose civilization the idea of the twelve signs of the Zodiac has long been embedded, is divided into only twelve types? Can we honestly believe that it is really as simple as that? If so, there must be pretty wide ranges of variation within each type. And if, to explain the variation, we call in heredity and environment, experiences in early childhood, the thyroid and other glands, and also the four functions of the mind together with extroversion and introversion, then one begins to wonder if the original classification was worth making at all. No sensible person believes that his favorite system explains everything. But even so, he will not find the system much use at all if it does not even save him the trouble of bothering with the others.

In the same way, if we were to put every person under only one sign of the Zodiac, the system becomes too rigid and unlike life. Besides, it was never intended to be used like that. It may be convenient to have only twelve types, but we know that in practice there is every possible gradation between aggressiveness and timidity, or between conscientiousness and laziness. How, then, do we account for this?

A person born under any given Sun sign can be mainly influenced by one or two of the other signs that appear in their individual horoscope. For instance, famous persons born under the sign of Gemini include Henry VIII, whom nothing and no one could have induced to abdicate, and Edward VIII, who did just that. Obviously, then, the sign Gemini does not fully explain the complete character of either of them.

Again, under the opposite sign, Sagittarius, were both Stalin, who was totally consumed with the notion of power, and Charles V, who freely gave up an empire because he preferred to go into a monastery. And we find under Scorpio many uncompromising characters such as Luther, de Gaulle, Indira Gandhi, and Montgomery, but also Petain, a successful commander whose name later became synonymous with collaboration.

A single sign is therefore obviously inadequate to explain the differences between people; it can only explain resemblances, such as the combativeness of the Scorpio group, or the far-reaching devotion of Charles V and Stalin to their respective ideals—the Christian heaven and the Communist utopia.

But very few people have only one sign in their horoscope chart.

In addition to the month of birth, the day and, even more, the hour to the nearest minute if possible, ought to be considered. Without this, it is impossible to have an actual horoscope, for the word horoscope literally means "a consideration of the hour."

The month of birth tells you only which sign of the Zodiac was occupied by the Sun. The day and hour tell you what sign was occupied by the Moon. And the minute tells you which sign was rising on the eastern horizon. This is called the Ascendant, and, as some astrologers believe, it is supposed to be the most important thing in the whole horoscope.

The Sun is said to signify one's heart, that is to say, one's deepest desires and inmost nature. This is quite different from the Moon, which signifies one's superficial way of behaving. When the ancient Romans referred to the Emperor Augustus as a Capricorn, they meant that he had the Moon in Capricorn. Or, to take another example, a modern astrologer would call Disraeli a Scorpion because he had Scorpio Rising, but most people would call him Sagittarius because he had the Sun there. The Romans would have called him Leo because his Moon was in Leo.

So if one does not seem to fit one's birth month, it is always worthwhile reading the other signs, for one may have been born at a time when any of them were rising or occupied by the Moon. It also seems to be the case that the influence of the Sun develops as life goes on, so that the month of birth is easier to guess in people over the age of forty. The young are supposed to be influenced mainly by their Ascendant, the Rising sign, which characterizes the body and physical personality as a whole.

It is nonsense to assume that all people born at a certain time will exhibit the same characteristics, or that they will even behave in the same manner. It is quite obvious that, from the very moment of its birth, a child is subject to the effects of its environment, and that this in turn will influence its character and heritage to a decisive extent. Also to be taken into account are education and economic conditions, which play a very important part in the formation of one's character as well.

People have, in general, certain character traits and qualities which, according to their environment, develop in either a positive or a negative manner. Therefore, selfishness (inherent selfishness, that is) might emerge as unselfishness; kindness and consideration as cruelty and lack of consideration toward others. In the same way, a naturally constructive person may, through frustration, become destructive, and so on. The latent characteristics with which people are born can, therefore, through environment and good or bad training, become something that would appear to be its opposite, and so give the lie to the astrologer's description of their character.

But this is not the case. The true character is still there, but it is buried deep beneath these external superficialities.

Careful study of the character traits of various signs of the Zodiac are of immeasurable help, and can render beneficial service to the intelligent person. Undoubtedly, the reader will already have discovered that, while he is able to get on very well with some people, he just "cannot stand" others. The causes sometimes seem inexplicable. At times there is intense dislike, at other times immediate sympathy. And there is, too, the phenomenon of love at first sight, which is also apparently inexplicable. People appear to be either sympathetic or unsympathetic toward each other for no apparent reason.

Now if we look at this in the light of the Zodiac, we find that people born under different signs are either compatible or incompatible with each other. In other words, there are good and bad interrelating factors among the various signs. This does not, of course, mean that humanity can be divided into groups of hostile camps. It would be quite wrong to be hostile or indifferent toward people who happen to be born under an incompatible sign. There is no reason why everybody should not, or cannot, learn to control and adjust their feelings and actions, especially after they are aware of the positive qualities of other people by studying their character analyses, among other things.

Every person born under a certain sign has both positive and negative qualities, which are developed more or less according to our free will. Nobody is entirely good or entirely bad, and it is up to each of us to learn to control ourselves on the one hand and at the same time to endeavor to learn about ourselves and others.

It cannot be emphasized often enough that it is free will that determines whether we will make really good use of our talents and abilities. Using our free will, we can either overcome our failings or allow them to rule us. Our free will enables us to exert sufficient willpower to control our failings so that they do not harm ourselves or others.

Astrology can reveal our inclinations and tendencies. Astrology can tell us about ourselves so that we are able to use our free will to overcome our shortcomings. In this way astrology helps us do our best to become needed and valuable members of society as well as helpmates to our family and our friends. Astrology also can save us a great deal of unhappiness and remorse.

Yet it may seem absurd that an ancient philosophy could be a prop to modern men and women. But below the materialistic surface of modern life, there are hidden streams of feeling and thought. Symbology is reappearing as a study worthy of the scholar; the psychosomatic factor in illness has passed from the writings of the crank to those of the specialist; spiritual healing in all its forms is no longer a pious hope but an accepted phenomenon. And it is into this context that we consider astrology, in the sense that it is an analysis of human types.

Astrology and medicine had a long journey together, and only parted company a couple of centuries ago. There still remain in medical language such astrological terms as "saturnine," "choleric," and "mercurial," used in the diagnosis of physical tendencies. The herbalist, for long the handyman of the medical profession, has been dominated by astrology since the days of the Greeks. Certain herbs traditionally respond to certain planetary influences, and diseases must therefore be treated to ensure harmony between the medicine and the disease.

But the stars are expected to foretell and not only to diagnose.

Astrological forecasting has been remarkably accurate, but often it is wide of the mark. The brave person who cares to predict world events takes dangerous chances. Individual forecasting is less clear cut; it can be a help or a disillusionment. Then we come to the nagging question: if it is possible to foreknow, is it right to foretell? This is a point of ethics on which it is hard to pronounce judgment. The doctor faces the same dilemma if he finds that symptoms of a mortal disease are present in his patient and that he can only prognosticate a steady decline. How much to tell an individual in a crisis is a problem that has perplexed many distinguished scholars. Honest and conscientious astrologers in this modern world, where so many people are seeking guidance, face the same problem.

Five hundred years ago it was customary to call in a learned man who was an astrologer who was probably also a doctor and a philosopher. By his knowledge of astrology, his study of planetary influences, he felt himself qualified to guide those in distress. The world has moved forward at a fantastic rate since then, and yet people are still uncertain of themselves. At first sight it seems fantastic in the light of modern thinking that they turn to the most ancient of all studies, and get someone to calculate a horoscope for them. But is it really so fantastic if you take a second look? For astrology is concerned with tomorrow, with survival. And in a world such as ours, tomorrow and survival are the keywords for the twenty-first century.

ASTROLOGICAL BRIDGE TO THE 21st CENTURY

Themes connecting past, present, and future are in play as new planetary cycles form the bridge to the twenty-first century and its broad horizons. The first decade reveals hidden paths and personal hints for achieving your potential, for making the most of your message from the planets.

With the dawning of the twenty-first century look first to Jupiter, the planet of good fortune. Each new yearly Jupiter cycle follows the natural progression of the Zodiac. First is Jupiter in Aries and in Taurus through spring 2000, next Jupiter is in Gemini to summer 2001, then in Cancer to midsummer 2002, in Leo to late summer 2003, in Virgo to early autumn 2004, in Libra to midautumn 2005, and so on through Jupiter in Pisces through June 2010. The beneficent planet Jupiter promotes your professional and educational goals while urging informed choice and deliberation, providing a rich medium for creativity. Planet Jupiter's influence is protective, the generous helper that comes to the rescue just in the nick of time. And while safeguarding good luck, Jupiter can turn unusual risks into achievable aims.

In order to take advantage of luck and opportunity, to gain wisdom from experience, to persevere against adversity, look to beautiful planet Saturn. Saturn, planet of reason and responsibility, began a new cycle in earthy Taurus at the turn of the century. Saturn in Taurus until spring 2001 inspires industry and affection, blends practicality and imagination, all the while inviting caution and care. Saturn in Taurus lends beauty, order, and structure to your life. Then Saturn is in Gemini, the sign of mind and communication, until June 2003. Saturn in Gemini gives a lively intellectual capacity, so the limits of creativity can be stretched and boundaries broken. Saturn in Gemini holds the promise of fruitful endeavor through sustained study, learning, and application. Saturn in Cancer from early June 2003 to mid-July 2005 poses issues of long-term security versus immediate gratification. Rely on deliberation and choice to make sense out of diversity and change. Saturn in Cancer can be a revealing cycle, leading to the desired outcomes of growth and maturity. Saturn in Leo from mid-July 2005 to early September 2007 can be a test of boldness versus caution. Here every challenge must be met with benevolent authority, cool organizational skills must be matched by a caring and generous outlook. Saturn in Leo can be the hallmark of success and power in the realm of business and profession.

Uranus, planet of innovation and surprise, started an important new cycle in January of 1996. At that time Uranus entered its natural home in airy Aquarius. Uranus in Aquarius into the year 2003 has a profound effect on your personality and the lens through which you see the world. A basic change in the way you project yourself is just one impact of Uranus in Aquarius. More significantly, a whole new consciousness is evolving. Winds of change blowing your way emphasize movement and freedom. Uranus in Aquarius poses involvement in the larger community beyond self, family, friends, lovers, associates. Radical ideas and progressive thought signal a journey of liberation. As the new century begins, follow Uranus on the path of humanitarianism. A new Uranus cycle begins March 2003 when Uranus visits Pisces, briefly revisits Aquarius, then returns late in 2003 to Pisces where it will stay into May 2010. Uranus in Pisces, a strongly intuitive force, urges work and service for the good of humankind to make the world a better place for all people.

Neptune, planet of vision and mystery, is enjoying a long cycle that excites creativity and imaginative thinking. Neptune is in airy Aquarius from November 1998 to February of 2012. Neptune in Aquarius, the sign of the Water Bearer, represents two sides of the coin of wisdom: inspiration and reason. Here Neptune stirs powerful currents bearing a rich and varied harvest, the fertile breeding ground for idealistic aims and practical considerations. Neptune's fine intuition tunes in to your dreams, your imagination, your spirituality. You can never turn your back on the mysteries of life. Uranus and Neptune, the planets of enlightenment and idealism, give you glimpses into the future, letting you peek through secret doorways into the twenty-first century.

Pluto, planet of beginnings and endings, began a new cycle of growth and learning late in 1995. Pluto entered fiery Sagittarius and remains there into the year 2008. Pluto in Sagittarius during its long stay over twelve years can create significant change. The great power of Pluto in Sagittarius is already starting its transformation of your character and lifestyle. Pluto in Sagittarius takes you on a new journey of exploration and learning. The awakening you experience on intellectual and artistic levels heralds a new cycle of growth. Uncompromising Pluto, seeker of truth, challenges your identity, persona, and self-expression. Uncovering the real you, Pluto holds the key to understanding and meaningful communication. Pluto in Sagittarius can be the guiding light illuminating the first decade of the twenty-first century. Good luck is riding on the waves of change.

THE SIGNS OF THE ZODIAC

Dominant Characteristics

Aries: March 21–April 20

The Positive Side of Aries

The Aries has many positive points to his character. People born under this first sign of the Zodiac are often quite strong and enthusiastic. On the whole, they are forward-looking people who are not easily discouraged by temporary setbacks. They know what they want out of life and they go out after it. Their personalities are strong. Others are usually quite impressed by the Ram's way of doing things. Quite often they are sources of inspiration for others traveling the same route. Aries men and women have a special zest for life that can be contagious; for others, they are a fine example of how life should be lived.

The Aries person usually has a quick and active mind. He is imaginative and inventive. He enjoys keeping busy and active. He generally gets along well with all kinds of people. He is interested in mankind, as a whole. He likes to be challenged. Some would say he thrives on opposition, for it is when he is set against that he often does his best. Getting over or around obstacles is a challenge he generally enjoys. All in all, Aries is quite positive and young-thinking. He likes to keep abreast of new things that are happening in the world. Aries are often fond of speed. They like things to be done quickly, and this sometimes aggravates their slower colleagues and associates.

The Aries man or woman always seems to remain young. Their whole approach to life is youthful and optimistic. They never say die, no matter what the odds. They may have an occasional setback, but it is not long before they are back on their feet again.

The Negative Side of Aries

Everybody has his less positive qualities—and Aries is no exception. Sometimes the Aries man or woman is not very tactful in communicating with others; in his hurry to get things done he is apt to be a little callous or inconsiderate. Sensitive people are likely to find him somewhat sharp-tongued in some situations. Often in his eagerness to get the show on the road, he misses the mark altogether and cannot achieve his aims.

At times Aries can be too impulsive. He can occasionally be stubborn and refuse to listen to reason. If things do not move quickly enough to suit the Aries man or woman, he or she is apt to become rather nervous or irritable. The uncultivated Aries is not unfamiliar with moments of doubt and fear. He is capable of being destructive if he does not get his way. He can overcome some of his emotional problems by steadily trying to express himself as he really is, but this requires effort.

Taurus: April 21–May 20

The Positive Side of Taurus

The Taurus person is known for his ability to concentrate and for his tenacity. These are perhaps his strongest qualities. The Taurus man or woman generally has very little trouble in getting along with others; it's his nature to be helpful toward people in need. He can always be depended on by his friends, especially those in trouble.

Taurus generally achieves what he wants through his ability to persevere. He never leaves anything unfinished but works on something until it has been completed. People can usually take him at his word; he is honest and forthright in most of his dealings. The Taurus person has a good chance to make a success of his life because of his many positive qualities. The Taurus who aims high seldom falls short of his mark. He learns well by experience. He is thorough and does not believe in shortcuts of any kind. The Bull's thoroughness pays off in the end, for through his deliberateness he learns how to rely on himself and what he has learned. The Taurus person tries to get along with others, as a rule. He is not overly critical and likes people to be themselves. He is a tolerant person and enjoys peace and harmony—especially in his home life.

Taurus is usually cautious in all that he does. He is not a person

who believes in taking unnecessary risks. Before adopting any one line of action, he will weigh all of the pros and cons. The Taurus person is steadfast. Once his mind is made up it seldom changes. The person born under this sign usually is a good family person—reliable and loving.

The Negative Side of Taurus

Sometimes the Taurus man or woman is a bit too stubborn. He won't listen to other points of view if his mind is set on something. To others, this can be quite annoying. Taurus also does not like to be told what to do. He becomes rather angry if others think him not too bright. He does not like to be told he is wrong, even when he is. He dislikes being contradicted.

Some people who are born under this sign are very suspicious of others—even of those persons close to them. They find it difficult to trust people fully. They are often afraid of being deceived or taken advantage of. The Bull often finds it difficult to forget or forgive. His love of material things sometimes makes him rather avaricious and petty.

Gemini: May 21–June 20
The Positive Side of Gemini

The person born under this sign of the Heavenly Twins is usually quite bright and quick-witted. Some of them are capable of doing many different things. The Gemini person very often has many different interests. He keeps an open mind and is always anxious to learn new things.

Gemini is often an analytical person. He is a person who enjoys making use of his intellect. He is governed more by his mind than by his emotions. He is a person who is not confined to one view; he can often understand both sides to a problem or question. He knows how to reason, how to make rapid decisions if need be.

He is an adaptable person and can make himself at home almost anywhere. There are all kinds of situations he can adapt to. He is a person who seldom doubts himself; he is sure of his talents and his ability to think and reason. Gemini is generally most satisfied when he is in a situation where he can make use of his intellect. Never

short of imagination, he often has strong talents for invention. He is rather a modern person when it comes to life; Gemini almost always moves along with the times—perhaps that is why he remains so youthful throughout most of his life.

Literature and art appeal to the person born under this sign. Creativity in almost any form will interest and intrigue the Gemini man or woman.

The Gemini is often quite charming. A good talker, he often is the center of attraction at any gathering. People find it easy to like a person born under this sign because he can appear easygoing and usually has a good sense of humor.

The Negative Side of Gemini

Sometimes the Gemini person tries to do too many things at one time—and as a result, winds up finishing nothing. Some Twins are easily distracted and find it rather difficult to concentrate on one thing for too long a time. Sometimes they give in to trifling fancies and find it rather boring to become too serious about any one thing. Some of them are never dependable, no matter what they promise.

Although the Gemini man or woman often appears to be well-versed on many subjects, this is sometimes just a veneer. His knowledge may be only superficial, but because he speaks so well he gives people the impression of erudition. Some Geminis are sharp-tongued and inconsiderate; they think only of themselves and their own pleasure.

Cancer: June 21–July 20

The Positive Side of Cancer

The Moon Child's most positive point is his understanding nature. On the whole, he is a loving and sympathetic person. He would never go out of his way to hurt anyone. The Cancer man or woman is often very kind and tender; they give what they can to others. They hate to see others suffering and will do what they can to help someone in less fortunate circumstances than themselves. They are often very concerned about the world. Their interest in people generally goes beyond that of just their own families and close friends; they have a deep sense of community and respect humanitarian values. The Moon Child means what he says, as a rule; he is honest about his feelings.

The Cancer man or woman is a person who knows the art of patience. When something seems difficult, he is willing to wait until the situation becomes manageable again. He is a person who knows how to bide his time. Cancer knows how to concentrate on one thing at a time. When he has made his mind up he generally sticks with what he does, seeing it through to the end.

Cancer is a person who loves his home. He enjoys being surrounded by familiar things and the people he loves. Of all the signs, Cancer is the most maternal. Even the men born under this sign often have a motherly or protective quality about them. They like to take care of people in their family—to see that they are well loved and well provided for. They are usually loyal and faithful. Family ties mean a lot to the Cancer man or woman. Parents and in-laws are respected and loved. Young Cancer responds very well to adults who show faith in him. The Moon Child has a strong sense of tradition. He is very sensitive to the moods of others.

The Negative Side of Cancer

Sometimes Cancer finds it rather hard to face life. It becomes too much for him. He can be a little timid and retiring, when things don't go too well. When unfortunate things happen, he is apt to just shrug and say, "Whatever will be will be." He can be fatalistic to a fault. The uncultivated Cancer is a bit lazy. He doesn't have very much ambition. Anything that seems a bit difficult he'll gladly leave to others. He may be lacking in initiative. Too sensitive, when he feels he's been injured, he'll crawl back into his shell and nurse his imaginary wounds. The immature Moon Child often is given to crying when the smallest thing goes wrong.

Some Cancers find it difficult to enjoy themselves in environments outside their homes. They make heavy demands on others, and need to be constantly reassured that they are loved. Lacking such reassurance, they may resort to sulking in silence.

Leo: July 21–August 21

The Positive Side of Leo

Often Leos make good leaders. They seem to be good organizers and administrators. Usually they are quite popular with others. Whatever group it is that they belong to, the Leo man or woman is almost sure to be or become the leader. Loyalty, one of the Lion's noblest traits, enables him or her to maintain this leadership position.

Leo is generous most of the time. It is his best characteristic. He or she likes to give gifts and presents. In making others happy, the Leo person becomes happy himself. He likes to splurge when spending money on others. In some instances it may seem that the Lion's generosity knows no boundaries. A hospitable person, the Leo man or woman is very fond of welcoming people to his house and entertaining them. He is never short of company.

Leo has plenty of energy and drive. He enjoys working toward some specific goal. When he applies himself correctly, he gets what he wants most often. The Leo person is almost never unsure of himself. He has plenty of confidence and aplomb. He is a person who is direct in almost everything he does. He has a quick mind and can make a decision in a very short time.

He usually sets a good example for others because of his ambitious manner and positive ways. He knows how to stick to something once he's started. Although Leo may be good at making a joke, he is not superficial or glib. He is a loving person, kind and thoughtful.

There is generally nothing small or petty about the Leo man or woman. He does what he can for those who are deserving. He is a person others can rely upon at all times. He means what he says. An honest person, generally speaking, he is a friend who is valued and sought out.

The Negative Side of Leo

Leo, however, does have his faults. At times, he can be just a bit too arrogant. He thinks that no one deserves a leadership position except him. Only he is capable of doing things well. His opinion of himself is often much too high. Because of his conceit, he is

sometimes rather unpopular with a good many people. Some Leos are too materialistic; they can only think in terms of money and profit.

Some Leos enjoy lording it over others—at home or at their place of business. What is more, they feel they have the right to. Egocentric to an impossible degree, this sort of Leo cares little about how others think or feel. He can be rude and cutting.

Virgo: August 22–September 22

The Positive Side of Virgo

The person born under the sign of Virgo is generally a busy person. He knows how to arrange and organize things. He is a good planner. Above all, he is practical and is not afraid of hard work.

Often called the sign of the Harvester, Virgo knows how to attain what he desires. He sticks with something until it is finished. He never shirks his duties, and can always be depended upon. The Virgo person can be thoroughly trusted at all times.

The man or woman born under this sign tries to do everything to perfection. He doesn't believe in doing anything halfway. He always aims for the top. He is the sort of a person who is always learning and constantly striving to better himself—not because he wants more money or glory, but because it gives him a feeling of accomplishment.

The Virgo man or woman is a very observant person. He is sensitive to how others feel, and can see things below the surface of a situation. He usually puts this talent to constructive use.

It is not difficult for the Virgo to be open and earnest. He believes in putting his cards on the table. He is never secretive or underhanded. He's as good as his word. The Virgo person is generally plainspoken and down to earth. He has no trouble in expressing himself.

The Virgo person likes to keep up to date on new developments in his particular field. Well-informed, generally, he sometimes has a keen interest in the arts or literature. What he knows, he knows well. His ability to use his critical faculties is well-developed and sometimes startles others because of its accuracy.

Virgos adhere to a moderate way of life; they avoid excesses. Virgo is a responsible person and enjoys being of service.

The Negative Side of Virgo

Sometimes a Virgo person is too critical. He thinks that only he can do something the way it should be done. Whatever anyone else does is inferior. He can be rather annoying in the way he quibbles over insignificant details. In telling others how things should be done, he can be rather tactless and mean.

Some Virgos seem rather emotionless and cool. They feel emotional involvement is beneath them. They are sometimes too tidy, too neat. With money they can be rather miserly. Some Virgos try to force their opinions and ideas on others.

Libra: September 23–October 22

The Positive Side of Libra

Libras love harmony. It is one of their most outstanding character traits. They are interested in achieving balance; they admire beauty and grace in things as well as in people. Generally speaking, they are kind and considerate people. Libras are usually very sympathetic. They go out of their way not to hurt another person's feelings. They are outgoing and do what they can to help those in need.

People born under the sign of Libra almost always make good friends. They are loyal and amiable. They enjoy the company of others. Many of them are rather moderate in their views; they believe in keeping an open mind, however, and weighing both sides of an issue fairly before making a decision.

Alert and intelligent, Libra, often known as the Lawgiver, is always fair-minded and tries to put himself in the position of the other person. They are against injustice; quite often they take up for the underdog. In most of their social dealings, they try to be tactful and kind. They dislike discord and bickering, and most Libras strive for peace and harmony in all their relationships.

The Libra man or woman has a keen sense of beauty. They appreciate handsome furnishings and clothes. Many of them are artistically inclined. Their taste is usually impeccable. They know how to use color. Their homes are almost always attractively arranged and inviting. They enjoy entertaining people and see to it that their guests always feel at home and welcome.

Libra gets along with almost everyone. He is well-liked and socially much in demand.

The Negative Side of Libra

Some people born under this sign tend to be rather insincere. So eager are they to achieve harmony in all relationships that they will even go so far as to lie. Many of them are escapists. They find facing the truth an ordeal and prefer living in a world of make-believe.

In a serious argument, some Libras give in rather easily even when they know they are right. Arguing, even about something they believe in, is too unsettling for some of them.

Libras sometimes care too much for material things. They enjoy possessions and luxuries. Some are vain and tend to be jealous.

Scorpio: October 23–November 22

The Positive Side of Scorpio

The Scorpio man or woman generally knows what he or she wants out of life. He is a determined person. He sees something through to the end. Scorpio is quite sincere, and seldom says anything he doesn't mean. When he sets a goal for himself he tries to go about achieving it in a very direct way.

The Scorpion is brave and courageous. They are not afraid of hard work. Obstacles do not frighten them. They forge ahead until they achieve what they set out for. The Scorpio man or woman has a strong will.

Although Scorpio may seem rather fixed and determined, inside he is often quite tender and loving. He can care very much for others. He believes in sincerity in all relationships. His feelings about someone tend to last; they are profound and not superficial.

The Scorpio person is someone who adheres to his principles no matter what happens. He will not be deterred from a path he believes to be right.

Because of his many positive strengths, the Scorpion can often achieve happiness for himself and for those that he loves.

He is a constructive person by nature. He often has a deep understanding of people and of life, in general. He is perceptive and unafraid. Obstacles often seem to spur him on. He is a positive person who enjoys winning. He has many strengths and resources; challenge of any sort often brings out the best in him.

The Negative Side of Scorpio

The Scorpio person is sometimes hypersensitive. Often he imagines injury when there is none. He feels that others do not bother to recognize him for his true worth. Sometimes he is given to excessive boasting in order to compensate for what he feels is neglect.

Scorpio can be proud, arrogant, and competitive. They can be sly when they put their minds to it and they enjoy outwitting persons or institutions noted for their cleverness.

Their tactics for getting what they want are sometimes devious and ruthless. They don't care too much about what others may think. If they feel others have done them an injustice, they will do their best to seek revenge. The Scorpion often has a sudden, violent temper; and this person's interest in sex is sometimes quite unbalanced or excessive.

Sagittarius: November 23–December 20

The Positive Side of Sagittarius

People born under this sign are honest and forthright. Their approach to life is earnest and open. Sagittarius is often quite adult in his way of seeing things. They are broad-minded and tolerant people. When dealing with others the person born under the sign of the Archer is almost always open and forthright. He doesn't believe in deceit or pretension. His standards are high. People who associate with Sagittarius generally admire and respect his tolerant viewpoint.

The Archer trusts others easily and expects them to trust him. He is never suspicious or envious and almost always thinks well of others. People always enjoy his company because he is so friendly and easygoing. The Sagittarius man or woman is often good-humored. He can always be depended upon by his friends, family, and coworkers.

The person born under this sign of the Zodiac likes a good joke every now and then. Sagittarius is eager for fun and laughs, which makes him very popular with others.

A lively person, he enjoys sports and outdoor life. The Archer is fond of animals. Intelligent and interesting, he can begin an ani-

mated conversation with ease. He likes exchanging ideas and discussing various views.

He is not selfish or proud. If someone proposes an idea or plan that is better than his, he will immediately adopt it. Imaginative yet practical, he knows how to put ideas into practice.

The Archer enjoys sport and games, and it doesn't matter if he wins or loses. He is a forgiving person, and never sulks over something that has not worked out in his favor.

He is seldom critical, and is almost always generous.

The Negative Side of Sagittarius

Some Sagittarius are restless. They take foolish risks and seldom learn from the mistakes they make. They don't have heads for money and are often mismanaging their finances. Some of them devote much of their time to gambling.

Some are too outspoken and tactless, always putting their feet in their mouths. They hurt others carelessly by being honest at the wrong time. Sometimes they make promises which they don't keep. They don't stick close enough to their plans and go from one failure to another. They are undisciplined and waste a lot of energy.

Capricorn: December 21–January 19

The Positive Side of Capricorn

The person born under the sign of Capricorn, known variously as the Mountain Goat or Sea Goat, is usually very stable and patient. He sticks to whatever tasks he has and sees them through. He can always be relied upon and he is not averse to work.

An honest person, Capricorn is generally serious about whatever he does. He does not take his duties lightly. He is a practical person and believes in keeping his feet on the ground.

Quite often the person born under this sign is ambitious and knows how to get what he wants out of life. The Goat forges ahead and never gives up his goal. When he is determined about something, he almost always wins. He is a good worker—a hard worker. Although things may not come easy to him, he will not complain, but continue working until his chores are finished.

He is usually good at business matters and knows the value of money. He is not a spendthrift and knows how to put something away for a rainy day; he dislikes waste and unnecessary loss.

Capricorn knows how to make use of his self-control. He can apply himself to almost anything once he puts his mind to it. His ability to concentrate sometimes astounds others. He is diligent and does well when involved in detail work.

The Capricorn man or woman is charitable, generally speaking, and will do what is possible to help others less fortunate. As a friend, he is loyal and trustworthy. He never shirks his duties or responsibilities. He is self-reliant and never expects too much of the other fellow. He does what he can on his own. If someone does him a good turn, then he will do his best to return the favor.

The Negative Side of Capricorn

Like everyone, Capricorn, too, has faults. At times, the Goat can be overcritical of others. He expects others to live up to his own high standards. He thinks highly of himself and tends to look down on others.

His interest in material things may be exaggerated. The Capricorn man or woman thinks too much about getting on in the world and having something to show for it. He may even be a little greedy.

He sometimes thinks he knows what's best for everyone. He is too bossy. He is always trying to organize and correct others. He may be a little narrow in his thinking.

Aquarius: January 20–February 18

The Positive Side of Aquarius

The Aquarius man or woman is usually very honest and forthright. These are his two greatest qualities. His standards for himself are generally very high. He can always be relied upon by others. His word is his bond.

Aquarius is perhaps the most tolerant of all the Zodiac personalities. He respects other people's beliefs and feels that everyone is entitled to his own approach to life.

He would never do anything to injure another's feelings. He is never unkind or cruel. Always considerate of others, the Water

Bearer is always willing to help a person in need. He feels a very strong tie between himself and all the other members of mankind.

The person born under this sign, called the Water Bearer, is almost always an individualist. He does not believe in teaming up with the masses, but prefers going his own way. His ideas about life and mankind are often quite advanced. There is a saying to the effect that the average Aquarius is fifty years ahead of his time.

Aquarius is community-minded. The problems of the world concern him greatly. He is interested in helping others no matter what part of the globe they live in. He is truly a humanitarian sort. He likes to be of service to others.

Giving, considerate, and without prejudice, Aquarius have no trouble getting along with others.

The Negative Side of Aquarius

Aquarius may be too much of a dreamer. He makes plans but seldom carries them out. He is rather unrealistic. His imagination has a tendency to run away with him. Because many of his plans are impractical, he is always in some sort of a dither.

Others may not approve of him at all times because of his unconventional behavior. He may be a bit eccentric. Sometimes he is so busy with his own thoughts that he loses touch with the realities of existence.

Some Aquarius feel they are more clever and intelligent than others. They seldom admit to their own faults, even when they are quite apparent. Some become rather fanatic in their views. Their criticism of others is sometimes destructive and negative.

Pisces: February 19–March 20

The Positive Side of Pisces

Known as the sign of the Fishes, Pisces has a sympathetic nature. Kindly, he is often dedicated in the way he goes about helping others. The sick and the troubled often turn to him for advice and assistance. Possessing keen intuition, Pisces can easily understand people's deepest problems.

He is very broad-minded and does not criticize others for their faults. He knows how to accept people for what they are. On the whole, he is a trustworthy and earnest person. He is loyal to his friends and will do what he can to help them in time of need. Generous and good-natured, he is a lover of peace; he is often willing to help others solve their differences. People who have taken a wrong turn in life often interest him and he will do what he can to persuade them to rehabilitate themselves.

He has a strong intuitive sense and most of the time he knows how to make it work for him. Pisces is unusually perceptive and often knows what is bothering someone before that person, himself, is aware of it. The Pisces man or woman is an idealistic person, basically, and is interested in making the world a better place in which to live. Pisces believes that everyone should help each other. He is willing to do more than his share in order to achieve cooperation with others.

The person born under this sign often is talented in music or art. He is a receptive person; he is able to take the ups and downs of life with philosophic calm.

The Negative Side of Pisces

Some Pisces are often depressed; their outlook on life is rather glum. They may feel that they have been given a bad deal in life and that others are always taking unfair advantage of them. Pisces sometimes feel that the world is a cold and cruel place. The Fishes can be easily discouraged. The Pisces man or woman may even withdraw from the harshness of reality into a secret shell of his own where he dreams and idles away a good deal of his time.

Pisces can be lazy. He lets things happen without giving the least bit of resistance. He drifts along, whether on the high road or on the low. He can be lacking in willpower.

Some Pisces people seek escape through drugs or alcohol. When temptation comes along they find it hard to resist. In matters of sex, they can be rather permissive.

Sun Sign Personalities

ARIES: Hans Christian Andersen, Pearl Bailey, Marlon Brando, Wernher Von Braun, Charlie Chaplin, Joan Crawford, Da Vinci, Bette Davis, Doris Day, W.C. Fields, Alec Guinness, Adolf Hitler, William Holden, Thomas Jefferson, Nikita Khrushchev, Elton John, Arturo Toscanini, J.P. Morgan, Paul Robeson, Gloria Steinem, Sarah Vaughn, Vincent van Gogh, Tennessee Williams

TAURUS: Fred Astaire, Charlotte Brontë, Carol Burnett, Irving Berlin, Bing Crosby, Salvador Dali, Tchaikovsky, Queen Elizabeth II, Duke Ellington, Ella Fitzgerald, Henry Fonda, Sigmund Freud, Orson Welles, Joe Louis, Lenin, Karl Marx, Golda Meir, Eva Peron, Bertrand Russell, Shakespeare, Kate Smith, Benjamin Spock, Barbra Streisand, Shirley Temple, Harry Truman

GEMINI: Ruth Benedict, Josephine Baker, Rachel Carson, Carlos Chavez, Walt Whitman, Bob Dylan, Ralph Waldo Emerson, Judy Garland, Paul Gauguin, Allen Ginsberg, Benny Goodman, Bob Hope, Burl Ives, John F. Kennedy, Peggy Lee, Marilyn Monroe, Joe Namath, Cole Porter, Laurence Olivier, Harriet Beecher Stowe, Queen Victoria, John Wayne, Frank Lloyd Wright

CANCER: "Dear Abby," Lizzie Borden, David Brinkley, Yul Brynner, Pearl Buck, Marc Chagall, Princess Diana, Babe Didrikson, Mary Baker Eddy, Henry VIII, John Glenn, Ernest Hemingway, Lena Horne, Oscar Hammerstein, Helen Keller, Ann Landers, George Orwell, Nancy Reagan, Rembrandt, Richard Rodgers, Ginger Rogers, Rubens, Jean-Paul Sartre, O.J. Simpson

LEO: Neil Armstrong, James Baldwin, Lucille Ball, Emily Brontë, Wilt Chamberlain, Julia Child, William J. Clinton, Cecil B. De Mille, Ogden Nash, Amelia Earhart, Edna Ferber, Arthur Goldberg, Alfred Hitchcock, Mick Jagger, George Meany, Annie Oakley, George Bernard Shaw, Napoleon, Jacqueline Onassis, Henry Ford, Francis Scott Key, Andy Warhol, Mae West, Orville Wright

VIRGO: Ingrid Bergman, Warren Burger, Maurice Chevalier, Agatha Christie, Sean Connery, Lafayette, Peter Falk, Greta Garbo, Althea Gibson, Arthur Godfrey, Goethe, Buddy Hackett, Michael Jackson, Lyndon Johnson, D.H. Lawrence, Sophia Loren, Grandma Moses, Arnold Palmer, Queen Elizabeth I, Walter Reuther, Peter Sellers, Lily Tomlin, George Wallace

LIBRA: Brigitte Bardot, Art Buchwald, Truman Capote, Dwight D. Eisenhower, William Faulkner, F. Scott Fitzgerald, Gandhi, George Gershwin, Micky Mantle, Helen Hayes, Vladimir Horowitz, Doris Lessing, Martina Navratalova, Eugene O'Neill, Luciano Pavarotti, Emily Post, Eleanor Roosevelt, Bruce Springsteen, Margaret Thatcher, Gore Vidal, Barbara Walters, Oscar Wilde

SCORPIO: Vivien Leigh, Richard Burton, Art Carney, Johnny Carson, Billy Graham, Grace Kelly, Walter Cronkite, Marie Curie, Charles de Gaulle, Linda Evans, Indira Gandhi, Theodore Roosevelt, Rock Hudson, Katherine Hepburn, Robert F. Kennedy, Billie Jean King, Martin Luther, Georgia O'Keeffe, Pablo Picasso, Jonas Salk, Alan Shepard, Robert Louis Stevenson

SAGITTARIUS: Jane Austen, Louisa May Alcott, Woody Allen, Beethoven, Willy Brandt, Mary Martin, William F. Buckley, Maria Callas, Winston Churchill, Noel Coward, Emily Dickinson, Walt Disney, Benjamin Disraeli, James Doolittle, Kirk Douglas, Chet Huntley, Jane Fonda, Chris Evert Lloyd, Margaret Mead, Charles Schulz, John Milton, Frank Sinatra, Steven Spielberg

CAPRICORN: Muhammad Ali, Isaac Asimov, Pablo Casals, Dizzy Dean, Marlene Dietrich, James Farmer, Ava Gardner, Barry Goldwater, Cary Grant, J. Edgar Hoover, Howard Hughes, Joan of Arc, Gypsy Rose Lee, Martin Luther King, Jr., Rudyard Kipling, Mao Tse-tung, Richard Nixon, Gamal Nasser, Louis Pasteur, Albert Schweitzer, Stalin, Benjamin Franklin, Elvis Presley

AQUARIUS: Marian Anderson, Susan B. Anthony, Jack Benny, John Barrymore, Mikhail Baryshnikov, Charles Darwin, Charles Dickens, Thomas Edison, Clark Gable, Jascha Heifetz, Abraham Lincoln, Yehudi Menuhin, Mozart, Jack Nicklaus, Ronald Reagan, Jackie Robinson, Norman Rockwell, Franklin D. Roosevelt, Gertrude Stein, Charles Lindbergh, Margaret Truman

PISCES: Edward Albee, Harry Belafonte, Alexander Graham Bell, Chopin, Adelle Davis, Albert Einstein, Golda Meir, Jackie Gleason, Winslow Homer, Edward M. Kennedy, Victor Hugo, Mike Mansfield, Michelangelo, Edna St. Vincent Millay, Liza Minelli, John Steinbeck, Linus Pauling, Ravel, Renoir, Diana Ross, William Shirer, Elizabeth Taylor, George Washington

The Signs and Their Key Words

		POSITIVE	NEGATIVE
ARIES	self	courage, initiative, pioneer instinct	brash rudeness, selfish impetuosity
TAURUS	money	endurance, loyalty, wealth	obstinacy, gluttony
GEMINI	mind	versatility	capriciousness, unreliability
CANCER	family	sympathy, homing instinct	clannishness, childishness
LEO	children	love, authority, integrity	egotism, force
VIRGO	work	purity, industry, analysis	faultfinding, cynicism
LIBRA	marriage	harmony, justice	vacillation, superficiality
SCORPIO	sex	survival, regeneration	vengeance, discord
SAGITTARIUS	travel	optimism, higher learning	lawlessness
CAPRICORN	career	depth	narrowness, gloom
AQUARIUS	friends	human fellowship, genius	perverse unpredictability
PISCES	confine-ment	spiritual love, universality	diffusion, escapism

The Elements and Qualities of The Signs

Every sign has both an *element* and a *quality* associated with it. The element indicates the basic makeup of the sign, and the quality describes the kind of activity associated with each.

Element	Sign	Quality	Sign
FIRE	ARIES	CARDINAL	ARIES
	LEO		LIBRA
	SAGITTARIUS		CANCER
			CAPRICORN
EARTH	TAURUS		
	VIRGO		
	CAPRICORN	FIXED	TAURUS
			LEO
			SCORPIO
AIR	GEMINI		AQUARIUS
	LIBRA		
	AQUARIUS		
		MUTABLE	GEMINI
WATER	CANCER		VIRGO
	SCORPIO		SAGITTARIUS
	PISCES		PISCES

Signs can be grouped together according to their element and quality. Signs of the same element share many basic traits in common. They tend to form stable configurations and ultimately harmonious relationships. Signs of the same quality are often less harmonious, but they share many dynamic potentials for growth as well as profound fulfillment.

Further discussion of each of these sign groupings is provided on the following pages.

The Fire Signs

SAGITTARIUS

ARIES

LEO

This is the fire group. On the whole these are emotional, volatile types, quick to anger, quick to forgive. They are adventurous, powerful people and act as a source of inspiration for everyone. They spark into action with immediate exuberant impulses. They are intelligent, self-involved, creative, and idealistic. They all share a certain vibrancy and glow that outwardly reflects an inner flame and passion for living.

The Earth Signs

CAPRICORN

TAURUS   VIRGO

This is the earth group. They are in constant touch with the material world and tend to be conservative. Although they are all capable of spartan self-discipline, they are earthy, sensual people who are stimulated by the tangible, elegant, and luxurious. The thread of their lives is always practical, but they do fantasize and are often attracted to dark, mysterious, emotional people. They are like great cliffs overhanging the sea, forever married to the ocean but always resisting erosion from the dark, emotional forces that thunder at their feet.

The Air Signs

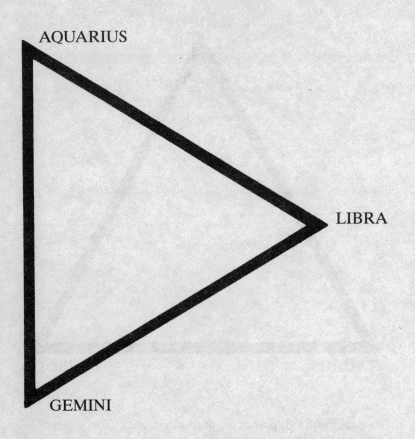

This is the air group. They are light, mental creatures desirous of contact, communication, and relationship. They are involved with people and the forming of ties on many levels. Original thinkers, they are the bearers of human news. Their language is their sense of word, color, style, and beauty. They provide an atmosphere suitable and pleasant for living. They add change and versatility to the scene, and it is through them that we can explore new territory of human intelligence and experience.

The Water Signs

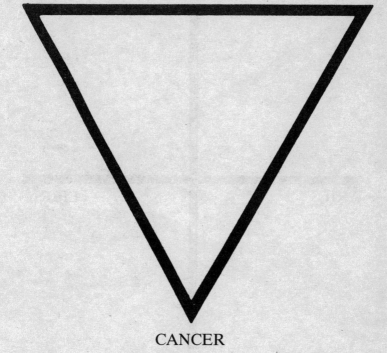

PISCES

SCORPIO

CANCER

This is the water group. Through the water people, we are all joined together on emotional, nonverbal levels. They are silent, mysterious types whose magic hypnotizes even the most determined realist. They have uncanny perceptions about people and are as rich as the oceans when it comes to feeling, emotion, or imagination. They are sensitive, mystical creatures with memories that go back beyond time. Through water, life is sustained. These people have the potential for the depths of darkness or the heights of mysticism and art.

The Cardinal Signs

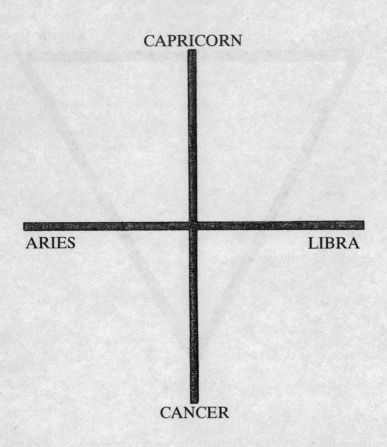

Put together, this is a clear-cut picture of dynamism, activity, tremendous stress, and remarkable achievement. These people know the meaning of great change since their lives are often characterized by significant crises and major successes. This combination is like a simultaneous storm of summer, fall, winter, and spring. The danger is chaotic diffusion of energy; the potential is irrepressible growth and victory.

The Fixed Signs

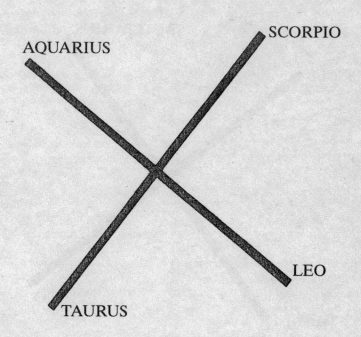

Fixed signs are always establishing themselves in a given place or area of experience. Like explorers who arrive and plant a flag, these people claim a position from which they do not enjoy being deposed. They are staunch, stalwart, upright, trusty, honorable people, although their obstinacy is well-known. Their contribution is fixity, and they are the angels who support our visible world.

The Mutable Signs

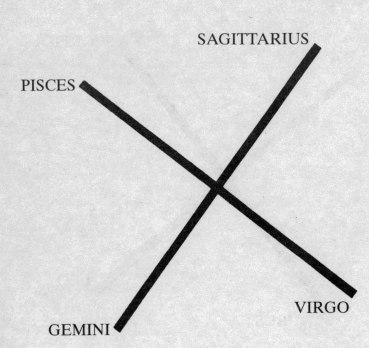

Mutable people are versatile, sensitive, intelligent, nervous, and deeply curious about life. They are the translators of all energy. They often carry out or complete tasks initiated by others. Combinations of these signs have highly developed minds; they are imaginative and jumpy and think and talk a lot. At worst their lives are a Tower of Babel. At best they are adaptable and ready creatures who can assimilate one kind of experience and enjoy it while anticipating coming changes.

THE PLANETS
OF THE SOLAR SYSTEM

This section describes the planets of the solar system. In astrology, both the Sun and the Moon are considered to be planets. Because of the Moon's influence in our day-to-day lives, the Moon is described in a separate section following this one.

The Planets and the Signs They Rule

The signs of the Zodiac are linked to the planets in the following way. Each sign is governed or ruled by one or more planets. No matter where the planets are located in the sky at any given moment, they still rule their respective signs, and when they travel through the signs they rule, they have special dignity and their effects are stronger.

Following is a list of the planets and the signs they rule. After looking at the list, read the definitions of the planets and see if you can determine how the planet ruling *your* Sun sign has affected your life.

SIGNS	RULING PLANETS
Aries	Mars, Pluto
Taurus	Venus
Gemini	Mercury
Cancer	Moon
Leo	Sun
Virgo	Mercury
Libra	Venus
Scorpio	Mars, Pluto
Sagittarius	Jupiter
Capricorn	Saturn
Aquarius	Saturn, Uranus
Pisces	Jupiter, Neptune

Characteristics of the Planets

The following pages give the meaning and characteristics of the planets of the solar system. They all travel around the Sun at different speeds and different distances. Taken with the Sun, they all distribute individual intelligence and ability throughout the entire chart.

The planets modify the influence of the Sun in a chart according to their own particular natures, strengths, and positions. Their positions must be calculated for each year and day, and their function and expression in a horoscope will change as they move from one area of the Zodiac to another.

We start with a description of the sun.

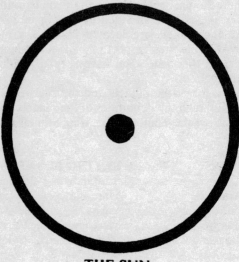

THE SUN

SUN

This is the center of existence. Around this flaming sphere all the planets revolve in endless orbits. Our star is constantly sending out its beams of light and energy without which no life on Earth would be possible. In astrology it symbolizes everything we are trying to become, the center around which all of our activity in life will always revolve. It is the symbol of our basic nature and describes the natural and constant thread that runs through everything that we do from birth to death on this planet.

To early astrologers, the Sun seemed to be another planet because it crossed the heavens every day, just like the rest of the bodies in the sky.

It is the only star near enough to be seen well—it is, in fact, a dwarf star. Approximately 860,000 miles in diameter, it is about ten times as wide as the giant planet Jupiter. The next nearest star is nearly 300,000 times as far away, and if the Sun were located as far away as most of the bright stars, it would be too faint to be seen without a telescope.

Everything in the horoscope ultimately revolves around this singular body. Although other forces may be prominent in the charts of some individuals, still the Sun is the total nucleus of being and symbolizes the complete potential of every human being alive. It is vitality and the life force. Your whole essence comes from the position of the Sun.

You are always trying to express the Sun according to its position by house and sign. Possibility for all development is found in the Sun, and it marks the fundamental character of your personal radiations all around you.

It is the symbol of strength, vigor, wisdom, dignity, ardor, and generosity, and the ability for a person to function as a mature individual. It is also a creative force in society. It is consciousness of the gift of life.

The underdeveloped solar nature is arrogant, pushy, undependable, and proud, and is constantly using force.

MERCURY

Mercury is the planet closest to the Sun. It races around our star, gathering information and translating it to the rest of the system. Mercury represents your capacity to understand the desires of your own will and to translate those desires into action.

In other words it is the planet of mind and the power of communication. Through Mercury we develop an ability to think, write, speak, and observe—to become aware of the world around us. It colors our attitudes and vision of the world, as well as our capacity to communicate our inner responses to the outside world. Some people who have serious disabilities in their power of verbal communication have often wrongly been described as people lacking intelligence.

Although this planet (and its position in the horoscope) indicates your power to communicate your thoughts and perceptions to the world, intelligence is something deeper. Intelligence is distributed throughout all the planets. It is the relationship of the planets to each other that truly describes what we call intelligence. Mercury rules speaking, language, mathematics, draft and design, students, messengers, young people, offices, teachers, and any pursuits where the mind of man has wings.

VENUS

Venus is beauty. It symbolizes the harmony and radiance of a rare and elusive quality: beauty itself. It is refinement and delicacy, softness and charm. In astrology it indicates grace, balance, and the aesthetic sense. Where Venus is we see beauty, a gentle drawing in of energy and the need for satisfaction and completion. It is a special touch that finishes off rough edges. It is sensitivity, and affection, and it is always the place for that other elusive phenomenon: love. Venus describes our sense of what is beautiful and loving. Poorly developed, it is vulgar, tasteless, and self-indulgent. But its ideal is the flame of spiritual love—Aphrodite, goddess of love, and the sweetness and power of personal beauty.

MARS

Mars is raw, crude energy. The planet next to Earth but outward from the Sun is a fiery red sphere that charges through the horoscope with force and fury. It represents the way you reach out for new adventure and new experience. It is energy and drive, initiative, courage, and daring. It is the power to start something and see it through. It can be thoughtless, cruel and wild, angry and hostile, causing cuts, burns, scalds, and wounds. It can stab its way through a chart, or it can be the symbol of healthy spirited adventure, well-channeled constructive power to begin and keep up the drive. If you have trouble starting things, if you lack the get-up-and-go to start the ball rolling, if you lack aggressiveness and self-confidence, chances are there's another planet influencing your Mars. Mars rules soldiers, butchers, surgeons, salesmen—any field that requires daring, bold skill, operational technique, or self-promotion.

JUPITER

This is the largest planet of the solar system. Scientists have recently learned that Jupiter reflects more light than it receives from the Sun. In a sense it is like a star itself. In astrology it rules good luck and good cheer, health, wealth, optimism, happiness, success, and joy. It is the symbol of opportunity and always opens the way for new possibilities in your life. It rules exuberance, enthusiasm, wisdom, knowledge, generosity, and all forms of expansion in general. It rules actors, statesmen, clerics, professional people, religion, publishing, and the distribution of many people over large areas.

Sometimes Jupiter makes you think you deserve everything, and you become sloppy, wasteful, careless and rude, prodigal and lawless, in the illusion that nothing can ever go wrong. Then there is the danger of overconfidence, exaggeration, undependability, and overindulgence.

Jupiter is the minimization of limitation and the emphasis on spirituality and potential. It is the thirst for knowledge and higher learning.

SATURN

Saturn circles our system in dark splendor with its mysterious rings, forcing us to be awakened to whatever we have neglected in the past. It will present real puzzles and problems to be solved, causing delays, obstacles, and hindrances. By doing so, Saturn stirs our own sensitivity to those areas where we are laziest.

Here we must patiently develop *method*, and only through painstaking effort can our ends be achieved. It brings order to a horoscope and imposes reason just where we are feeling least reasonable. By creating limitations and boundary, Saturn shows the consequences of being human and demands that we accept the changing cycles inevitable in human life. Saturn rules time, old age, and sobriety. It can bring depression, gloom, jealousy, and greed, or serious acceptance of responsibilities out of which success will develop. With Saturn there is nothing to do but face facts. It rules laborers, stones, granite, rocks, and crystals of all kinds.

THE OUTER PLANETS:
URANUS, NEPTUNE, PLUTO

Uranus, Neptune, Pluto are the outer planets. They liberate human beings from cultural conditioning, and in that sense are the law-breakers. In early times it was thought that Saturn was the last planet of the system—the outer limit beyond which we could never go. The discovery of the next three planets ushered in new phases of human history, revolution, and technology.

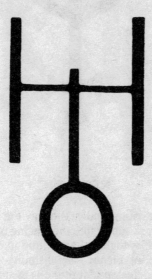

URANUS

Uranus rules unexpected change, upheaval, revolution. It is the symbol of total independence and asserts the freedom of an individual from all restriction and restraint. It is a breakthrough planet and indicates talent, originality, and genius in a horoscope. It usually causes last-minute reversals and changes of plan, unwanted separations, accidents, catastrophes, and eccentric behavior. It can add irrational rebelliousness and perverse bohemianism to a personality or a streak of unaffected brilliance in science and art. It rules technology, aviation, and all forms of electrical and electronic advancement. It governs great leaps forward and topsy-turvy situations, and *always* turns things around at the last minute. Its effects are difficult to predict, since it rules sudden last-minute decisions and events that come like lightning out of the blue.

NEPTUNE

Neptune dissolves existing reality the way the sea erodes the cliffs beside it. Its effects are subtle like the ringing of a buoy's bell in the fog. It suggests a reality higher than definition can usually describe. It awakens a sense of higher responsibility often causing guilt, worry, anxieties, or delusions. Neptune is associated with all forms of escape and can make things seem a certain way so convincingly that you are absolutely sure of something that eventually turns out to be quite different.

It is the planet of illusion and therefore governs the invisible realms that lie beyond our ordinary minds, beyond our simple factual ability to prove what is "real." Treachery, deceit, disillusionment, and disappointment are linked to Neptune. It describes a vague reality that promises eternity and the divine, yet in a manner so complex that we cannot really fathom it at all. At its worst Neptune is a cheap intoxicant; at its best it is the poetry, music, and inspiration of the higher planes of spiritual love. It has dominion over movies, photographs, and much of the arts.

PLUTO

Pluto lies at the outpost of our system and therefore rules finality in a horoscope—the final closing of chapters in your life, the passing of major milestones and points of development from which there is no return. It is a final wipeout, a closeout, an evacuation. It is a distant, subtle but powerful catalyst in all transformations that occur. It creates, destroys, then recreates. Sometimes Pluto starts its influence with a minor event or insignificant incident that might even go unnoticed. Slowly but surely, little by little, everything changes, until at last there has been a total transformation in the area of your life where Pluto has been operating. It rules mass thinking and the trends that society first rejects, then adopts, and finally outgrows.

Pluto rules the dead and the underworld—all the powerful forces of creation and destruction that go on all the time beneath, around, and above us. It can bring a lust for power with strong obsessions.

It is the planet that rules the metamorphosis of the caterpillar into a butterfly, for it symbolizes the capacity to change totally and forever a person's lifestyle, way of thought, and behavior.

THE MOON IN EACH SIGN

The Moon is the nearest planet to the Earth. It exerts more observable influence on us from day to day than any other planet. The effect is very personal, very intimate, and if we are not aware of how it works it can make us quite unstable in our ideas. And the annoying thing is that at these times we often see our own instability but can do nothing about it. A knowledge of what can be expected may help considerably. We can then be prepared to stand strong against the Moon's negative influences and use its positive ones to help us to get ahead. Who has not heard of going with the tide?

The Moon reflects, has no light of its own. It reflects the Sun—the life giver—in the form of vital movement. The Moon controls the tides, the blood rhythm, the movement of sap in trees and plants. Its nature is inconstancy and change so it signifies our moods, our superficial behavior—walking, talking, and especially thinking. Being a true reflector of other forces, the Moon is cold, watery like the surface of a still lake, brilliant and scintillating at times, but easily ruffled and disturbed by the winds of change.

The Moon takes about 27⅓ days to make a complete transit of the Zodiac. It spends just over 2¼ days in each sign. During that time it reflects the qualities, energies, and characteristics of the sign and, to a degree, the planet which rules the sign. When the Moon in its transit occupies a sign incompatible with our own birth sign, we can expect to feel a vague uneasiness, perhaps a touch of irritableness. We should not be discouraged nor let the feeling get us down, or, worse still, allow ourselves to take the discomfort out on others. Try to remember that the Moon has to change signs within 55 hours and, provided you are not physically ill, your mood will probably change with it. It is amazing how frequently depression lifts with the shift in the Moon's position. And, of course, when the Moon is transiting a sign compatible or sympathetic to yours, you will probably feel some sort of stimulation or just be plain happy to be alive.

In the horoscope, the Moon is such a powerful indicator that competent astrologers often use the sign it occupied at birth as the birth sign of the person. This is done particularly when the Sun is on the cusp, or edge, of two signs. Most experienced astrologers, however, coordinate both Sun and Moon signs by reading and confirming from one to the other and secure a far more accurate and personalized analysis.

For these reasons, the Moon tables which follow this section (see pages 86–92) are of great importance to the individual. They show the days and the exact times the Moon will enter each sign of the Zodiac for the year. Remember, you have to adjust the indicated times to local time. The corrections, already calculated for most of the main cities, are at the beginning of the tables. What follows now is a guide to the influences that will be reflected to the Earth by the Moon while it transits each of the twelve signs. The influence is at its peak about 26 hours after the Moon enters a sign. As you read the daily forecast, check the Moon sign for any given day and glance back at this guide.

MOON IN ARIES

This is a time for action, for reaching out beyond the usual self-imposed limitations and faint-hearted cautions. If you have plans in your head or on your desk, put them into practice. New ventures, applications, new jobs, new starts of any kind—all have a good chance of success. This is the period when original and dynamic impulses are being reflected onto Earth. Such energies are extremely vital and favor the pursuit of pleasure and adventure in practically every form. Sick people should feel an improvement. Those who are well will probably find themselves exuding confidence and optimism. People fond of physical exercise should find their bodies growing with tone and well-being. Boldness, strength, determination should characterize most of your activities with a readiness to face up to old challenges. Yesterday's problems may seem petty and exaggerated—so deal with them. Strike out alone. Self-reliance will attract others to you. This is a good time for making friends. Business and marriage partners are more likely to be impressed with the man and woman of action. Opposition will be overcome or thrown aside with much less effort than usual. CAUTION: Be dominant but not domineering.

MOON IN TAURUS

The spontaneous, action-packed person of yesterday gives way to the cautious, diligent, hardworking "thinker." In this period ideas will probably be concentrated on ways of improving finances. A great deal of time may be spent figuring out and going over schemes and plans. It is the right time to be careful with detail. People will find themselves working longer than usual at their desks. Or devoting more time to serious thought about the future. A strong desire to put order into business and financial arrangements may cause extra work. Loved ones may complain of being neglected and may fail to appreciate that your efforts are for their ultimate benefit. Your desire for system may extend to criticism of arrangements in the home and lead to minor upsets. Health may be affected through overwork. Try to secure a reasonable amount of rest and relaxation, although the tendency will be to "keep going" despite good advice. Work done conscientiously in this period should result in a solid contribution to your future security. CAUTION: Try not to be as serious with people as the work you are engaged in.

MOON IN GEMINI

The humdrum of routine and too much work should suddenly end. You are likely to find yourself in an expansive, quicksilver world of change and self-expression. Urges to write, to paint, to experience the freedom of some sort of artistic outpouring, may be very strong. Take full advantage of them. You may find yourself finishing something you began and put aside long ago. Or embarking on something new which could easily be prompted by a chance meeting, a new acquaintance, or even an advertisement. There may be a yearning for a change of scenery, the feeling to visit another country (not too far away), or at least to get away for a few days. This may result in short, quick journeys. Or, if you are planning a single visit, there may be some unexpected changes or detours on the way. Familiar activities will seem to give little satisfaction unless they contain a fresh element of excitement or expectation. The inclination will be toward untried pursuits, particularly those that allow you to express your inner nature. The accent is on new faces, new places. CAUTION: Do not be too quick to commit yourself emotionally.

MOON IN CANCER

Feelings of uncertainty and vague insecurity are likely to cause problems while the Moon is in Cancer. Thoughts may turn frequently to the warmth of the home and the comfort of loved ones. Nostalgic impulses could cause you to bring out old photographs and letters and reflect on the days when your life seemed to be much more rewarding and less demanding. The love and understanding of parents and family may be important, and, if it is not forthcoming, you may have to fight against bouts of self-pity. The cordiality of friends and the thought of good times with them that are sure to be repeated will help to restore you to a happier frame of mind. The desire to be alone may follow minor setbacks or rebuffs at this time, but solitude is unlikely to help. Better to get on the telephone or visit someone. This period often causes peculiar dreams and upsurges of imaginative thinking which can be helpful to authors of occult and mystical works. Preoccupation with the personal world of simple human needs can overshadow any material strivings. CAUTION: Do not spend too much time thinking—seek the company of loved ones or close friends.

MOON IN LEO

New horizons of exciting and rather extravagant activity open up. This is the time for exhilarating entertainment, glamorous and lavish parties, and expensive shopping sprees. Any merrymaking that relies upon your generosity as a host has every chance of being a spectacular success. You should find yourself right in the center of the fun, either as the life of the party or simply as a person whom happy people like to be with. Romance thrives in this heady atmosphere and friendships are likely to explode unexpectedly into serious attachments. Children and younger people should be attracted to you and you may find yourself organizing a picnic or a visit to a fun-fair, the movies, or the beach. The sunny company and vitality of youthful companions should help you to find some unsuspected energy. In career, you could find an opening for promotion or advancement. This should be the time to make a direct approach. The period favors those engaged in original research. CAUTION: Bask in popularity, not in flattery.

MOON IN VIRGO

Off comes the party cap and out steps the busy, practical worker. He wants to get his personal affairs straight, to rearrange them, if necessary, for more efficiency, so he will have more time for more work. He clears up his correspondence, pays outstanding bills, makes numerous phone calls. He is likely to make inquiries, or sign up for some new insurance and put money into gilt-edged investment. Thoughts probably revolve around the need for future security—to tie up loose ends and clear the decks. There may be a tendency to be "finicky," to interfere in the routine of others, particularly friends and family members. The motive may be a genuine desire to help with suggestions for updating or streamlining their affairs, but these will probably not be welcomed. Sympathy may be felt for less fortunate sections of the community and a flurry of some sort of voluntary service is likely. This may be accompanied by strong feelings of responsibility on several fronts and health may suffer from extra efforts made. CAUTION: Everyone may not want your help or advice.

MOON IN LIBRA

These are days of harmony and agreement and you should find yourself at peace with most others. Relationships tend to be smooth and sweet-flowing. Friends may become closer and bonds deepen in mutual understanding. Hopes will be shared. Progress by cooperation could be the secret of success in every sphere. In business, established partnerships may flourish and new ones get off to a good start. Acquaintances could discover similar interests that lead to congenial discussions and rewarding exchanges of some sort. Love, as a unifying force, reaches its optimum. Marriage partners should find accord. Those who wed at this time face the prospect of a happy union. Cooperation and tolerance are felt to be stronger than dissension and impatience. The argumentative are not quite so loud in their bellowings, nor as inflexible in their attitudes. In the home, there should be a greater recognition of the other point of view and a readiness to put the wishes of the group before selfish insistence. This is a favorable time to join an art group. CAUTION: Do not be too independent—let others help you if they want to.

MOON IN SCORPIO

Driving impulses to make money and to economize are likely to cause upsets all around. No area of expenditure is likely to be spared the ax, including the household budget. This is a time when the desire to cut down on extravagance can become near fanatical. Care must be exercised to try to keep the aim in reasonable perspective. Others may not feel the same urgent need to save and may retaliate. There is a danger that possessions of sentimental value will be sold to realize cash for investment. Buying and selling of stock for quick profit is also likely. The attention turns to organizing, reorganizing, tidying up at home and at work. Neglected jobs could suddenly be done with great bursts of energy. The desire for solitude may intervene. Self-searching thoughts could disturb. The sense of invisible and mysterious energies in play could cause some excitability. The reassurance of loves ones may help. CAUTION: Be kind to the people you love.

MOON IN SAGITTARIUS

These are days when you are likely to be stirred and elevated by discussions and reflections of a religious and philosophical nature. Ideas of faraway places may cause unusual response and excitement. A decision may be made to visit someone overseas, perhaps a person whose influence was important to your earlier character development. There could be a strong resolution to get away from present intellectual patterns, to learn new subjects, and to meet more interesting people. The superficial may be rejected in all its forms. An impatience with old ideas and unimaginative contacts could lead to a change of companions and interests. There may be an upsurge of religious feeling and metaphysical inquiry. Even a new insight into the significance of astrology and other occult studies is likely under the curious stimulus of the Moon in Sagittarius. Physically, you may express this need for fundamental change by spending more time outdoors: sports, gardening, long walks appeal. CAUTION: Try to channel any restlessness into worthwhile study.

MOON IN CAPRICORN
Life in these hours may seem to pivot around the importance of gaining prestige and honor in the career, as well as maintaining a spotless reputation. Ambitious urges may be excessive and could be accompanied by quite acquisitive drives for money. Effort should be directed along strictly ethical lines where there is no possibility of reproach or scandal. All endeavors are likely to be characterized by great earnestness, and an air of authority and purpose which should impress those who are looking for leadership or reliability. The desire to conform to accepted standards may extend to sharp criticism of family members. Frivolity and unconventional actions are unlikely to amuse while the Moon is in Capricorn. Moderation and seriousness are the orders of the day. Achievement and recognition in this period could come through community work or organizing for the benefit of some amateur group. CAUTION: Dignity and esteem are not always self-awarded.

MOON IN AQUARIUS
Moon in Aquarius is in the second last sign of the Zodiac where ideas can become disturbingly fine and subtle. The result is often a mental "no-man's land" where imagination cannot be trusted with the same certitude as other times. The dangers for the individual are the extremes of optimism and pessimism. Unless the imagination is held in check, situations are likely to be misread, and rosy conclusions drawn where they do not exist. Consequences for the unwary can be costly in career and business. Best to think twice and not speak or act until you think again. Pessimism can be a cruel self-inflicted penalty for delusion at this time. Between the two extremes are strange areas of self-deception which, for example, can make the selfish person think he is actually being generous. Eerie dreams which resemble the reality and even seem to continue into the waking state are also possible. CAUTION: Look for the fact and not just for the image in your mind.

MOON IN PISCES

Everything seems to come to the surface now. Memory may be crystal clear, throwing up long-forgotten information which could be valuable in the career or business. Flashes of clairvoyance and intuition are possible along with sudden realizations of one's own nature, which may be used for self-improvement. A talent, never before suspected, may be discovered. Qualities not evident before in friends and marriage partners are likely to be noticed. As this is a period in which the truth seems to emerge, the discovery of false characteristics is likely to lead to disenchantment or a shift in attachments. However, when qualities are accepted, it should lead to happiness and deeper feeling. Surprise solutions could bob up for old problems. There may be a public announcement of the solving of a crime or mystery. People with secrets may find someone has "guessed" correctly. The secrets of the soul or the inner self also tend to reveal themselves. Religious and philosophical groups may make some interesting discoveries. CAUTION: Not a time for activities that depend on secrecy.

NOTE: When you read your daily forecasts, use the Moon Sign Dates that are provided in the following section of Moon Tables. Then you may want to glance back here for the Moon's influence in a given sign.

MOON TABLES

CORRECTION FOR NEW YORK TIME, FIVE HOURS WEST OF GREENWICH

Atlanta, Boston, Detroit, Miami, Washington, Montreal,
  Ottawa, Quebec, Bogota, Havana, Lima, Santiago ... Same time
Chicago, New Orleans, Houston, Winnipeg, Churchill,
  Mexico City .... Deduct 1 hour
Albuquerque, Denver, Phoenix, El Paso, Edmonton,
  Helena .... Deduct 2 hours
Los Angeles, San Francisco, Reno, Portland,
  Seattle, Vancouver .... Deduct 3 hours
Honolulu, Anchorage, Fairbanks, Kodiak .... Deduct 5 hours
Nome, Samoa, Tonga, Midway .... Deduct 6 hours
Halifax, Bermuda, San Juan, Caracas, La Paz,
  Barbados .... Add 1 hour
St. John's, Brasilia, Rio de Janeiro, Sao Paulo,
  Buenos Aires, Montevideo .... Add 2 hours
Azores, Cape Verde Islands .... Add 3 hours
Canary Islands, Madeira, Reykjavik .... Add 4 hours
London, Paris, Amsterdam, Madrid, Lisbon,
  Gibraltar, Belfast, Raba .... Add 5 hours
Frankfurt, Rome, Oslo, Stockholm, Prague,
  Belgrade .... Add 6 hours
Bucharest, Beirut, Tel Aviv, Athens, Istanbul, Cairo,
  Alexandria, Cape Town, Johannesburg .... Add 7 hours
Moscow, Leningrad, Baghdad, Dhahran,
  Addis Ababa, Nairobi, Teheran, Zanzibar .... Add 8 hours
Bombay, Calcutta, Sri Lanka .... Add 10½
Hong Kong, Shanghai, Manila, Peking, Perth ...... Add 13 hours
Tokyo, Okinawa, Darwin, Pusan .... Add 14 hours
Sydney, Melbourne, Port Moresby, Guam .... Add 15 hours
Auckland, Wellington, Suva, Wake .... Add 17 hours

2006 MOON SIGN DATES—
NEW YORK TIME

JANUARY Day Moon Enters		FEBRUARY Day Moon Enters		MARCH Day Moon Enters	
1. Aquar.	7:15 am	1. Aries	5:57 pm	1. Aries	4:20 am
2. Aquar.		2. Aries		2. Aries	
3. Pisces	7:45 am	3. Taurus	8:32 pm	3. Taurus	5:23 am
4. Pisces		4. Taurus		4. Taurus	
5. Aries	9:45 am	5. Taurus		5. Gemini	9:39 am
6. Aries		6. Gemini	2:33 am	6. Gemini	
7. Taurus	2:10 pm	7. Gemini		7. Cancer	5:39 pm
8. Taurus		8. Cancer	11:34 am	8. Cancer	
9. Gemini	9:00 pm	9. Cancer		9. Cancer	
10. Gemini		10. Leo	10:45 pm	10. Leo	4:43 am
11. Gemini		11. Leo		11. Leo	
12. Cancer	5:51 am	12. Leo		12. Virgo	5:25 pm
13. Cancer		13. Virgo	11:14 am	13. Virgo	
14. Leo	4:32 pm	14. Virgo		14. Virgo	
15. Leo		15. Virgo		15. Libra	6:14 am
16. Leo		16. Libra	12:10 am	16. Libra	
17. Virgo	4:50 am	17. Libra		17. Scorp.	6:00 pm
18. Virgo		18. Scorp.	12:12 pm	18. Scorp.	
19. Libra	5:50 pm	19. Scorp.		19. Scorp.	
20. Libra		20. Sagitt.	9:39 pm	20. Sagitt.	3:44 am
21. Libra		21. Sagitt.		21. Sagitt.	
22. Scorp.	5:30 am	22. Sagitt.		22. Capric.	10:37 am
23. Scorp.		23. Capric.	3:17 am	23. Capric.	
24. Sagitt.	1:39 am	24. Capric.		24. Aquar.	2:22 pm
25. Sagitt.		25. Aquar.	5:16 am	25. Aquar.	
26. Capric.	5:32 pm	26. Aquar.		26. Pisces	3:34 pm
27. Capric.		27. Pisces	4:57 am	27. Pisces	
28. Aquar.	6:10 pm	28. Pisces		28. Aries	3:32 pm
29. Aquar.				29. Aries	
30. Pisces	5:33 pm			30. Taurus	4:02 pm
31. Pisces				31. Taurus	

Daylight saving time to be considered where applicable.

2006 MOON SIGN DATES—
NEW YORK TIME

APRIL		MAY		JUNE	
Day Moon Enters		**Day Moon Enters**		**Day Moon Enters**	
1. Gemini	6:50 pm	1. Cancer	10:18 am	1. Leo	
2. Gemini		2. Cancer		2. Virgo	3:18 pm
3. Gemini		3. Leo	7:19 pm	3. Virgo	
4. Cancer	1:16 am	4. Leo		4. Virgo	
5. Cancer		5. Leo		5. Libra	4:10 am
6. Leo	11:26 am	6. Virgo	7:21 am	6. Libra	
7. Leo		7. Virgo		7. Scorp.	3:42 pm
8. Leo		8. Libra	8:11 pm	8. Scorp.	
9. Virgo	12:00 am	9. Libra		9. Scorp.	
10. Virgo		10. Libra		10. Sagitt.	12:06 am
11. Libra	12:48 pm	11. Scorp.	7:26 am	11. Sagitt.	
12. Libra		12. Scorp.		12. Capric.	5:20 am
13. Libra		13. Sagitt.	3:57 pm	13. Capric.	
14. Scorp.	12:09 am	14. Sagitt.		14. Aquar.	8:33 am
15. Scorp.		15. Capric.	10:00 pm	15. Aquar.	
16. Sagitt.	9:21 am	16. Capric.		16. Pisces	11:06 am
17. Sagitt.		17. Capric.		17. Pisces	
18. Capric.	4:14 pm	18. Aquar.	2:20 am	18. Aries	1:55 pm
19. Capric.		19. Aquar.		19. Aries	
20. Aquar.	8:57 pm	20. Pisces	5:40 am	20. Taurus	5:24 pm
21. Aquar.		21. Pisces		21. Taurus	
22. Pisces	11:44 pm	22. Aries	8:25 am	22. Gemini	9:50 pm
23. Pisces		23. Aries		23. Gemini	
24. Pisces		24. Taurus	11:02 am	24. Gemini	
25. Aries	1:13 am	25. Taurus		25. Cancer	3:49 am
26. Aries		26. Gemini	2:20 pm	26. Cancer	
27. Taurus	2:28 am	27. Gemini		27. Leo	12:10 pm
28. Taurus		28. Cancer	7:35 pm	28. Leo	
29. Gemini	4:59 am	29. Cancer		29. Virgo	11:16 pm
30. Gemini		30. Cancer		30. Virgo	
		31. Leo	3:53 am		

Daylight saving time to be considered where applicable.

2006 MOON SIGN DATES—
NEW YORK TIME

JULY Day Moon Enters		AUGUST Day Moon Enters		SEPTEMBER Day Moon Enters	
1. Virgo		1. Scorp.	8:09 am	1. Sagitt.	
2. Libra	12:07 pm	2. Scorp.		2. Capric.	9:36 am
3. Libra		3. Sagitt.	6:14 pm	3. Capric.	
4. Libra		4. Sagitt.		4. Aquar.	1:16 pm
5. Scorp.	12:14 am	5. Sagitt.		5. Aquar.	
6. Scorp.		6. Capric.	12:21 am	6. Pisces	1:58 pm
7. Sagitt.	9:15 am	7. Capric.		7. Pisces	
8. Sagitt.		8. Aquar.	2:49 am	8. Aries	1:24 pm
9. Capric.	2:26 pm	9. Aquar.		9. Aries	
10. Capric.		10. Pisces	3:11 am	10. Taurus	1:31 pm
11. Aquar.	4:47 pm	11. Pisces		11. Taurus	
12. Aquar.		12. Aries	3:23 am	12. Gemini	4:00 pm
13. Pisces	6:01 pm	13. Aries		13. Gemini	
14. Pisces		14. Taurus	5:01 am	14. Cancer	9:55 pm
15. Aries	7:40 pm	15. Taurus		15. Cancer	
16. Aries		16. Gemini	9:08 am	16. Cancer	
17. Taurus	10:45 pm	17. Gemini		17. Leo	7:16 am
18. Taurus		18. Cancer	4:04 pm	18. Leo	
19. Taurus		19. Cancer		19. Virgo	7:08 pm
20. Gemini	3:39 am	20. Cancer		20. Virgo	
21. Gemini		21. Leo	1:34 am	21. Virgo	
22. Cancer	10:29 am	22. Leo		22. Libra	8:07 am
23. Cancer		23. Virgo	1:09 pm	23. Libra	
24. Leo	7:26 pm	24. Virgo		24. Scorp.	8:55 pm
25. Leo		25. Virgo		25. Scorp.	
26. Leo		26. Libra	2:02 am	26. Scorp.	
27. Virgo	6:37 am	27. Libra		27. Sagitt.	8:17 am
28. Virgo		28. Scorp.	2:57 pm	28. Sagitt.	
29. Libra	7:28 pm	29. Scorp.		29. Capric.	5:02 pm
30. Libra		30. Scorp.		30. Capric.	
31. Libra		31. Sagitt.	2:01 am		

Daylight saving time to be considered where applicable.

2006 MOON SIGN DATES—
NEW YORK TIME

OCTOBER		NOVEMBER		DECEMBER	
Day Moon Enters		**Day Moon Enters**		**Day Moon Enters**	
1. Aquar.	10:25 pm	1. Pisces		1. Taurus	8:27 pm
2. Aquar.		2. Aries	10:47 am	2. Taurus	
3. Aquar.		3. Aries		3. Gemini	10:06 pm
4. Pises	12:34 am	4. Taurus	11:06 am	4. Gemini	
5. Pisces		5. Taurus		5. Gemini	
6. Aries	12:33 am	6. Gemini	11:47 am	6. Cancer	1:02 am
7. Aries		7. Gemini		7. Cancer	
8. Taurus	12:05 am	8. Cancer	2:47 pm	8. Leo	6:53 am
9. Taurus		9. Cancer		9. Leo	
10. Gemini	1:07 am	10. Leo	9:35 pm	10. Virgo	4:32 pm
11. Gemini		11. Leo		11. Virgo	
12. Cancer	5:22 am	12. Leo		12. Virgo	
13. Cancer		13. Virgo	8:20 am	13. Libra	5:02 am
14. Leo	1:39 pm	14. Virgo		14. Libra	
15. Leo		15. Libra	9:15 pm	15. Scorp.	5:44 pm
16. Leo		16. Libra		16. Scorp.	
17. Virgo	1:17 am	17. Libra		17. Scorp.	
18. Virgo		18. Scorp.	9:48 am	18. Sagitt.	4:11 am
19. Libra	2:20 pm	19. Scorp.		19. Sagitt.	
20. Libra		20. Sagitt.	8:16 pm	20. Capric.	11:40 am
21. Libra		21. Sagitt.		21. Capric.	
22. Scorp.	2:25 am	22. Sagitt.		22. Aquar.	4:50 pm
23. Scorp.		23. Capric.	4:26 am	23. Aquar.	
24. Sagitt.	1:54 pm	24. Capric.		24. Pisces	8:44 pm
25. Sagitt.		25. Aquar.	10:42 am	25. Pisces	
26. Capric.	10:48 pm	26. Aquar.		26. Pisces	
27. Capric		27. Pisces	3:22 pm	27. Aries	12:05 am
28. Capric.		28. Pisces		28. Aries	
29. Aquar.	5:18 am	29. Aries	6:31 pm	29. Taurus	3:09 am
30. Aquar.		30. Aries		30. Taurus	
31. Pisces	9:12 am			31. Gemini	6:17 am

Daylight saving time to be considered where applicable.

2006 PHASES OF THE MOON— NEW YORK TIME

New Moon	First Quarter	Full Moon	Last Quarter
Dec. 30 ('05)	Jan. 6	Jan. 14	Jan. 22
Jan. 29	Feb. 6	Feb. 13	Feb. 21
Feb. 27	March 6	March 14	March 22
March 29	April 5	April 13	April 20
April 27	May 5	May 13	May 20
May 27	June 3	June 11	June 18
June 25	July 3	July 10	July 17
July 25	August 2	August 9	August 15
August 23	August 31	Sept. 7	Sept. 14
Sept. 22	Sept. 30	Oct. 6	Oct. 13
Oct. 22	Oct. 29	Nov. 5	Nov. 12
Nov. 20	Nov. 28	Dec. 4	Dec. 12
Dec. 20	Dec. 27	Jan. 3 ('07)	Jan. 11 ('07)

Each phase of the Moon lasts approximately seven to eight days, during which the Moon's shape gradually changes as it comes out of one phase and goes into the next.

There will be a solar eclipse during the New Moon phase on March 29 and September 22.

There will be a lunar eclipse during the Full Moon phase on March 14 and September 7.

2006 FISHING GUIDE

	Good	Best
January	6–14–15–16–17–29	12–13–14
February	11–12–13–14–15–16–21	5–9–28
March	6–11–12–13–14–21–29	15–16–17
April	10–16–17	5–12–13–14–15–20–28
May	5–14–15–27	9–10–11–12–16–21
June	3–10–11–12–14–18	8–9–13–25
July	8–9–12–13–16–24	3–10–11–14
August	8–9–12–16–24	2–6–7–10–11
September	1–4–5–6–8–9–13	7–23–30
October	6–7–10–29	4–5–8–9–13–22
November	2–3–6–7–12	4–5–19–28
December	4–5–12–19–28	2–3–6–7

2006 PLANTING GUIDE

	Aboveground Crops	Root Crops
January	4–8–9–12–13–31	20–21–22–23–27–28
February	4–5–9–10–27–28	16–17–18–19–23–24
March	4–5–8–9–31	15–16–17–18–23–27–28
April	4–5–12–13–27–28	14–15–19–20–23–24
May	2–3–9–10–11–29–30	16–17–20–21–25
June	5–6–7–8–9–25–26	13–17–21–22
July	3–4–5–10–30–31	10–14–15–18–19–22–23
August	1–2–6–7–26–27–28–29–30	10–11–14–15–19–20
September	3–23–24–25–26–30	11–12–15–16
October	1–4–5–22–23–27–28	8–9–12–13–20
November	1–24–28–29	5–9–10–16–17–18
December	2–3–21–25–26–29–30	6–7–13–14–15–16

	Pruning	Weeds and Pests
January	23–24	15–16–17–18–25–26
February	19–20	14–15–21–22–25–26
March	18–19–27–28	21–25
April	15–23–24	17–21–22–25–26
May	21	14–15–18–19–23
June	16–17	15–19–20–23
July	13–14–22–23	12–13–16–17–20–21
August	10–11–19–20	12–13–16–17–21–22
September	15–16	9–13–14–17–18–19–20–21
October	12–13	7–10–11–15–16–17–18
November	9–10–19	7–11–12–13–14–15
December	6–7–16	4–5–8–9–10–11–12–18–19

MOON'S INFLUENCE OVER PLANTS

Centuries ago it was established that seeds planted when the Moon is in signs and phases called Fruitful will produce more growth than seeds planted when the Moon is in a Barren sign.

Fruitful Signs: Taurus, Cancer, Libra, Scorpio, Capricorn, Pisces
Barren Signs: Aries, Gemini, Leo, Virgo, Sagittarius, Aquarius
Dry Signs: Aries, Gemini, Sagittarius, Aquarius

Activity	Moon In
Mow lawn, trim plants	**Fruitful sign:** 1st & 2nd quarter
Plant flowers	**Fruitful sign:** 2nd quarter; best in Cancer and Libra
Prune	**Fruitful sign:** 3rd & 4th quarter
Destroy pests; spray	**Barren sign:** 4th quarter
Harvest potatoes, root crops	**Dry sign:** 3rd & 4th quarter; Taurus, Leo, and Aquarius

MOON'S INFLUENCE OVER YOUR HEALTH

ARIES   Head, brain, face, upper jaw
TAURUS   Throat, neck, lower jaw
GEMINI   Hands, arms, lungs, shoulders, nervous system
CANCER   Esophagus, stomach, breasts, womb, liver
LEO   Heart, spine
VIRGO   Intestines, liver
LIBRA   Kidneys, lower back
SCORPIO   Sex and eliminative organs
SAGITTARIUS   Hips, thighs, liver
CAPRICORN   Skin, bones, teeth, knees
AQUARIUS   Circulatory system, lower legs
PISCES   Feet, tone of being

Try to avoid work being done on that part of the body when the Moon is in the sign governing that part.

MOON'S INFLUENCE OVER DAILY AFFAIRS

The Moon makes a complete transit of the Zodiac every 27 days 7 hours and 43 minutes. In making this transit the Moon forms different aspects with the planets and consequently has favorable or unfavorable bearings on affairs and events for persons according to the sign of the Zodiac under which they were born.

When the Moon is in conjunction with the Sun it is called a New Moon; when the Moon and Sun are in opposition it is called a Full Moon. From New Moon to Full Moon, first and second quarter—which takes about two weeks—the Moon is increasing or waxing. From Full Moon to New Moon, third and fourth quarter, the Moon is decreasing or waning.

Activity	Moon In
Business: buying and selling new, requiring public support	Sagittarius, Aries, Gemini, Virgo 1st and 2nd quarter
meant to be kept quiet	3rd and 4th quarter
Investigation	3rd and 4th quarter
Signing documents	1st & 2nd quarter, Cancer, Scorpio, Pisces
Advertising	2nd quarter, Sagittarius
Journeys and trips	1st & 2nd quarter, Gemini, Virgo
Renting offices, etc.	Taurus, Leo, Scorpio, Aquarius
Painting of house/apartment	3rd & 4th quarter, Taurus, Scorpio, Aquarius
Decorating	Gemini, Libra, Aquarius
Buying clothes and accessories	Taurus, Virgo
Beauty salon or barber shop visit	1st & 2nd quarter, Taurus, Leo, Libra, Scorpio, Aquarius
Weddings	1st & 2nd quarter

Taurus

TAURUS

Character Analysis

Of all the signs of the Zodiac, Taurus is perhaps the most diligent and determined. Taurus are hard workers and stick with something once it's begun. They are thorough people and are careful to avoid making mistakes. Patient, the Bull knows how to bide his time. If something doesn't work out as scheduled, he or she will wait until the appropriate moment comes along, then forge ahead.

The person born under this sign is far from lazy. He will work hard to achieve whatever it is he desires. He is so determined that others often think of him as being unreasonably stubborn. He'll stick to a point he believes is right—nothing can force him to give up his chosen path once his mind is made up.

Taurus takes his time in whatever he does. He wants to make sure everything is done right. At times this may exasperate people who are quick about things. Still and all, a job done by a Taurus is generally a job well done. Careful, steady, and reliable, Taurus is just the opposite of high-strung. This person can take a lot upon himself. Sometimes his burdens or worries are of such proportions that others would find them impossible to carry, but somehow Taurus manages in his silent way.

Taurus may be even-tempered, but he puts up with nonsense from no one. Others had better not take advantage of his balanced disposition. If they do, they are apt to rue the day.

The Taurus man or woman plans well before taking any one line of action. He believes in being well-prepared before embarking on any one project. Others may see him as a sort of slowpoke, but he is not being slow—just sure. He is not the sort of person who would act on a whim or fancy. He wants to be certain of the ground he is standing on.

Material things make him feel comfortable and successful. Some have a definite love of luxury and the like. This may be the result of a slight feeling of inferiority. Material goods make him feel that he is doing well and that he is just as good as the next person.

Taurus is someone who can be trusted at all times. Once he has declared himself a friend, he remains so. He is loyal and considerate of others. In his circle of friends he is quite apt to be one of the successful people. Taurus admires success; he looks up to people who have made something of themselves.

On the whole, Taurus is a down-to-earth person. He is not pretentious or lofty, but direct and earnest. Things that are a bit abstract or far-fetched may not win his immediate approval. He believes in being practical. When he makes a decision, it is generally one with a lot of thought behind it.

Health

People born under this second sign of the Zodiac generally are quite fit physically. They are often gifted with healthy constitutions and can endure more than others in some circumstances. Taurus is often vigorous and strong. At times his strength may astonish others. He can put up with more pressure than most. Pain or the threat of it generally does not frighten him.

He can be proud of his good health. Even when ill, he would rather not give in to it or admit it. But when a disability becomes such that it cannot be ignored, Taurus becomes sad and depressed. For him it is a kind of insult to be ill. When he is laid up with an illness, it generally takes awhile to recover. Although his constitution is strong, when struck down by a disease, his powers for recuperation are not very great. Getting better is a slow and gradual process for the average Taurus.

Males born under this sign are often broad and stocky. They may be wide-shouldered and powerfully built. They are seldom short on muscle. As they age, they sometimes become fat.

Females born under the sign of Taurus are often attractive and charming. They are fond of pretty things and like to see to it that they look fashionable. Although they are often beautiful when young, as they grow older some of them tend to put on a little extra weight. They often have unusually attractive eyes, and their complexions are clear and healthy.

The weakest part of the Taurus body is the throat. If ever he is sick, this part of his body is often affected. Sore throats and the like are often common Taurus complaints.

Occupation

The Taurus man or woman can do a good job—no matter what the work is. They have the ability to be thorough and accurate. They never shirk their duties. They may be looked upon as being slow, especially when they begin a task; but after they are thoroughly familiar with what they are doing, they work at an even and reasonable pace. They are methodical, which counts a good deal. They are good at detail. They seldom overlook anything.

Not all Taurus are slow. Some are quick and brilliant. In many cases, it depends on the circumstances they have to deal with. In any event, they never forget anything once they have learned it.

They can be quite shrewd in business matters and are often highly valued in their place of business.

The average Taurus has plenty of get-up-and-go. He is never lazy or neglectful in his work. He enjoys working and does what he can to bring about favorable results.

In business, he will generally shy away from anything that involves what seems to be an unnecessary risk. He likes the path he trods to be a sure one, one that has been well laid out. When he has to make his own way, he sees to it that he is certain of every step of the route. This may often exasperate colleagues. His plodding ways generally pay off in the end, however. In spite of this, and because of his distrust of change, he often misses out on a good business deal. His work may become humdrum and dull due to his dislike of change in routine or schedule.

The Taurus man or woman does well in a position of authority. He is a good manager and knows how to keep everything in order. Discipline is no problem. He knows what scheme to follow and sticks to it. Because his own powers of self-control are so well developed, he has no problem in managing others. Taurus is not frightened by opposition. He knows how to forge ahead with his plans and will not stop until everything comes out according to plan.

Taurus is a stickler for detail. Every little point has to be thoroughly covered before he is satisfied. Because he is a patient person, he knows how to bide his time; he is the kind of person who will wait for the right opportunity to come along, if need be. This sort of person excels in a position where he can take his time in doing things. Any job that requires thoroughness and painstaking effort is one in which a Taurus is likely to do well. They make good managers and can handle certain technical and industrial jobs. Some Taurus are gifted with the ability to draw or design and do well in the world of architecture. Many of them are quite artistic, and it depends on the proper circumstances to bring this out. In most cases, however, Taurus is content with doing work that is sure and calculated. His creative ability may not have the proper chance to surface, and it is only through cultivation that he is able to make a broad use of it.

Although many people born under this sign work in the city, they prefer the peace and quiet of remote places to the hustle and bustle of the busy metropolis. Many of them do well in the area of agriculture. They have a way with growing things. A Taurus man or woman could easily become a successful dairy or poultry farmer. They find it easy to relate to things rural or rustic. Many of them are gifted with green thumbs.

When working with others, Taurus can be relied upon. His partner if possible should be similar in nature. The Bull may become annoyed if he works with someone who is always changing his mind or schedule. He doesn't care much for surprises or sudden changes. New ideas may not appeal to him at first; he has to have time to get used to them. Generally, he likes to think of something new as being a creation of his own. And by taking his time in approaching it, he comes to see it in that light. Taurus should be gently coaxed when working with others. He will give his consent to new ideas if his colleagues are subtle enough in their presentation.

Although the Taurus man or woman may not hold an important position in the place where he works, this does not disturb him. He doesn't mind working under others—especially if they are good and able leaders or managers. Taurus is a loyal worker. He can always be depended on to complete his tasks.

The Taurus man or woman understands the value of money and appreciates the things it can do. He may not be a millionaire, but he does know how to earn and save well enough so that he can acquire those material items he feels are important. Some people born under this sign can easily acquire a greedy streak if they don't watch out. So obsessed with material gain are some Taurus that they do not take time to relax and enjoy other things that life has to offer. Money-oriented, the ambitious Taurus sometimes turns into someone who is all work and no play. It is not surprising, then, that a great many bankers and financiers are born under this sign of the Zodiac.

The Taurus person is generally straightforward and well-meaning. If someone is in need, he will not hesitate to assist them financially. Taurus as children are sometimes stingy, but as they grow up and have enough money, they become reasonably free in their use of it. Still and all, the average Taurus will never invest all the money he has in anything. He always likes to keep a good portion of it aside for that inevitable rainy day. Although he may not be interested in taking many risks, the person born under this sign is often lucky. When he does take a chance and gambles, he quite often turns out the winner.

When a Taurus puts his best foot forward, he can achieve almost anything—even though it may take a little longer than it does with most. He has many hidden strengths and positive characteristics that help him to get ahead.

Home and Family

The Taurus person is a lover of home life. He likes to be surrounded by familiar and comfortable things. He is the kind of person who calls his home his castle. Generally, the home of a Taurus radiates comfort and hospitality. The Taurus woman knows how to decorate and arrange a house so that visitors feel immediately at home upon entering. The Taurus man is more often than not a good breadwinner. He sees to it that the members of his immediate family have everything they need.

The Taurus person usually likes the peace, quiet, and beauty of the country. If possible, he will see to it that he lives there—for part of the year if not for the whole year. The Taurus housewife has her work down to an efficient routine. She is interested in keeping everything neat and orderly. She is a very good hostess and knows how to make people feel at ease.

Being well-liked is important. Taurus likes to be surrounded by good friends. He admires important people and likes to include them in his social activities if possible. When entertaining, the Taurus woman usually outdoes herself in preparing all sorts of delicious items. She is skilled in the culinary arts. If ever she is poorly entertained or fed by others, she feels upset about it.

The Taurus man or woman usually has a tastefully furnished home. But what is more important to Taurus than beauty is comfort. His house must be a place where he can feel at home.

Taurus can be strict with their children and stand for no nonsense. They are interested in seeing that their children are brought up correctly. It is important for them that the youngsters reflect the good home they come from. Compliments from others about the behavior of their children make Taurus parents happy and proud. As the children grow older, however, and reach the teenage stage, some difficulties may occur in the beginning. The Taurus mother or father may resent the sudden change in the relationship as the child tries to assert his own individuality.

Social Relationships

Taurus generally does what he can to be popular among his friends. He is loyal and caring with people who are close to him. Because he is sincere and forthright, people generally seek him out as a friend. He makes a good talker as well as a listener. People in difficulties often turn to him for advice.

The Taurus person is genuinely interested in success, and there is nothing he admires more than someone who has achieved his goal. In making friends, it seems as though a person born under this sign gravitates toward people who have made a success of themselves or people on their way up. Influential people are admired by Taurus. Being surrounded by people who have met with some success in life makes the person born under this sign feel somewhat successful too.

The Taurus person is one who generally likes to keep his family matters to himself. He resents the meddling of friends—even close friends.

He is a person who sticks to his principles, and as a result he may make an enemy or two as he goes along.

Love and Marriage

In love matters, Taurus may go through a series of flings—many of them lighthearted—before settling down with the "right" person. By nature, Taurus is serious. In love matters, his feelings run deep; but he will take steps to guard himself against disappointment if he feels the affair won't be lasting. Taurus can be romantic. As with everything, once he has made up his mind about someone, nothing will stand in his way; he'll win the object of his affection if it's the last thing he does. Other suitors don't frighten him in the least.

Younger Taurus have nothing against light romances, but as they grow older they look for stability and deep affection in a love affair. Faithful in love as they are in most things, they look for partners who are apt to feel the way they do.

The Taurus in love does not generally attempt a coy approach. More likely than not he'll be direct in expressing his feelings. Once he has won the person he loves, the average Taurus is often possessive as well as protective.

Persons born under this sign generally do well in a marriage relationship. Matters at home go well as long as he is treated fairly by his mate. If conditions at home are not to his liking, he can be biting and mean.

There is no halfway in marriage as far as Taurus is concerned; it's a matter of two people giving themselves completely. As husbands and wives, they make ideal mates in many respects. They are usually quite considerate and generous. They like looking after the other members of their families. They are very family-oriented types, and nothing pleases them more than to be able to spend time at home with their loved ones.

Romance and the Taurus Woman

The Taurus woman has a charm and beauty that are hard to define. There is something elusive about her that attracts the opposite sex—something mysterious. Needless to say, she is much sought after. Men find her a delight. She is generally easygoing, relaxed, and good-natured. Men find her a joy to be with because they can be themselves. They don't have to try to impress her by being something they are not.

Although she may have a series of romances before actually settling down, every time she falls in love it is the real thing. She is not superficial or flighty in romance. When she gives her heart, she hopes it will be forever. When she does finally find the right person, she has no trouble in being true to him for the rest of her life.

In spite of her romantic nature, the female Taurus is quite practical, too, when it comes to love. She wants a man who can take care of her. Someone on whom she can depend. Someone who can provide her with the comforts she feels she needs. Some Taurus look for men who are well-to-do or who have already achieved success. To them, the practical side of marriage is just as important as the romantic. But most Taurus women are attracted to sincere, hardworking men who are good company and faithful in the relationship. A Taurus wife sticks by the man of her choice. She will do everything in her power to give her man the spiritual support he needs in order to advance in his career.

The Taurus woman likes pretty, gentle things. They enjoy making their home a comfortable and attractive one. They are quite artistic, and their taste in furnishings is often flawless. They know how to make a house comfortable and inviting. The Taurus woman is interested in material things. They make her feel secure and loved. Her house is apt to be filled with various objects that have an important meaning for her alone.

She is even-tempered and does what she can to get along with her mate or loved one, but once she is rubbed the wrong way she can become very angry and outspoken. The considerate mate or lover, however, has no problem with his Taurus woman. When treated well, she maintains her pleasant disposition, and is a delight to be with. She is a woman who is kind and warm when she is with the man of her choice. A man who is strong, protective, and financially sound is the sort of man who can help bring out the best in a woman born under this sign. She enjoys being flattered and being paid small attentions. It is not that she is excessively demanding, but just that she likes to have evidence from time to time that she is dearly loved.

The Taurus woman is very dependable and faithful. The man who wins her is indeed lucky. She wants a complete, comfortable, and correct home life. She seldom complains. She is quite flexible and can enjoy the good times or suffer the bad times with equal grace. Although she does enjoy luxury, if difficult times come about, she will not bicker but stick beside the man she loves. For her marriage is serious business. It is very unlikely that a Taurus woman would seek a divorce unless it was absolutely necessary.

A good homemaker, the Taurus woman knows how to keep the love of her man alive once she has won him. To her, love is a way of life. She will live entirely for the purpose of making her man happy. Men seldom have reason to be dissatisfied with a Taurus mate. Their affections never stray. Taurus women are determined people. When they put their minds to making a marriage or love relationship work, it seldom fails. They'll work as hard at romance as they will at anything else they want.

As a mother, the Taurus woman does what she can to see that her children are brought up correctly. She likes her children to be polite and obedient. She can be strict when she puts her mind to it. It is important to her that the youngsters learn the right things in life—even if they don't seem to want to. She is not at all permissive as a parent. Her children must respect her and do as she says. She won't stand for insolence or disobedience. She is well-meaning in her treatment of her children. Although the children may resent her strictness as they are growing up, in later life they see that she was justified in the way she handled them.

Romance and the Taurus Man

The Taurus man is as determined in love as he is in everything else. Once he sets his mind on winning a woman, he keeps at it until he has achieved his goal.

Women find him attractive. The Taurus man has a protective way about him. He knows how to make a woman feel wanted and taken care of. Taurus men are often fatherly, so women looking for protection and unwavering affection are attracted to them. Because of their he-man physiques, and sure ways, they have no trouble in romance. The opposite sex find their particular brand of charm difficult to resist.

He can be a very romantic person. The number of romances he is likely to have before actually settling down may be many. But he is faithful. He is true to the person he loves for as long as that relationship lasts. When he finds someone suited to him, he devotes the rest of his life to making her happy.

Married life agrees with the man born under the Taurus sign. They make good, dependable husbands and excellent, concerned fathers. The Taurus man is, of course, attracted to a woman who is good-looking and charming. But the qualities that most appeal to him often lie deeper than the skin. He is not interested in glamour alone. The girl of his choice must be a good homemaker, resourceful, and loving. Someone kind and considerate is apt to touch his heartstrings more than a pretty, one-dimensional face. He is looking for a woman to settle down with for a lifetime.

Marriage is important to him because it means stability and security, two things that are most important to Taurus. He is serious about marriage. He will do his best to provide for his family in a way he feels is correct and responsible. He is not one to shirk his family responsibilities. He likes to know that the woman he has married will stand beside him in all that he does.

The Taurus man believes that only he should be boss of the family. He may listen and even accept the advice of his spouse, but he is the one who runs things. He likes to feel that he is the king in his castle.

He likes his home to be comfortable and inviting. He has a liking for soft things; he likes to be babied a little by the woman he loves. He may be a strict parent, but he feels it is for the children's own good.

Woman—Man

TAURUS WOMAN
ARIES MAN

If you are attracted to a man born under the sign of the Ram, it is not certain as to how far the relationship would go. An Aries who has made his mark in the world and is somewhat steadfast in his outlook and attitudes could be quite a catch for you. On the other hand, Aries are swift-footed and quick-minded; their industrious manner may often fail to impress you, particularly when you become aware that their get-up-and-go sometimes leads nowhere. When it comes to a fine romance, you want a nice broad shoulder to lean on; you might find a relationship with someone who doesn't like to stay put for too long a time somewhat upsetting. Then, too, the Aries man is likely to misunderstand your interest in a slow-but-sure approach to most matters. He may see you as a stick-in-the-mud. What's more, he'll tell you so if you make him aware of it too often. Aries speak their minds, sometimes at the drop of a hat.

You may find a man born under this sign too demanding. He may give you the feeling that he wants you to be at all places at the same time. Even though he realizes that this is impossible, he may grumble at you for not at least having tried. You have a barrelful of patience at your disposal, and he may try every bit of it. Whereas you're a thorough person, he may overshoot something essential to a project or a relationship due to his eagerness to quickly achieve his end.

Being married to a Ram does not mean that you'll necessarily have a secure and safe life as far as finances are concerned. Aries are not rash with cash, but they lack the sound head that you have for putting something away for that inevitable rainy day. He'll do his best to see that you're well provided for though his efforts may leave something to be desired.

Although there will be a family squabble occasionally, you, with your steady nature and love of permanence, will learn to take it in your stride and make your marriage a success.

He'll love the children. Aries make wonderful fathers. Kids take to them like ducks to water, probably because of their quick minds and zestful behavior. Sometimes Aries fathers spoil their children, and here is where you'll have to step in. But don't be too strict with youngsters, or you'll drive most of their affection over to their father. When they reach the adolescent stage and become increasingly difficult to manage, it would perhaps be better for you to take a backseat and rely on your Aries husband's sympathy and understanding of this stage of life.

TAURUS WOMAN
TAURUS MAN

Although a man born under the same sign as you may seem like a "natural," better look twice before you leap. It can also be that he resembles you too closely to be compatible. You can be pretty set in your ways. When you encounter someone with just as much willpower or stubbornness, a royal fireworks display can be the result. When two Taurus lock horns it can be a very exhausting and totally frustrating get-together. But if the man of your dreams is one born under your sign and you're sure that no other will do, then proceed with extreme caution. Even though you know yourself well—or think you do—it does not necessarily mean that you will have an easy time understanding him. Since you both are practical, you should try a rational approach to your relationship. Put all the cards on the table, discuss the matter, and decide whether to cooperate, compromise, or call it quits.

If you both have your sights set on the same goals, a life together could be just what the doctor ordered. You both are affectionate and have a deep need for affection. Being loved, understood, and appreciated is vital for your mutual well-being.

Essentially, you are both looking for peace, security, and harmony in your lives. Working toward these goals together may be a good way of eventually attaining them, especially if you are honest and tolerant of each other.

If you should marry a Taurus man, you can be sure that the wolf will stay far away from the door. They are notoriously good providers and do everything to make their families comfortable and happy. He'll appreciate the way you make a home warm and inviting. Good food, all the comforts, and a few luxuries are essential ingredients. Although he may be a big lug of a guy, he'll be fond of gentle treatment and soft things. If you puff up his pillow and tuck him in at night, he won't complain. He'll eat it up and ask for more.

In friendships, you'll both be on even footing. You both tend to seek out friends who are successful or prominent. You admire people who work hard and achieve what they set out for. It helps to reassure your way of looking at things.

Taurus parents love their children very much and never sacrifice a show of affection even when scolding them. Since you both are excellent disciplinarians bringing up children, you should try to balance your tendency to be strict with a healthy amount of pampering and spoiling.

TAURUS WOMAN
GEMINI MAN

Gemini men, in spite of their charm and dash, may make even placid Taurus nervous. Some Twins do seem to lack the common sense you set so much store in. Their tendencies to start a half-dozen projects, then toss them up in the air out of boredom, may only exasperate you. You may be inclined to interpret their jumping around from here to there as childish if not downright psychotic. Gemini will never stay put. If you should take it into your head to try and make him sit still, he will resent it strongly.

On the other hand, he's likely to think you're a slowpoke and far too interested in security and material things. He's attracted to things that sparkle and bubble—not necessarily for a long time. You are likely to seem quite dull and uninteresting—with your practical head and feet firm on the ground—to the Gemini gadabout. If you're looking for a life of security and steadiness, then Mr. Right he ain't.

Chances are you'll be taken in by his charming ways and facile wit. Few women can resist Gemini charm. But after you've seen through his live-for-today, gossamer facade, you'll be most happy to turn your attention to someone more stable, even if he is not as interesting. You want a man who's there when you need him, someone on whom you can fully rely. Keeping track of Gemini's movements will make your head spin. Still, being a Taurus, you're a patient woman who can put up with almost anything if you think it will be worth the effort.

A successful and serious-minded Gemini could make you a very happy woman, perhaps, if you gave him half the chance. Although Gemini may impress you as being scatterbrained, he generally has a good head on his shoulders and can make efficient use of it when he wants. Some of them, who have learned the art of being steadfast, have risen to great professional heights.

Once you convince yourself that not all people born under the sign of the Twins are witless grasshoppers, you won't mind dating a few to support your newborn conviction. If you do walk down the aisle with one, accept the fact that married life with him will mean taking the bitter with the sweet.

Life with a Gemini man can be more fun than a barrel of clowns. You'll never experience a dull moment. You'd better see to it, though, that you get his paycheck every payday. If you leave the budgeting and bookkeeping to him you'll wind up behind the eight ball.

The Gemini father is apt to let children walk all over him, so you'd better take charge of them most of the time.

TAURUS WOMAN
CANCER MAN

The man born under the sign of Cancer may very well be the man after your own heart. Generally, Cancers are steady people. They share the Taurus interest in security and practicality. Despite their sometimes seemingly grouchy exterior, men born under the sign of the Crab are sensitive and kind. They are almost always hard workers and are very interested in making successes of themselves in business as well as socially. Their conservative outlook on many things often agrees with yours. He'll be a man on whom you can depend come rain or come shine. He'll never shirk his responsibilities as a provider and will always see to it that his mate and family never want.

Your patience will come in handy if you decide it's a Moon Child you want for a mate. He doesn't rush headlong into romance. He wants to be sure about love as you do. After the first couple of months of dating, don't jump to the conclusion that he's about to make his "great play."

Don't let his coolness fool you, though. Underneath his starched reserve is a very warm heart. He's just not interested in showing off as far as affection is concerned. For him, affection should only be displayed for two sets of eyes—yours and his. If you really want to see him warm up to you, you'd better send your roommate off, then bolt the doors and windows—to insure him that you won't be disturbed or embarrassed. He will never step out of line—he's too much of a gentleman for that, but it is likely that in such a sealed off atmosphere, he'll pull out an engagement ring (that belonged to his grandmother) and slip it on your finger.

Speaking of relatives, you'll have to get used to the fact that Cancers are overly fond of their mothers. When he says his mother's the most wonderful woman in the world, you'd better agree with him—that is, if you want to become his wife. It's a very touchy area for him. Say one wrong word about his mother or let him suspect that your interest in her is not real, and you'd better look for husband material elsewhere.

He'll always be a faithful husband; Cancers seldom tomcat around after they've taken that vow. They take their marriage responsibilities seriously. They see to it that everything in their homes runs smoothly. Bills will always be paid promptly. He'll take out all kinds of insurance policies on his family and property. He'll see to it that when retirement time rolls around, you'll both be very well off.

The Cancer father is patient, sensitive, and understanding, always protective of his children.

TAURUS WOMAN
LEO MAN

To know a man born under the sign of the Lion is not necessarily to love him—even though the temptation may be great. When he fixes most girls with his leonine double-whammy, it causes their hearts to throb and their minds to cloud over. But with you, the sensible Bull, it takes more than a regal strut and a roar to win you. There's no denying that Leo has a way with women, even practical Taurus women. Once he's swept you off your feet it may be hard to scramble upright again. Still, you're no pushover for romantic charm if you feel there may be no security behind it. He'll wine you and dine you in the fanciest places and shower you with diamonds if he can. Still, it would be wise to find out just how long the shower's going to last before consenting to be his wife.

Lions in love are hard to ignore, let alone brush off. Your "no" will have a way of nudging him on until he feels he has you completely under his spell. Once mesmerized by this romantic powerhouse, you will most likely find yourself doing things you never dreamed of. Leos can be like vain pussycats when involved in romance; they like to be cuddled and pampered and told how wonderful they are. This may not be your cup of tea, exactly. Still when you're romancing a Leo, you'll find yourself doing all kinds of things to make him purr. Although he may be sweet and gentle when trying to win you, he'll roar if he feels he's not getting the tender love and care he feels is his due. If you keep him well supplied with affection, you can be sure his eyes will never stray and his heart will never wander.

Leo men often turn out to be leaders. They're born to lord it over others in one way or another. If he is top banana in his firm, he'll most likely do everything he can to stay on top. And if he's not number one yet, then he's working on it, and will see to it that he's sitting on the throne before long.

You'll have more security than you can use if he's in a position to support you in the manner to which he feels you should be accustomed. He's apt to be too lavish, though. Although creditors may never darken your door, handle as much of the household bookkeeping as you can to put your mind at ease.

He's a natural-born friend-maker and entertainer. At a party, he will try to attract attention. Let him. If you allow him his occasional ego trips without quibbling, your married life will be one of warmth, wealth, and contentment.

When a little Lion or Lioness comes along, this Baby Leo will be brought up like one of the landed gentry if Papa Leo has anything to say about it.

TAURUS WOMAN
VIRGO MAN

Although the Virgo man may be a fussbudget at times, his seriousness and common sense may help you overlook his tendency to be too critical about minor things.

Virgo men are often quiet, respectable types who set great store in conservative behavior and levelheadedness. He'll admire you for your practicality and tenacity, perhaps even more than for your good looks. He's seldom bowled over by glamour. When he gets his courage up, he turns to a serious and reliable girl for romance. He'll be far from a Valentino while dating. In fact, you may wind up making all the passes. Once he does get his motor running, however, he can be a warm and wonderful fellow—to the right woman.

He's gradual about love. Chances are your romance with him will most likely start out looking like an ordinary friendship. Once he's sure you're no fly-by-night flirt and have no plans of taking him for a ride, he'll open up and rain sunshine over your heart.

Virgo men tend to marry late in life. He believes in holding out until he's met the right one. He may not have many names in his little black book; in fact, he may not even have a little black book. He's not interested in playing the field; leave that to men of the more flamboyant signs. The Virgo man is so particular that he may remain romantically inactive for a long period. His girl has to be perfect or it's no go. If you find yourself feeling weak-kneed for a Virgo, do your best to convince him that perfect is not so important when it comes to love. Help him to realize that he's missing out on a great deal by not considering the near-perfect or whatever you consider yourself to be. With your surefire perseverance, you'll make him listen to reason and he'll wind up reciprocating your romantic interests.

The Virgo man is no block of ice. He'll respond to what he feels to be the right feminine flame. Once your love life with a Virgo starts to bubble, don't give it a chance to fall flat. You may never have a second chance at romance with him.

If you should ever separate for a while, forget about patching up. He'd prefer to let the pieces lie scattered. Once married, though, he'll stay that way—even if it hurts. He's too conscientious to try to back out of a legal deal.

A Virgo man is as neat as a pin. He's thumbs down on sloppy housekeeping. An ashtray with even one used cigarette is apt to make him see red. Keep everything bright, neat, and shiny. Neatness goes for the children, too, at least by the time he gets home from work. But Daddy's little girl or boy will never lack for interesting playthings and learning tools.

TAURUS WOMAN
LIBRA MAN
Taurus may find Libra men too wrapped up in a dream world ever to come down to earth. Although he may be very careful about weighing both sides of an argument, that does not mean he will ever make a decision about anything. Decisions large and small are capable of giving Libra the willies. Don't ask him why. He probably doesn't know, himself. As a lover, you—who are interested in permanence and constancy in a relationship—may find him a puzzlement. One moment he comes on hard and strong with "I love you", the next moment he's left you like yesterday's mashed potatoes. It does no good to wonder "What did I do now?" You most likely haven't done anything. It's just one of Libra's ways.

On the other hand, you'll appreciate his admiration of harmony and beauty. If you're all decked out in your fanciest gown or have a tastefully arranged bouquet on the dining room table, you'll get a ready compliment—one that's really deserved. Libras don't pass out compliments to all and sundry. Generally, he's tactful enough to remain silent if he finds something disagreeable.

He may not be as ambitious as you would like your lover or husband to be. Where you do have drive and a great interest in getting ahead, Libra is often content to drift along. It is not that he is lazy or shiftless, it's just that he places greater value on aesthetic things than he does on the material. If he's in love with you, however, he'll do anything in his power to make you happy.

You may have to give him a good nudge now and again to get him to see the light. But he'll be happy wrapped up in his artistic dreams when you're not around to remind him that the rent is almost due.

If you love your Libra don't be too harsh or impatient with him. Try to understand him. Don't let him see the stubborn side of your nature too often, or you'll scare him away. Libras are peace-loving people and hate any kind of confrontation that may lead to an argument. Some of them will do almost anything to keep the peace—even tell little white lies, if necessary.

Although you possess gobs of patience, you may find yourself losing a little of it when trying to come to grips with your Libra. He may think you're too materialistic or mercenary, but he'll have the good grace not to tell you, for fear you'll perhaps chew his head off.

If you are deeply involved with a Libra, you'd better see to it that you help him manage his money. It's for his own good. Money will never interest him as much as it should, and he does have a tendency to be too generous when he shouldn't be.

Although Libra is a gentle and understanding father, he'll see to it that he never spoils his children.

TAURUS WOMAN
SCORPIO MAN

In the astrological scheme of things Scorpio is your zodiacal mate, but also your zodiacal opposite. If your heart is set on a Scorpio, you must figure him out to stay on his good side.

Many people have a hard time understanding a Scorpio man. Few, however, are able to resist his fiery charm. When angered, he can act like a nestful of wasps, and his sting is capable of leaving an almost permanent mark. Scorpios are straight to the point. They can be as sharp as a razor blade and just as cutting.

The Scorpio man is capable of being very blunt, and he can act like a brute or a cad. His touchiness may get on your nerves after a while. If it does, you'd better tiptoe away from the scene rather than chance an explosive confrontation.

It's quite likely that he will find your slow, deliberate manner a little irritating. He may misinterpret your patience for indifference. On the other hand, you're the kind of woman who can adapt to almost any sort of situation or circumstance if you put your mind and heart to it. Scorpio men are perceptive and intelligent. In some respects, they know how to use their brains more effectively and quicker than most. They believe in winning in everything; in business, they usually achieve the position they desire through drive and intellect.

Your interest in your home is not likely to be shared by him. No matter how comfortable you've managed to make the house, it will have very little influence on him as far as making him aware of his family responsibilities. He doesn't like to be tied down, generally. He would rather be out on the battlefield of life, belting away at what he feels is a just and worthy cause, than using leisure time at home.

He is passionate in his business affairs and political interests. He is just as passionate—if not more so—in romance. Most women are easily attracted to him—and the Taurus woman is no exception, that is, at least before she knows what she might be getting into. Those who allow their hearts to be stolen by a Scorpio man soon find that they're dealing with a cauldron of seething excitement.

Scorpio likes fathering a large family. He gets along well with children and is proud of them, but often he fails to live up to his responsibilities as a parent. When he takes his fatherly duties seriously, he is adept with youngsters. Whenever you have trouble understanding the kids, Scorpio's ability to see beneath the surface of things will be invaluable.

TAURUS WOMAN
SAGITTARIUS MAN

The Taurus woman who has her cap set for a Sagittarius man may have to apply large amounts of strategy before being able to make him pop that question. When visions of the altar enter the romance, Sagittarius are apt to get cold feet. Although you may become attracted to the Archer, because of his positive, winning manner, you may find the relationship loses some of its luster when it assumes a serious hue. Sagittarius are full of bounce—perhaps too much bounce to suit you. They are often hard to pin down and dislike staying put. If ever there's a chance to be on the move, he'll latch on to it post haste. They're quick people, both in mind and spirit. And sometimes because of their zip, they make mistakes. If you have good advice to offer, he'll tell you to keep it.

Sagittarius like to rely on their own wit whenever possible. His up-and-at-'em manner about most things is likely to drive you up the wall occasionally. Your cautious, deliberate manner is likely to make him impatient. And he can be resentful if you don't accompany him on his travel or sports ventures. He can't abide a slowpoke. At times, you'll find him too breezy and kiddish. However, don't mistake his youthful demeanor for premature senility. Sagittarius are equipped with first-class brain power and know well how to put it to use. They're often full of good ideas and drive. Generally they're very broad-minded people and are very much concerned with fair play and equality.

In romance, he's quite capable of loving you wholeheartedly while treating you like a good pal. His hail-fellow well-met manner in the arena of love is likely to scare a dainty damsel off. However, a woman who knows that his heart is in the right place won't mind his bluff, rambunctious style.

He's not much of a homebody. He's got ants in his pants and enjoys being on the move. Humdrum routine, especially at home, bores him to distraction. At the drop of a hat he may ask you to whip off your apron and dine out for a change instead. He's fond of coming up with instant surprises. He'll love to keep you guessing. His friendly, candid nature gains him many friends.

When it comes to children, you may find that you've been left holding the bag. Sagittarius feel helpless around little shavers. When children become older, he will develop a genuine interest in them.

TAURUS WOMAN
CAPRICORN MAN

A Taurus woman is often capable of bringing out the best in a Capricorn man. While other women are puzzled by his silent and slow ways, Taurus, with her patience and understanding, can lend him the confidence he perhaps needs in order to come out from behind the rock.

Quite often, the Capricorn man is not the romantic kind of lover that attracts most women. Still, behind his reserve and calm, he's a pretty warm guy. He is capable of giving his heart completely once he has found the right girl. The Taurus woman who is deliberate by nature and who believes in taking time to be sure will find her kind of man in a Capricorn. He is slow and deliberate about almost everything—even romance. He doesn't believe in flirting and would never let his heart be led on a merry chase. If you win his trust, he'll give you his heart on a platter. Quite often, it is the woman who has to take the lead when romance is in the air. As long as he knows you're making the advances in earnest he won't mind. In fact, he'll probably be grateful.

Don't think that he's all cold fish; he isn't. Although some Goats have no difficulty in expressing passion, when it comes to displaying affection, they're at sea. But with an understanding and patient Bull, he should have no trouble in learning to express himself, especially if you let him know how important affection is to you, and for the good of your relationship.

The Capricorn man is very interested in getting ahead. He's ambitious and usually knows how to apply himself well to whatever task he undertakes. He's far from a spendthrift and tends to manage his money with extreme care. But a Taurus woman with a knack for putting away money for that rainy day should have no trouble in understanding this.

The Capricorn man thinks in terms of future security. He wants to make sure that he and his wife have something to fall back on when they reach retirement age.

He'll want you to handle the household efficiently, but that's no problem for most Taurus. If he should check up on you from time to time about the price of this and the cost of that, don't let it irritate you. Once he is sure you can handle this area to his liking, he'll leave it all up to you.

Although he may be a hard man to catch when it comes to marriage, once he's made that serious step, he's quite likely to become possessive. Capricorns need to know that they have the support of their women in whatever they do, every step of the way. Your Capricorn man, because he's waited so long for for the right mate, may be considerably older than you.

Capricorn fathers never neglect their children and instinctively know what is good for them.

TAURUS WOMAN
AQUARIUS MAN

The Aquarius man in your life is perhaps the most broad-minded you have ever met. Still, you may think he is the most impractical. He's more of a dreamer than a doer. If you don't mind putting up with a man whose heart and mind are as wide as the sky but his head is almost always up in the clouds, then start dating that Aquarius man who somehow has captured your fancy. Maybe you, with your Taurus good sense, can bring him down to earth before he gets too starry-eyed.

He's no dumbbell; make no mistake about that. He can be busy making complicated and idealistic plans when he's got that out-to-lunch look in his eyes. But more than likely, he'll never execute them. After he's shared one or two of his progressive ideas with you, you may think he's a nut. But don't go jumping to any wrong conclusions. There's a saying that the Water Bearer is a half-century ahead of everybody else. If you do decide to say yes to his will-you-marry-me, you'll find out how right some of his zany whims are on your golden anniversary. Maybe the waiting will be worth it. Could be that you have an Einstein on your hands—and heart.

Life with an Aquarius won't be one of total despair for you if you learn to balance his airiness with your down-to-brass-tacks practicality. He won't gripe if you do. Being the open-minded man he is, the Water Bearer will entertain all your ideas and opinions. He may not agree with them, but he'll give them a trial airing out, anyway.

Don't tear your hair out when you find that it's almost impossible to hold a normal conversation with your Aquarius friend. He's capable of answering your how-do-you-do with a running commentary on some erudite topic. Always keep in mind that he means well. His broad-mindedness extends to your freedom and individuality, a modern idea indeed.

He'll be kind and generous as a husband and will never lower himself by quibbling over petty things. You take care of the budgeting and bookkeeping; that goes without saying. He'll be thankful that you do such a good job of tracking all the nickels and dimes that would otherwise burn a hole in his pocket.

In your relationship with a man born under Aquarius you'll have plenty of opportunities to put your legendary patience to good use. At times, you may feel like tossing in the towel and calling it quits, but try counting to ten before deciding it's the last straw.

Aquarius is a good family man. He's understanding with children and will overlook a naughty deed now and then or at least try to see it in its proper perspective.

TAURUS WOMAN
PISCES MAN

The Pisces man could be the man you've looked for high and low and thought never existed. He's terribly sensitive and terribly romantic. Still, he has a very strong individual character and is well aware that the moon is not made of green cheese. He'll be very considerate of your every wish and will do his best to see to it that your relationship is a happy one.

The Pisces man is great for showering the object of his affection with all kinds of gifts and tokens of his love.

He's just the right mixture of dreamer and realist; he's capable of pleasing most women's hearts. When it comes to earning bread and butter, the strong Pisces will do all right in the world. Quite often they are capable of rising to very high positions. Some do extremely well as writers or psychiatrists. He'll be as patient and understanding with you as you will undoubtedly be with him. One thing a Pisces man dislikes is pettiness. Anyone who delights in running another into the ground is almost immediately crossed off his list of possible mates. If you have any small grievances, don't tell him about them. He couldn't care less and will think less of you if you do.

If you fall in love with a weak Pisces man, don't give up your job before you get married. Better hang on to it a long time after the honeymoon; you may still need it. A funny thing about the man born under this sign is that he can be content almost anywhere. This is perhaps because he is inner-directed and places little value on material things. In a shack or in a palace, the Pisces man is capable of making the best of all possible adjustments. He won't kick up a fuss if the roof leaks and if the fence is in sad need of repair. He's got more important things on his mind, he'll tell you. At this point, you're quite capable of telling him to go to blazes. Still and all, the Pisces man is not shiftless or aimless, but it is important to understand that material gain is never an urgent goal for him.

Pisces men have a way with the sick and troubled. It's often his nature to offer his shoulder to anyone in the mood for a good cry. He can listen to one hard-luck story after another without seeming to tire. He often knows what's bothering a person before the person knows it himself.

As a lover, he'll be attentive. You'll never have cause to doubt his intentions or sincerity. Everything will be aboveboard in his romantic dealings with you.

Children are often delighted with the Pisces man because he spoils and pampers them no end.

Man—Woman

TAURUS MAN
ARIES WOMAN

The Aries woman may be a little too bossy and busy for you. Generally, Aries are ambitious creatures and can become impatient with people who are more thorough and deliberate than they are—especially when they feel it's taking too much time. Unlike you, the Aries woman is a fast worker. In fact, sometimes she's so fast, she forgets to look where she's going. When she stumbles or falls, it's a nice thing if you're there to grab her. She'll be grateful. Don't ever tell her "I told you so" when she errs.

Aries are proud and don't like people to naysay them. That can turn them into blocks of ice. And don't think that an Aries woman will always get tripped up in her plans because she lacks patience. Quite often they are capable of taking aim and hitting the bull's-eye. You'll be flabbergasted at times by their accuracy as well as by their ambition. On the other hand, because of your interest in being sure and safe, you're apt to spot many a mistake or flaw in your Aries friend's plans before she does.

In some respects, the Aries-Taurus relationship is like that of the tortoise and the hare. Although it may seem like plodding to the Ram, you're capable of attaining exactly what she has her sights set on. It may take longer but you generally do not make any mistakes along the way.

Taurus men are renowned lovers. With some, it's almost a way of life. When you are serious, you want your partner to be as earnest and as giving as you are. An Aries woman can be giving when she feels her partner is deserving. She needs a man she can look up to and be proud of. If the shoe fits, slip into it. If not, put your sneakers back on and tiptoe out of her sight. She can cause you plenty of heartache if you've made up your mind about her but she hasn't made up hers about you. Aries women are very demanding, or at least they can be if they feel it's worth their while. They're high-strung at times and can be difficult if they feel their independence is being restricted.

If you manage to get to first base with the Ram of your dreams, keep a pair of kid gloves in your back pocket. You'll need them for handling her. Not that she's all that touchy; it's just that your relationship will have a better chance of progressing if you handle her with tender loving care. Let her know that you like her for her brains as well as for her good looks. Don't even begin to admire a woman sitting opposite you in the bus. When your Aries date sees green, you'd better forget about a rosy future together.

Aries mothers believe in teaching their children initiative at a very early age. Unstructured play might upset your Taurus notion of tradition, but such experimentation encouraged by your Aries mate may be a perfect balance for the kids.

TAURUS MAN
TAURUS WOMAN

Although two Taurus may be able to understand each other and even love each other, it does not necessarily hold true that theirs will be a stable and pleasant relationship. The Taurus woman you are dating may be too much like you in character to ever be compatible. You can be set in your ways. When you encounter someone with just as much willpower or stubbornness, the results can be anything but pleasant.

Whenever two Bulls lock horns it can be a very exhausting and unsatisfactory get-together. However, if you are convinced that no other will do, then proceed—but with caution. Even though you know yourself well—or, at least, think you do—it does not necessarily mean that you will have an easy time understanding your Taurus mate. However, since both of you are basically practical people, you should try a rational approach to your relationship: put your cards on the table, talk it over, then decide whether you should or could cooperate, compromise, or call it a day. If you both have your sights set on the same goal, life together could be just what the doctor ordered.

Both of you are very affectionate people and have a deep need for affection. Being loved, understood, and appreciated are very important for your well-being. You need a woman who is not stingy with her love because you're very generous with yours. In the Taurus woman you'll find someone who is attuned to your way of feeling when it comes to romance. Taurus people, although practical and somewhat deliberate in almost everything they do, are very passionate. They are capable of being very warm and loving when they feel that the relationship is an honest one and that their feelings will be reciprocated.

In home life, two Bulls should hit it off very well. Taurus wives are very good at keeping the household shipshape. They know how to market wisely, how to budget, and how to save. If you and your Taurus wife decide on a particular amount of money for housekeeping each month, you can bet your bottom dollar that she'll stick to it right up to the last penny.

You're an extremely ambitious person—all Bulls are—and your chances for a successful relationship with a Taurus woman will perhaps be better if she is a woman of some standing. It's not that you're a social climber or that you are cold and calculating when it comes to love, but you are well aware that it is just as easy to fall in love with a rich or socially prominent woman as it is with a poor one.

Both of you should be careful in bringing up your children. Taurus has a tendency to be strict. When your children grow up and become independent, they could turn against you as a result.

TAURUS MAN
GEMINI WOMAN

The Gemini woman may be too much of a flirt ever to take your honest heart too seriously. Then again, it depends on what kind of a mood she's in. Gemini women can change from hot to cold quicker than a cat can wink its eye. Chances are her fluctuations will tire you after a time, and you'll pick up your heart—if it's not already broken into small pieces—and go elsewhere.

Women born under the sign of the Twins have the talent of being able to change their moods and attitudes as frequently as they change their party dresses. They're good-time gals who like to whoop it up and burn the candle to the wick. You'll always see them at parties, surrounded by men of all types, laughing gaily or kicking up their heels at every opportunity. Wallflowers they're not. The next day you may bump into her at the library, and you'll hardly recognize her. She'll probably have five or six books under her arms—on five or six different subjects. In fact, she may even work there. Don't come on like an instant critic. She may know more about everything than you would believe possible. She is one smart lady.

You'll probably find her a dazzling and fascinating creature—for a time, at any rate—just as the majority of men do. But when it comes to being serious, sparkling Gemini may leave quite a bit to be desired. It's not that she has anything against being serious, it's just that she might find it difficult trying to be serious with you. At one moment she'll praise you for your steadfast and patient ways, the next moment she'll tell you in a cutting way that you're an impossible stick-in-the-mud.

Don't even try to fathom the depths of her mercurial soul—it's full of false bottoms. She'll resent close investigation, anyway, and will make you rue the day you ever took it into your head to try to learn more about her than she feels is necessary. Better keep the relationship fancy-free and full of fun until she gives you the go-ahead sign. Take as much of her as she's willing to give and don't ask for more. If she does take a serious interest in you and makes up her fickle mind about herself and you, then she'll come across with the goods.

There will come a time when the Gemini girl will realize that she can't spend her entire life at the ball and that the security and warmth you offer is just what she needs in order to be a happy, ful-filled woman.

Don't try to cramp her individuality; she'll never try to cramp yours.

A Gemini mother enjoys her children, which can be the truest form of love. Like them, she's often restless, adventurous, and eas-ily bored. She will never complain about their fleeting interests because she understands the changes the youngsters will go through as they mature.

TAURUS MAN
CANCER WOMAN

The Cancer woman needs to be protected from the cold, cruel world. She'll love you for your masculine yet gentle manner; you make her feel safe and secure. You don't have to pull any he-man or heroic stunts to win her heart; that's not what interests her. She's will be impressed by your sure, steady ways—the way you have of putting your arm around her and making her feel that she's the only girl in the world. When she's feeling glum and tears begin to well up in her eyes, you have that knack of saying just the right thing. You know how to calm her fears, no matter how silly some of them may seem.

The Moon Child is inclined to have her ups and downs. You have the talent for smoothing out the ruffles in her sea of life. She'll most likely worship the ground you walk on or put you on a terribly high pedestal. Don't disappoint her if you can help it. She'll never disap-point you. She will take great pleasure in devoting the rest of her natural life to you. She'll darn your socks, mend your overalls, scrub floors, wash windows, shop, cook, and do just about anything short of murder in order to please you and to let you know that she loves you. Sounds like that legendary good old-fashioned girl, doesn't it? Contrary to popular belief, there are still a good number of them around—and many of them are Cancers.

Of all the signs in the Zodiac, the women under Cancer are the most maternal. In caring for and bringing up children, they know just how to combine the right amount of tenderness with the proper dash of discipline. A child couldn't ask for a better mother. Cancer women are sympathetic, affectionate, and patient with children.

While we're on the subject of motherhood, there's one thing you should be warned about: never be unkind to your mother-in-law. It will be the only golden rule your Cancer wife will probably expect you to live up to. No mother-in-law jokes in the presence of your mate, please. With her, they'll go over like a lead balloon. Mother is something special for her. She may be the crankiest, nosiest old bat, but if she's your wife's mother, you'd better treat her like royalty. Sometimes this may be difficult. But if you want to keep your home together and your wife happy, you'd better learn to grin and bear it.

Your Cancer wife will prove to be a whiz in the kitchen. She'll know just when you're in the mood for your favorite dish or snack, and she can whip it up in a jiffy.

Treat your Cancer wife fairly, and she'll treat you like a king.

TAURUS MAN
LEO WOMAN

The Leo woman can make most men roar like lions. If any woman in the Zodiac has that indefinable something that can make men lose their heads and find their hearts, it's the Leo woman. She's got more than her share of charm and glamour, and she knows how to put them to good use. Jealous men either lose their sanity or at least their cool when trying to woo a woman born under the sign of the Lion.

She likes to kick up her heels quite often and doesn't care who knows it. She often makes heads turn and tongues wag. You don't necessarily have to believe any of what you hear—it's most likely just jealous gossip or wishful thinking.

This vamp makes the blood rush to your head, and you momentarily forget all of the things that you thought were important and necessary in your life. When you come back down to earth and are out of her bewitching presence, you'll conclude that although this vivacious creature can make you feel pretty wonderful, she just isn't the kind of girl you'd planned to bring home to mother. Although Leo will certainly do her best to be a good wife for you, she may not live up to your idea of what your wife should be like.

If you're planning on not going as far as the altar with that Leo woman who has you flipping your lid, you'd better be financially equipped for some very expensive dating. Be prepared to shower her with expensive gifts, take her dining and dancing in the smartest nightspots in town. Promise her the moon, if you're in a position to go that far. Luxury and glamour are two things that are bound to lower a Leo's resistance. She's got expensive tastes, and you'd better cater to them if you expect to get to first base with this gal.

If you've got an important business deal to clinch and you have doubts as to whether it will go over well or not, bring your Leo partner along to that business luncheon. It will be a cinch that you'll have that contract—lock, stock, and barrel—in your pocket before the meeting is over. She won't have to say or do anything—just be there at your side. The grouchiest oil magnate can be transformed into a gushing, obedient schoolboy if there's a charm-studded Leo woman in the room.

Easygoing and friendly, the Leo mother loves to pal around with the children and proudly show them off. She can be so proud of her kids that she sometimes is blind to their faults. Yet when she wants the children to learn and to take their rightful place in society, the Leo mother is a strict but patient teacher.

TAURUS MAN
VIRGO WOMAN

The Virgo woman is particular about choosing her men friends. She's not interested in just going out with anybody. She has her own idea of what a boyfriend or prospective husband should be, and it's possible that image has something of you in it. Generally, Virgo is quiet and refined. She doesn't believe that nonsense has any place in a love affair. She's serious and will expect you to be. She's looking for a man who has both of his feet on the ground—someone who can take care of himself as well as take care of her. She knows the value of money and how to get the most out of a dollar. She's far from being a spendthrift. Throwing money around unnerves her, even if it isn't her money that's being tossed to the winds.

She'll most likely be very shy about romancing. Even the simple act of holding hands may make her blush—on the first couple of dates. You'll have to make all the advances, which is how you feel it should be. You'll have to be careful not to make any wrong moves. She's capable of showing anyone who oversteps the boundaries of common decency the door. It may even take a long time before she'll accept that goodnight kiss. Don't give up. You're exactly the kind of man who can bring out the woman in her. There is warmth and tenderness underneath Virgo's seemingly frigid facade. It will take a patient and understanding man to bring her enjoyment of sex to full bloom.

You'll find Virgo a very sensitive partner, perhaps more sensitive than is good for her. You can help her overcome this by treating her with gentleness and affection.

When a Virgo has accepted you as a lover or mate, she won't stint on giving her love in return. With her, it's all or nothing at all. You'll be surprised at the transformation your earnest attention can bring about in this quiet kind of woman. When in love, Virgos only listen to their hearts, not to what the neighbors say.

Virgo women are honest in love once they've come to grips with it. They don't appreciate hypocrisy, particularly in romance. They believe in being honest to their hearts, so much so that once they've learned the ropes and they find that their hearts have stumbled on another fancy, they will be true to the new heart-throb and leave you standing in the rain. But if you're earnest about your interest in her, she'll know and reciprocate your affection. Do her wrong once, however, and you can be sure she'll snip the soiled ribbon of your relationship.

The Virgo mother encourages her children to develop practical skills in order to stand on their own two feet. If she is sometimes short on displays of affection, here is where you come in to demonstrate warmth and cuddling.

TAURUS MAN
LIBRA WOMAN

It is a woman's prerogative to change her mind. This is a woman born under the sign of Libra. Her changeability, in spite of its undeniable charm, could actually drive even a man of your patience up the wall. She's capable of smothering you with love and kisses one day, and the next day she's apt to avoid you like the plague. If you think you're a man of steel nerves, perhaps you can tolerate her sometimeness without suffering too much. However, if you own up to the fact that you're only a mere mortal of flesh and blood, then you'd better try to fasten your attention on someone more constant.

But don't get the wrong idea: a love affair with a Libra is not all bad. In fact, it has an awful lot of positives. Libra women are soft, very feminine, and warm. She doesn't have to vamp in order to gain a man's attention. Her delicate presence is enough to warm the cockles of any man's heart. One smile and you're a piece of putty in the palm of her hand.

She can be fluffy and affectionate, things you like in a girl. On the other hand, her indecision about what dress to wear, what to cook for dinner, or whether or not to redo the house could make you tear your hair out. What will perhaps be more exasperating is her flat denial that she can't make a simple decision when you accuse her of this. The trouble is she wants to be fair and thinks the only way to do this is to weigh both sides of the situation before coming to a decision. A Libra can go on weighing things for days, months, or years if allowed the time.

The Libra woman likes to be surrounded with beautiful things. Money is no object when beauty is concerned. There'll always be plenty of flowers around her apartment. She'll know how to arrange them tastefully, too. Women under this sign are fond of beautiful clothes and furnishings. They'll run up bills without batting an eye, if given the chance, in order to surround themselves with luxury.

Once she's cottoned to you, the Libra woman will do everything in her power to make you happy. She'll wait on you hand and foot when you're sick, bring you breakfast in bed, and even read you the funny papers if you're too sleepy to open your eyes. She'll be very thoughtful about anything that concerns you. If anyone dares suggest you're not the grandest man in the world, your Libra wife will give him or her a good talking to.

The Libra woman, ruled by the lovely planet Venus as you are, will share with you the joys and burdens of parenthood. She works wonders in bringing up children, although you most always will come first in her affections. The Libra mother understands that youngsters need both guidance and encouragement. Her children will never lack anything that could make their lives easier and richer.

TAURUS MAN
SCORPIO WOMAN

Scorpio is the true zodiacal mate and partner for a Taurus, but is also your zodiacal opposite. The astrological link between Taurus and Scorpio draws you both together in the hopes of an ideal partnership, blessed by the stars. But the Taurus man with a placid disposition and a staid demeanor may find the woman born under the sign of Scorpio too intense and moody.

When a Scorpio woman gets upset, be prepared to run for cover. There is nothing else to do. When her temper flies, so does everything else that's not bolted down. On the other hand, when she chooses to be sweet, she can put you in a hypnotic spell of romance. She can be as hot as a tamale or as cool as a cucumber, but whatever mood she happens to be in, it's for real. She doesn't believe in poses or hypocrisy. The Scorpio woman is often seductive and sultry. Her femme fatale charm can pierce through the hardest of hearts like a laser ray. She doesn't have to look like Mata Hari—

many resemble the tomboy next door—but once you've looked into those tantalizing eyes, you're a goner.

The Scorpio woman can be a whirlwind of passion, perhaps too much passion to suit even a hot-blooded Taurus. Life with a girl born under this sign will not be all smiles and smooth sailing. When prompted, she can unleash a gale of venom. If you think you can handle a woman who purrs like a pussycat when treated correctly but spits bullets once her fur is ruffled, then try your luck. Your stable and steady nature will have a calming effect on her. But never cross her, even on the smallest thing. If you do, you'll be in the doghouse.

Generally, the Scorpio woman will keep family battles within the walls of your home. When company visits, she's apt to give the impression that married life is one great big joyride. It's just her way of expressing loyalty to you, at least in front of others. She may fight you tooth and nail in the confines of your living room, but at the ball or during an evening out, she'll hang on your arm and have stars in her eyes. She doesn't consider this hypocrisy, she just believes that family quarrels are a private matter and should be kept so. She's pretty good at keeping secrets. She may even keep a few from you if she feels like it.

By nature, you're a calm and peace-loving man. You value dependability highly. A Scorpio may be too much of a pepperpot for your love diet; you might wind up a victim of chronic heartburn. She's an excitable and touchy woman. You're looking to settle down with someone whose emotions are more steady and reliable. You may find a relationship with a Scorpio too draining.

Never give your Scorpio partner reason to think you've betrayed her. She's an eye-for-an-eye woman. She's not keen on forgiveness when she feels she's been done wrong.

If you've got your sights set on a shapely Scorpio siren, you'd better be prepared to take the bitter with the sweet.

The Scorpio mother secretly idolizes her children, although she will never put them on a pedestal or set unrealistic expectations for them. She will teach her children to be courageous and steadfast. Astrologically linked, the Taurus-Scorpio couple make wonderful parents together. Both of you will share the challenges and responsibilities for bringing up gracious yet gifted youngsters.

TAURUS MAN
SAGITTARIUS WOMAN
The Sagittarius woman is hard to keep track of. First she's here, then she's there. She's a woman with a severe case of itchy feet. She'll win you over with her hale-fellow-well-met manner and

breezy charm. She's constantly good-natured and almost never cross. She will strike up a palsy-walsy relationship with you, but you might not be interested in letting it go any further. She probably won't sulk if you leave it on a friendly basis. Treat her like a kid sister, and she'll love you all the more for it.

She'll probably be attracted to you because of your restful, self-assured manner. She'll need a friend like you to rely on and will most likely turn to you frequently for advice.

There's nothing malicious about the female Archer. She'll be full of bounce and good cheer. Her sunshiny disposition can be relied upon even on the rainiest of days. No matter what she'll ever say or do, you'll know that she means well. Sagittarius are often short on tact and say literally anything that comes into their heads, no matter what the occasion. Sometimes the words that tumble out of their mouths seem downright cutting and cruel. She never meant it that way, however. She is capable of losing her friends, and perhaps even yours, through a careless slip of the lip. On the other hand, you will appreciate her honesty and good intentions.

She's not a date you might be interested in marrying, but she'll certainly be a lot of fun to pal around with. Quite often, Sagittarius women are the outdoor type. They're crazy about hiking, fishing, white-water canoeing, and even mountain climbing. She's a busy little lady, and no one could ever accuse her of being a slouch. She's great company most of the time and can be more fun than a three-ring circus when treated fairly. You'll like her for her candid and direct manner. On the whole, Sagittarius are very kind and sympathetic women.

If you do wind up marrying this girl-next-door type, you'll perhaps never regret it. Still, there are certain areas of your home life that you'll have to put yourself in charge of just to keep matters on an even keel. One area is savings. Sagittarius often do not have heads for money and as a result can let it run through their fingers like sand before they realize what has happened to it.

Another area is children. She loves kids so much, she's apt to spoil them silly. If you don't step in, she'll give them all of the freedom they think they need. But the Sagittarius mother trusts her youngsters to learn from experience and know right from wrong.

TAURUS MAN
CAPRICORN WOMAN

You'll probably not have any difficulty in understanding the woman born under the sign of Capricorn. In some ways, she's just like you. She is faithful, dependable, and systematic in just about everything that she undertakes. She is concerned with security and sees to it that every penny she spends is spent wisely. She is very economical in using her time, too. She doesn't believe in whittling away her energy in a scheme that is bound not to pay off.

Ambitious themselves, they're often attracted to ambitious men—men who are interested in getting somewhere in life. If a man of this sort wins her heart, she'll stick by him and do all she can to see to it that he gets to the top. The Capricorn woman is almost always diplomatic and makes an excellent hostess. She can be very influential with your business acquaintances.

She's not the most romantic woman of the Zodiac, but she's far from being frigid when she meets the right man. She believes in true love and doesn't appreciate getting involved in flings. To her, they're just a waste of time. She's looking for a man who means business—in life as well as in love. Although she can be very affectionate with her boyfriend or mate, she tends to let her head govern her heart. That is not to say that she is a cool, calculating cucumber. On the contrary, she just feels she can be more honest about love if she consults her brains first. She'll want to size up the situation first before throwing her heart in the ring. She wants to make sure that it won't get crushed.

A Capricorn woman is concerned and proud about her family tree. Relatives are important to her, particularly if they've been able to make their mark in life. Never say a cross word about her family members. That can really go against her grain, and she won't talk to you for days on end.

She's generally thorough in whatever she undertakes: cooking, cleaning, entertaining. Capricorn women are well-mannered and gracious, no matter what their background. They seem to have it in their natures always to behave properly.

If you should marry a Capricorn, you need never worry about her going on a wild shopping spree. The Goat understands the value of money better than most women. If you turn over your paycheck to her at the end of the week, you can be sure that a good hunk of it will go into the bank and that all the bills will be paid on time.

With children, the Capricorn mother is both loving and correct. She will teach the youngsters to be polite and kind, and to honor tradition as much as you do. The Capricorn mother is very ambitious for the children. An earth sign like you, she wants the children to have every advantage and to benefit from things she perhaps lacked as a child.

TAURUS MAN
AQUARIUS WOMAN

The woman born under the sign of the Water Bearer can be odd and eccentric at times. Some say that this is the source of her mysterious charm. You may think she's nutty, and you may be fifty percent right. Aquarius women have their heads full of dreams, and stars in their eyes. By nature, they are often unconventional and have their own ideas about how the world should be run. Sometimes their ideas may seem pretty weird, but more likely than not they are just a little too progressive for their time. There's a saying that runs: the way Aquarius thinks, so will the world in fifty years.

If you find yourself falling in love with an Aquarius, you'd better fasten your safety belt. It may take some time before you really know what she's like and even then you may have nothing more to go on but a string of vague hunches. She can be like a rainbow, full of dazzling colors. She's like no other girl you've ever known. There's something about her that is definitely charming, yet elusive; you'll never be able to put your finger on it. She seems to radiate adventure and magic without even half trying. She'll most likely be the most tolerant and open-minded woman you've ever encountered.

If you find that she's too much mystery and charm for you to handle—and being a Taurus, chances are you might—just talk it out with her and say that you think it would be better if you called it quits. She'll most likely give you a peck on the cheek and say you're one hundred percent right but still there's no reason why you can't remain friends. Aquarius women are like that. And perhaps you'll both find it easier to get along in a friendship than in a romance.

It is not difficult for her to remain buddy-buddy with someone she has just broken off with. For many Aquarius, the line between friendship and romance is a fuzzy one.

She's not a jealous person and, while you're romancing her, she'll expect you not to be, either. You'll find her a free spirit most of the time. Just when you think you know her inside out, you'll discover that you don't really know her at all. She's a very sympathetic and warm person. She can be helpful to people in need of assistance and advice.

She's a chameleon and can fit in anywhere. She'll seldom be suspicious even when she has every right to be. If the man she loves slips and allows himself a little fling, chances are she'll just turn her head the other way and pretend not to notice that the gleam in his eye is not meant for her.

The Aquarius mother is generous and seldom refuses her children anything. You may feel the youngsters need a bit more discipline and practicality. But you will appreciate the Aquarius mother's wordly views, which prepare the youngsters to get along in life. Her open-minded attitude is easily transmitted to the children. They will grow up to be respectful and tolerant.

TAURUS MAN
PISCES WOMAN

The Pisces woman places great value on love and romance. She's gentle, kind, and romantic. Perhaps she's that girl you've been dreaming about all these years. Like you, she has very high ideals; she will only give her heart to a man who she feels can live up to her expectations.

Many a man dreams of an alluring Pisces woman. You are no exception. She's soft and cuddly and very domestic. She'll let you be the brains of the family; she's contented to play a behind-the-scenes role in order to help you achieve your goals. The illusion that you are the master of the household is the kind of magic that the Pisces woman is adept at creating.

She can be very ladylike and proper. Your business associates and friends will be dazzled by her warmth and femininity. Although she's a charmer, there is a lot more to her than just a pretty exterior. There is a brain ticking away behind that soft, womanly facade. You may never become aware of it—that is, until you're married to her. It's no cause for alarm, however, she'll most likely never use it against you, only to help you and possibly set you on a more sucessful path.

If she feels you're botching up your married life through careless behavior or if she feels you could be earning more money than you do, she'll tell you about it. But any wife would really. She will never try to usurp your position as head and breadwinner of the family.

No one had better dare say one uncomplimentary word about you in her presence. It's likely to cause her to break into tears. Pisces women are usually very sensitive beings. Their reaction to adversity, frustration, or anger is just a plain, good, old-fashioned cry. They can weep buckets when inclined.

She can do wonders with a house. She is very fond of dramatic and beautiful things. There will always be plenty of fresh-cut flowers around the house. She will choose charming artwork and antiques, if they are affordable. She'll see to it that the house is decorated in a dazzling yet welcoming style.

She'll have an extra special dinner prepared for you when you come home from an important business meeting. Don't dwell on the boring details of the meeting, though. But if you need that grand vision, the big idea, to seal a contract or make a conquest, your Pisces woman is sure to confide a secret that will guarantee your success. She is canny and shrewd with money, and once you are on her wavelength you can manage the intricacies on your own.

If you are patient and kind, you can keep a Pisces woman happy for a lifetime. She, however, is not without her faults. Her sensitivity may get on your nerves after a while. You may find her lacking in practicality and good old-fashioned stoicism. You may even feel that she uses her tears as a method of getting her own way.

Treat her with tenderness, and your relationship will be an enjoyable one. Pisces women are generally fond of sweets, so keep her in chocolates (and flowers, of course) and you'll have a very happy wife. Never forget birthdays, anniversaries, and the like. These are important occasions for her. If you ever let such a thing slip your mind, you can be sure of sending her off in a huff.

Your Taurus talent for patience and gentleness can pay off in your relationship with a Pisces woman. Chances are she'll never make you sorry that you placed that band of gold on her finger.

There is usually a strong bond between a Pisces mother and her children. She'll try to give them things she never had as a child and is apt to spoil them as a result. She can deny herself in order to fill their needs. But the Pisces mother will teach her youngsters the value of service to the community while not letting them lose their individuality.

TAURUS
LUCKY NUMBERS 2006

Lucky numbers and astrology can be linked through the movements of the Moon. Each phase of the thirteen Moon cycles vibrates with a sequence of numbers for your Sign of the Zodiac over the course of the year. Using your lucky numbers is a fun system that connects you with tradition.

New Moon	First Quarter	Full Moon	Last Quarter
Dec. 30 ('05)	Jan. 6	Jan. 14	Jan. 22
9 6 1 0	4 8 2 9	1 9 5 3	4 4 8 5
Jan. 29	Feb. 6	Feb. 13	Feb. 21
2 6 9 0	0 7 5 5	1 1 3 4	7 2 8 5
Feb. 27	March 6	March 14	March 22
9 3 4 1	1 0 8 4	6 7 2 4	4 1 7 2
March 29	April 5	April 13	April 20
5 6 3 1	1 1 6 8	8 9 4 1	7 4 8 2
April 27	May 5	May 13	May 20
6 3 9 7	7 3 5 6	9 1 0 7	4 8 1 5
May 27	June 3	June 11	June 18
8 6 6 2	2 4 5 9	4 6 3 7	1 5 8 5
June 25	July 3	July 10	July 17
1 3 8 1	1 2 6 3	1 9 4 7	2 5 3 2
July 25	August 2	August 9	August 15
2 7 9 1	1 5 2 8	7 3 6 1	1 7 4 2
August 23	August 31	Sept. 7	Sept. 14
2 2 4 5	9 6 3 7	2 1 5 8	8 6 6 2
Sept. 22	Sept. 30	Oct. 6	Oct. 13
2 5 6 0	7 4 8 2	5 3 9 7	7 7 3 5
Oct. 22	Oct. 29	Nov. 5	Nov. 12
5 6 4 1	7 2 5 0	0 6 3 1	1 6 8 9
Nov. 20	Nov. 28	Dec. 4	Dec. 12
9 4 4 0	5 8 3 9	3 6 4 9	9 2 3 7
Dec. 20	Dec. 27	Jan. 3 ('07)	Jan. 11 ('07)
7 4 6 0	4 8 5 2	1 9 5 7	7 8 3 9

TAURUS
YEARLY FORECAST 2006

Forecast for 2006 Concerning Business
and Financial Affairs, Job Prospects,
Travel, Health, Romance and Marriage
for Persons Born with the Sun
in the Zodiacal Sign of Taurus.
April 21–May 20

For those born under the influence of the Sun in the zodiacal sign of Taurus, ruled by Venus, planet of love and beauty, this year of strengthening and tempering promises to sustain you in the face of change. This could be your lucky year in terms of meeting important newcomers and making fortunate connections with them as well as with the people you already know and trust. Your dream of personal success continues to inspire and light your way.

Play the cards right and a gravy train might pull in to your station in the guise of wealthy customers and clients who can't seem to get enough of what you're selling. Satisfied purchasers are the best advertising that money can buy, so go the extra mile to give service that's remarked upon and not forgotten. Remembering names will make all the difference for return business. Aim to further your reach in the marketplace by word of mouth and personal recommendation. There will be tests along the way. It could be easy to lose sight of long-term goals in February and March. At that time you may be serving the wrong master or trusting in the wrong characters. When you're approached with schemes for easy profits, just remember that a fool and his money are easily parted. Handing your financial responsibilities over to someone you hardly know can be a recipe for disaster. Even if it takes all year, it's better to wait for the right adviser, manager, or partner. This person is genuinely likely to come your way in November. Be wary of lazy and greedy individuals elbowing their way into your success formula, siphoning off the cream. Maintaining standards can be tough in the face of domestic concerns and relentless competition. You're likely to be sorely tested in June and October, but don't give in or give up.

Taurus singles who are getting married or committing to another type of long-term relationship might do well to look into a prenuptial agreement where finances are concerned. The same goes for business partnerships, which will be much safer if dollar issues are clearly spelled out. To avoid trouble, make other people responsible for their use of joint resources. Real estate and rentals could be a big earner for you, or you could finally receive a handsome bonus for long service. Don't hold your breath for an anticipated inheritance, as it may not eventuate until next year. Watch the periods when wily Mercury retrograde makes commercial life a merry dance for Taurus. March 2–25 may require renegotiating wages or prices. July 4–28 may see communication breakdowns and delays with documentation, negotiations, travel, and transport. And October 28–November 17 is a precarious time, as the most important deals and decisions of the year may hang in the balance.

With Venus retrograde until the start of February, there could be initial uncertainty as to the outcome of a job or to your application for a new position. Constructive foundations for real progress can be laid from late March into April. At that time the main focus is the right connections and a stable living environment in the right territory. The second half of the year offers far more social potential of meeting the right people, promoting your abilities and accomplishments, and hooking into a network that's going somewhere. The crunch comes in late October, when a choice is essential between one person, or one group, and another. Look for signs of positive fresh growth, rather than powerful circumstances that have peaked and are now in decay or are being consumed by struggles for control. By mid-November it will be clear whether you're moving with a happening crew.

While you imagine the heights of your potential accomplishments, bear in mind that determined rivals and competitors can be just as stubborn and determined as you. If you wait for them to come around to your side, it may be too late. The future is on your side, and that means investing time and energy in what's on the cutting edge of your chosen trade or profession. Reinvent yourself to stay one step ahead, rising with the inevitable tides of change. Don't let personal responsibilities or fears hold you back or become excuses for remaining stagnant and accepting less than your best. September and November are the most likely periods for finding work that's in line with your hopes and plans. Fields that offer promise include real estate and property management, psychology, childcare, event planning and organization, and corporate integration of digital technology.

A solar eclipse at the end of March marks an important travel decision for this year. Or there may be a journey of dramatic necessity that involves commerce or personal financial matters. Another possibility is that it may be due to the health of someone significant in your life. Some Taurus people could decide to undertake a pilgrimage as an act of faith, possibly with others who hold the same beliefs and persuasion. Family ties and heritage could have a lot to do with such a decision. You may decide that a long flight is out of the question, but that leaves your whole country for cruising and exploring. Natural wonders and beauty appeal greatly to earthy Taurus people. Planning a summer vacation near a body of water would be ideal. Either late June or late July is the best time for departure. Don't forget the joy and exhilaration of ice and snow if you're taking a break during the winter months. If you must go abroad, perhaps for family concerns or study purposes, January, February, and December are the best periods for traveling. However, you're likely to get homesick quickly. Do everything possible to stay in touch with the love and familiarity of home and hearth. Small totems and reminders will keep you tuned to home when distance seems unbearable. If dreaming of a honeymoon or of a romantic trip away with a special companion, be patient until November, but it will be well worth the wait.

If this year begins with you feeling your age or worse for wear, make a solid commitment to yourself that you're going to do all that you can to improve. Then change your ways health-wise to keep this promise. During January some Taurus people may be out of action due to accident, illness, or enforced recuperation. Accept this as a wake-up call, and let yourself recover fully before once again taking on work and normal duties. This might really be a blessing in disguise, allowing you to get the treatment always needed and to truly know the state of your physical well-being. There's also the possible scenario of unconsciously getting sick just to have a long break from the world. Career stress and the complications of juggling life's many commitments demand peak performance and vitality. Nothing beats fresh air, clean water, nutritious food, and regular relaxation. Supplemental vitamins and minerals, acupuncture, homoeopathy, and aromatherapy could assist as preventive maintenance. Stay away from carriers of colds, flu, and other contagions because your immune level remains vulnerable.

Taurus singles may have found the one person with whom sharing a life is not only possible, but supremely preferable. Planning on a life together will become uppermost. Relationships and families need security and space, making the purchase of a house or the long-term lease of an apartment a definite priority. First of all it's important to decide exactly where to live. Work, transport, and education are key considerations. Your early hopes might founder against the hard rocks of reality, when trust proves elusive and mutual agreement becomes a maze of readjustment and counterproposals. Stick to the essence of original plans, and be consciously patient and enduring in order to build a personal dream. A division of labor is necessary, whether it's in bouncing the baby, raising the kids, or caring for aging parents. If you can't cope on your own, look into hiring help.

This is also a year of new friendship and an ever-widening social network, which will give you the human contact that everyone needs. At least one individual could become one of your greatest lifelong friends, but to see this potential you need to do more than merely scratch the surface. Taurus singles will be popular. Your company will highly sought after, yet this may not translate into a permanent lover. Have heaps of fun playing the field as long as you play fair. The option of living in solitary circumstances may be very appealing, whether you're a loner by disposition or are taking time out to recover from a terminated relationship. June and late October may see a dramatic showdown and fateful outcome to hoped-for dreams, along with discovered betrayals or exasperated last chances. Knowing what is happening will actually open up new doors for your long-term happiness.

TAURUS
DAILY FORECAST

January–December 2006

JANUARY

1. SUNDAY. Puzzling. Venus, custodian planet of Taurus, opens this year in reverse gear, appearing to be going backward in the Zodiac. This has been going on since last Christmas Eve. A celestial body goes retro to signify that there is an opportunity to reconsider, sometimes even repeat, certain past events. For Taurus people now, a lucky break can lead to a change regarding life's direction. A prior prospect may return, giving you a second chance. This time take it seriously. A matter related to a previous happening, possibly involving one or more family members, may surface once again and have to be handled in a different way.

2. MONDAY. Disquieting. Black-and-white styles of mood switching, one minute finding you full of high spirits and then getting in a huff the next, is not your usual mode of operation. Unstable ups and downs could have you wondering how to stay in control, but don't get paranoid. Everyone can expect mood swings now and then. Right now, the cross-purposes of seesaw dynamics are simply making their presence felt. Take some time out, breathe deeply, equalize. Locate the appropriate remedy, something that's good for your own soul. Just be yourself. A quiet talk in a private setting can reveal much wisdom.

3. TUESDAY. Pleasant. As a Taurus you're noted for being a people person, and today offers proof. The company of good companions with simpatico spirits is sure to be uplifting. Newcomers could be highly inspiring, offering mind-expanding ideas and special insights within the context of simply having an entertaining time. Be open to spontaneous ideas. Generous, encouraging individuals may awaken in you a new path to follow. Fresh and unexpected friendship can be seeded and sealed at present. Meaningful interactions are apt to develop effortlessly and without prior planning, giving you a whole new view of what could be.

4. WEDNESDAY. Excellent. Taurus people who are involved in leading or motivating a group are likely to be effective and efficient. In getting down to work, draw on your excellent practical skills and apply logical organization and thought. Getting fired up about a cause or a principle is possible. In fact, ideal cosmic patterns appear to support the best possible outcomes to legal processes. You can slice through a lot of red tape. If you desire to learn anything important, real inroads can be made in researching. It is said that the teacher will find the student when the student is ready. This can be a day of encountering the right guide for any path on which you wish to journey.

5. THURSDAY. Reflecting. The Venus-ruled need regular beauty sleep, although you can sometimes be prone to letting irrational interruptions disturb your peace. Worries and anxieties could have led to a degree of tossing and turning through the wee small hours of last night. Whether you are well rested or not, your mental abilities are galvanized. Handle the day one step at a time. A personal connection with someone who is senior to you, possibly an extension of your family, can provide valuable support. Connect with the past, from the heritage of ancestry to the reunion on an old group. A lot can be learned right now by reflecting deeply on what has gone before.

6. FRIDAY. Positive. You may experience a sense of pressure to get something mobilized, due in part to formation of a waxing square of the Moon. Mixing the physical with the creative could be an excellent way of channeling internal stress. Focus on dynamic arts and sports, where the expressive meets the athletic. This is a positive time for Taurus people engaged in industries related to beauty, creative arts, or pleasure. Inspirational, otherworldly glamour is in the air, ideal for putting on any kind of show or special event. Personal faith and beliefs may get a public airing and be delivered charismatically, perhaps on television or in a magazine. Be open to new ideas.

7. SATURDAY. Pleasurable. If you have ever wondered why some supposedly earthiest of the earthy star children become the looniest of space cadets, here's an explanation you can believe or not. The Moon has always been very important to your Sun sign, which is said to exalt her. When the Moon assumes this comfortable cosmic position, it's no surprise if emotional sensitivity is up, with a tendency to focus on the self. There could be an urge to pamper yourself, or for some kind of sweet stuff. Massage, a beauty treatment, or any hands-on indulgence of the senses is a good option. Of course, a big bowl of ice cream and a foreign movie could also be your indulgence of choice. Whatever you do, be good to your Taurus self.

8. SUNDAY. Joyous. The enthusiastic times augured today should leave the imprint of a few fine memories. Many of your interactions will be loaded with oomph and pizzazz. If it's not your own love of fun, then likely it belongs to someone close to you. In fact, everyone could give as good as they get, generating a very lively day. Taurus singles, especially the most flirtatious, are sure to be on stage and the center of attention at least at some point during the day. Be alert for a debate escalating from the joy of expression into an unwieldy free-for-all, especially if drinks are being consumed. Stay out of discussions about religion, politics, and other flash points that you know will arouse controversy.

9. MONDAY. Disenchanting. The necessity of having to admit the state of your bank balance could lead to applying the brakes to gallivanting about. Dues always have to paid eventually, especially outstanding bills. Having to take stock of what's still in the coffers is a sure way to bring any high-flying Taurus back down to earth. Bulls aren't known to have wings, but sometimes you can borrow them. Mercenary as it sounds, it's money and security that usually lift the most grounded of the Venus-ruled into flight. When you realize the situation and make adjustments, you can comfortably resume the journey of life. Dealings with international rules and regulations, such as foreign currency exchange, might be unavoidable.

10. TUESDAY. Complicated. Both borrowing and lending could lead to turmoil, particularly if it involves a friend or a group of acquaintances. A prized possession might be broken or mislaid, which can be even more damaging to a personal relationship. Any major material transactions done now should produce the best outcome if you are prepared to enlist the help of an expert. Someone smart who is seasoned by time and experience is likely to help with all sorts of practical proceedings. Renovators, landscapers, and home builders can look forward to a lot of constructive accomplishment. In particular, there are good astro contacts for the laying of a firm new foundation.

11. WEDNESDAY. Visionary. A little creative visualization never hurts. Great fulfillments begin with an original dream. Fantasies and imaginings about life's path and future direction could infiltrate your mental musings. You may suddenly realize fully that there's more to life than simply following a goal totally concerned with earning money. Never discount what truly suits you and turns you on. Although often difficult to weave together, inspiration and success are the combination most likely to achieve dreams. A career based on creative ability and otherworldly leanings might get an illuminating break. There could be recognition, sponsorship, or a notable new job contract.

12. THURSDAY. Variable. A celestial body can move through the heavens and keep to itself by not astrologically plugging in to other planets. This is called being void-of-course. It is similar to a car coasting along in neutral gear with the engine turned off. The Moon will do this for a good part of today, signifying a starred time for reverie. Stay with what's most familiar rather than flying into any new beginnings. Potentially nothing will come of ideas and matters initiated at this point. However, radically disparate dynamics can enter later, when electrical Uranus is finally plugged in. Then there's an acceleration in pace and much unexpected movement in your favor.

13. FRIDAY. Favorable. Any Taurus people who are at all superstitious about this so-called unlucky day can forget worrying. From the start the heavens are not out of sorts. In fact, they look especially favorable for you. Fairly deluxe star contacts are forming through today and tomorrow, ideal if you are seeking love. Empathy may be heightened as a sumptuous Full Moon begins to make its presence truly felt. Generally good regard is in the air, which should make for some very pleasant personal interactions. People you loved in the past, lost loves, can enter your world in some way. It might be that this person finally returns from a trip or an assignment. The first thing to do is actively make contact, putting any past problems out of mind.

14. SATURDAY. Enlightening. Relations with other people are set to intensify, demanding an objective focus on the situation. You could lose your head and become very turned on by someone's words. There should be a sense of camaraderie and good-natured exchange of ideas. Humor may even be injected into any conflict, as a filter capable of turning animosity into something worth laughing at. Guard against buying into a negative drama. You can become your own life coach and a positive motivator, uplifting those who are anxiety-prone or downtrodden. Today speaks of realizations, in terms of what's given and what's received in return.

15. SUNDAY. Cloistered. The familiar, something of a Taurus specialty, is likely to rule over the unfamiliar. Perhaps a visit to places from the past, such as where you grew up or went to school, should be on your agenda. Or it could be that you find yourself in a position of reminiscing and reflecting on times long gone. The urge to be a hermit, or at least a hermit with a loved one, might be just what you want. Taurus couch potatoes may be hard-pressed to get any more active than necessary. Self-motivation may be at a low ebb. When it comes to any outside stimulus, maybe the best that can be had right now is professional entertainment.

16. MONDAY. Sensitive. Sleeping can be almost addictive, especially in order to stay with a great dream you are having. Being physically drained has finally caught up with you, and it's time to rebalance by getting extra rest. A contributing factor may be your heightened sensitivity to the outer world, making crowds not at all appealing. You can seem as if you're on your own unrelated flight path, with no route mapped out. It's no surprise that you don't want to be a part of any of daily life. Those engaged in an at-home business, or dealing with real estate, could have extra work to do due to juggling legalities and morality.

17. TUESDAY. Bittersweet. The fervent attention of someone to you might dominate quite a lot of today. Or perhaps the tables are turned and it's you who wants to take full advantage of time spent with a special someone. A separation of sorts is augured, and is likely to be underpinning certain motivations. A visitor from afar might be returning to their origin, but most likely temporarily. Roses come with thorns, and love can be ill-starred. Maybe you will be lucky at cards. Fortune is apt to arrive disguised and backhanded, as quirky flukes come and go quickly. Taurus gamblers must be wary and wise. If a wager pays off, don't be greedy; know when to take your profit and run.

18. WEDNESDAY. Determined. Mars, brave warrior planet, is in your sign and is quite active at present. Using your personal initiative will keep circumstances in your favor. Due to confusion, or an ineffective superior, you could be left holding reins weighted down with greater responsibility. You can rally to the occasion, especially if you have your own capable lieutenant. Mars, the red planet, in Taurus may also make for the proverbial bull in a china shop. Remain mindful of being too forceful or bombastic in expressing your views. Toes inadvertently stepped on today might return to kick you tomorrow. Keep in mind Venus, that peace planet to which you're supposed to be attuned.

19. THURSDAY. Cautious. Maintenance of health and improvement of your overall well-being need extra attention. This goes not only for the state of your body but also for the fitness of your spirit and soul. Problems may occur when it comes to the functioning of everything, but especially the mechanisms of just being human and living life to the fullest. What you hope to ultimately achieve is beneficial to ponder. The body is the ultimate messenger for all earth signs, and Taurus qualifies the most. Don't ignore these signals. Lovers of alien and unusual animals may be turned on when passing a pet shop window. However, it's best to think twice, and research the nature of becoming the custodian of something strange.

20. FRIDAY. Rewarding. Work and ambition may fall into line, potentially allowing you to gain a more viable career path. At least realizing and setting a new goal might happen. Today the important light of the Sun begins to pass through the career and life-direction sector of your solar horoscope. An achievement is well on its way to culmination, possibly encompassing a rise in status such as an on-the-job promotion. If you have been solidly advancing toward attaining better credentials and an enhanced reputation, you may find yourself thrust into the spotlight. Recognition following a test of character is in the ethers, and this is apt to be an addition to enhancing your social profile.

21. SATURDAY. Frustrating. Distorted, unreal prospects always set up disappointments. Ideals can be high, particularly when it comes to the expectations of how other people should act. Be wary of waiting for someone to make certain changes in order for a situation to become better. At the end of the day, somebody else doing the changing isn't going to fix what's probably your own inner turmoil. A fundamental difference in beliefs and values could be undermining the cement in a partnership. It's possible someone's not listening, already filled to the brim with their own opinions. This is a good time to ponder and reflect, rather than launch into action and attempt to be heard.

22. SUNDAY. Expansive. Foreign themes enter into today's experiences. Travelers from afar may appear on your doorstep. Or you may experience a desire to jump on a plane and just go. At least visit a travel agent. For some Taurus people this urge may be part of a message or call from overseas. Lovelorn Taurus might be yearning for what will once again be. Venus and Mars line up nicely for you. These two planets together are a very sensual combination. They often signify that the body and its appetites rule, rather than the rational clarity of your mind. Seeds that lead to a great romance can be planted, but how they will grow in times to come is the wild card.

23. MONDAY. Mixed. Check to see if you're too full of yourself, parading around in the proverbial emperor's new clothes. Beware, because you know wheels can fall off, especially in high places. Pride eventually goes, when illusion is exposed. Venus and Mars, the well-aligned planetary pair, are maintaining their desirous contact and are highlighted once again. These are perfect stars for embarking on a new relationship this evening. If nothing else, finally get up the nerve to ask out a person you have long admired from a distance. Romantics could pen a poem or a letter, which can be good therapy if not a good move.

24. TUESDAY. Lucky. Wheelings and dealings are favored, including negotiating with power brokers and moving large amounts of resources. Entrepreneurs can get on with pursuing goals and setting up good outcomes. Negotiations with those in any hierarchy are likely to be cut-and-dried, primed to go well. Just ensure that your transactions are with professionals who possess a proven track record in their field of expertise. Be willing to pay for their advice. Restructuring with insurance companies or other large institutions could be productive. Family heirlooms or an inheritance might be in focus. The successful recycling of something old is sure to be satisfying and may be lucrative.

25. WEDNESDAY. Interesting. The joining of what does not ordinarily come together or interact is an unusual potential today. In particular, the old and the new can attempt to come to terms with each other. In some fashion, tradition and custom can blend with innovation and independence. An equalizing truce may form between unrelated individuals who are usually miles apart in their thinking or acting. The same could develop regarding a family member and a large organization. Whatever the degree of stabilization, dynamics of the unexpected may actually wait in ambush at certain times. Help lies in being flexible and taking a positive approach to contingencies. An unexpected mentor waits in the wings, if needed.

26. THURSDAY. Opportune. Gear up for action. When it comes to personal investments or material possessions, you need to decide if you should diversify. Ask yourself whether it's better to keep all eggs in one basket or spread the collection out. The choice exists between narrowing the focus to a specialized area or to explore variety. This same principle pertains if you are in a course of study or are planning any type of long journey, including an overseas trip. Getting to talk to a person you respect is sure to help you gain clarity and make decisions. Indulgent vibes are building as the hours pass. The night's right for an exclusive tryst with that special person in your life.

27. FRIDAY. Tricky. Wishes can be granted at the moment, whether you ask or not. It's true, however, about not getting something for nothing. Usually what's attracted somehow reflects deeper inner worth and value. Bear in mind that everyone's magnet, including yours, is tuned to different levels and subjects. An unusual encounter and attending a quirky social occasion could figure in your social world. A unique, rebellious individual may inspire excitement and change, but do not be too quick to go along with this person's ideas.

28. SATURDAY. Constructive. Your Sun sign isn't noted for instigating action. However, once it gets started, Taurus is highly commended for determination and stamina. Today there can be an injection of motivating energy that helps you get a lot accomplished, especially in the morning. You may have to expend more and more physical power as time goes by. Knowing when to stop moving along stubbornly, even destructively, is often a hard lesson. The Moon goes void from today's second half until tomorrow, and also reaches its dark phase. This marks a traditional period of withdrawal and rest, so take advantage of it.

29. SUNDAY. Promising. Your vocational sector contains the New Moon catching the Sun in Aquarius, with somber Saturn also in play. Although subdued in tone, this heralds a fresh new cycle over the following month. You can now turn serious focus upon your life path and reputation. Significant connections, with the fitting people for getting ahead, can take place in certain social sectors. Turning points are in the air. A major new vision can be considered, such as moving to a new home, even to a different state or country. Taurus people who have been away from their roots may return, possibly for a reason involving family lineage or celebration.

30. MONDAY. Volatile. Star-crossed patterns enter the heavens, cutting some fuses down to the shortest levels and potentially making for volatile scenes. Anger may be on the rise. Offensive and defensive dynamics are primed to charge you, as well as others, and certainly will rile your normally placid self. Wanting your way, or no way, is not advisable. It could actually sow the seeds that signal the end to certain affiliations. Turn off the brooding, which won't lead to anything anyway. Some intimate bonds are in for transformative times. A good friend might score an unexpected stroke of luck, which could even benefit you.

31. TUESDAY. Refreshing. Silence is certainly golden. For fortunate Taurus people, today can commence in a luxurious kind of quiet space. After the tension in yesterday's astrology, time out is the best remedy. Don't look a gift horse in the mouth. Take full advantage, since such rare peace is destined for a short life. Sooner rather than later, more frenetic energy will once again permeate your world. Communication gadgets may go out of action all at once, making you all too well aware that it doesn't rain but comes down in torrents. Although completely disruptive, interruptions and interactions promise stimulating future times and a break from what has become usual routine.

FEBRUARY

1. WEDNESDAY. Energetic. Today's formations of great star patterns can help you put visions into action and become inspired to initiate a new project. Although your energy and drive should be high, it's probably only a short burst. However, that doesn't mean nothing can be achieved. Attempt not to procrastinate if you want quick results. Aim to strike while you're all fired up. This is a time filled with glaring exposés as well as veiled illusions. Focus on activity that pertains to bringing a matter that's been kept under wraps out into the open. On the other hand, what is very public can be secreted away and not seen for what it is.

2. THURSDAY. Changeable. Retro Venus finally decides to change her gears into forward motion. This is reasonably significant since Venus is your ruling planet. Generally this kind of cosmic shift relates to the dynamics of returning, releasing, and the stirring of sleeping dogs. Sometimes it signifies last chances being offered for reworking and redoing something of importance before it's too late. Any long-standing delays, especially involving expanding experience and getting ahead, are likely to be overcome during the next couple of weeks. Opportunities seeded earlier should begin to display their potential for blossoming. Satisfaction is long overdue.

3. FRIDAY. Troublesome. Your overly active mind, stirred up by many thoughts and the stimulating talk of other people, could have had you up for most of last night. Being stuck on the same mental track, grinding the same self-talk over and over, is apt to persist into today. Take care that gossip and hearsay are not fueling pointless obsession. Capricious, volatile, out-of-the-blue dynamics may pepper your experiences. You might find it hard to suppress an emotional outburst, finally releasing the toxins of a past event. Although intense, an abrasive moment can be a blessing in disguise, creating a clean slate and allowing you to move forward once again.

4. SATURDAY. Spirited. Taurus types are said to be basically creatures of habit and routine. At present, however, molds and stereotypes can be broken. A choice may have to be made regarding where to direct your time and personal energy. Social invitations and community events offer a variety of possibilities. Within the domestic and family sphere, ordinary commitments are primed to bog down your spirits. No prizes will be awarded for guessing your preference! There may be a reason to step out of the comfort of your own culture, and pleasantly so, to have a meeting with a foreigner or to enjoy food and entertainment filled with international themes.

5. SUNDAY. Successful. There's nothing wrong with taking action first, and in your own interests. That's exactly what you might feel like doing right now. Getting out and about, being in the midst of beautiful objects and good design, may please your aesthetic eye and inspire you to make a purchase. Searching for new adornments for yourself, such as clothing, accessories, and jewelry, will be sure to please you. Just watch that you do not stretch the budget if shopping in exclusive surroundings. It's probably better to browse and live to spend another day. Energy is available for raw physical exertion. A personal best can be attained.

6. MONDAY. Significant. Name droppers and diehard fans are in for a treat. The degrees of separation may narrow between yourself and someone you very much admire and respect. You could even encounter an icon, possibly even meet personally. This doesn't necessarily mean a famous individual, since there are different role models in differing contexts. This might even refer to an important family member, possibly a parent. Compelling inspiration can be offered from on high, wherever and whatever on high is. Influential and mind-opening discussions are likely. Fast incisive decisions will ensue.

7. TUESDAY. Receptive. If you are hoping to make a notable decision, relying on other people for clarity and straight talking may let you down. Your intuition might be more worthy of respect, especially if keenly felt. Guidance could somehow be presented, illuminating positive opportunity in regard to your own chosen path. A beneficial interaction with a higher-up can become more bonded as certain boundaries and biases unravel. Perhaps you can have drinks with the boss or attend a meeting with notables. Generally and ideally, a better awareness of personal validity and of how you relate to authority is evolving. There might be discussion of a promotion, or some improvement to your job description.

8. WEDNESDAY. Frustrating. Not many can dig in their heels and refuse to budge like the Taurus can. A polarized standoff may reach a crystallized point, where something has to give. Otherwise a lack of bending may produce a break. In general, holding stubborn ideas about principles and values is apt to be the culprit when it comes to any bad blood. A legal battle concerning money and shared resources might reach an impasse, frustrating all concerned. Resolution and solutions to any bottleneck lie in the ability to listen and to be open to compromise and mediation. Don't block assimilating new information.

9. THURSDAY. Convivial. Gatherings, interactions, and social matters fill the structure of the day. Your calendar and dance card may fill up rapidly. It's important to keep tabs on messages. Networkers, advertisers, and those involved with communications in any way are sure to experience progress. Activities involving crowds are one of today's hallmarks, either relating to associates and friends or to a particular institution. International contacts are to be expected, possibly even personal travel. If you are in a relationship, you may be required to spend extra quality time with your beloved. Spontaneous, easygoing interaction is sure to be memorable.

10. FRIDAY. Stirring. Variety and the variable come on the scene. Collective occasions related to youthful themes are in the air. Taurus parents might be dealing with an organization that's built on the patronage of youngsters. Changes and new information within a group may require a response, even a formal meeting or other get-together. Actions could suffer mistiming. This gives rise to the potential of an accident, particularly while you are in transit and running around from place to place. Rather than rushing, where haste will make waste, proceed in a slow and steady manner. Such a typical Taurus pace will be most beneficial.

11. SATURDAY. Serene. Staying close to home base, and probably happily so, is a likely scenario. Doing a bit of housework can be approached as a therapeutic exercise. Not only will your environment become more orderly, but your inner self can regroup, satisfied and ready to take it easy. There's extra energy for going beyond the call of duty, perhaps launching into an early spring cleaning or some home handiwork. Take advantage of this energy. An old object may be unearthed and turn out to be of some value, materially or sentimentally. Family elders, or those who currently exercise domestic authority, appear deserving of a thoughtful gesture.

12. SUNDAY. Confusing. Vague qualities permeate the atmosphere. It can seem like being in a dream state when it comes to trying to make conversation or decisions. When it comes to certain substances being ingested, whether medicine, alcohol, or food, there could be a vulnerability that causes an adverse physical reaction of some type. Be aware of any sensitivity and remain prudent. Seeking a quiet place of peace is a way of containing the self. Imagined or spiritual pursuits suit your current mood. Tonight's Full Moon might draw you out into the public, oddly enough in an effort to get away from it all.

13. MONDAY. Problematic. Pleasure rather than business, or maybe mixing both, is sure to spice up the day. However, devoting resources to what's deemed enjoyable may draw the unwary Taurus into a web of debt or even emotional guilt. That doesn't mean you should avoid chasing what promises pleasure, but just watch how you go after it. Be even more cautious if the generosity and resources of another person are actually at stake. News might be received that contains the potential to inject a change of direction to your visions of the future. This is a time to ponder. Brilliant ideas are apt to come to mind. However, do not act on this first day of Full Moon.

14. TUESDAY. Starred. Venus-ruled Taurus are destined for a Valentine's Day full of sensual indulgences and validation. The planet of love is also making clear contact with optimistic Jupiter, which is in your house of relationships. In addition, the Moon is in the middle of an astro area concerned with sex and fun. With this lineup, any astrologer would recognize the likelihood of having a good time, ideally with a special person at your side. The evening is capable of producing especially memorable moments. Ironically, today's stars also reflect a theme of apartness, which could feel quite raw in some cases. The phone is helpful if distance is a problem.

15. WEDNESDAY. Lucky. It's not what you know but who you know, at least this is potentially true now. As a Taurus you have been going through a phase where encounters with the right people can greatly help you in getting ahead. This is one of those fortunate times. Goodwill and generosity are yours for the asking. Opportunity is present. Lucky breaks are likely to come from those holding positions of status and control, who know you and what you can offer. The romantic vibes of yesterday continue. Interactions with a love interest can be prolonged or, if missed before, may happen this evening.

16. THURSDAY. Pressured. This is a time to be like the ant, not the grasshopper. Remember that fable? Parties and playtime aren't on the agenda. Focus on maintaining practical security for times to come. Extra work of some variety could be taken on. If you already have many obligations, you are the type most likely to add more to your schedule. The diligent may happily bring work home and industriously get it done in record time. Extra pay, or at least kudos, will probably be the motivating factor. It's best to create your own light at the end of the tunnel. For some the day can revolve around household chores and a working bee. Diligent effort will pay off.

17. FRIDAY. Significant. The heavens open the door to the Taurus sector concerned with worth, value, and money. The celestial body full of initiative that comes trundling into the arena is red planet Mars. Where this planet goes, it's an astrological resource with an energy reservoir. Offense, defense, and conflict also belong under the god of war's banner. In this case there may be lots of words, both spoken and written. As this phase starts, get proactive and think about what's motivating your material choices. Make sure communications are clear. Read the fine print of any document you are asked to sign.

18. SATURDAY. Trying. Something of a serious, possibly formal, nature may take place. This is apt to be linked to a relationship, possibly involving family members. There is also the likelihood of some kind of celebration or important event, perhaps a wedding or anniversary gala. The early days of partnership may now be over, leading to a change in status from wishes to commitment. You could finally meet the family of your significant other. Major discussions are in the cards regarding where your life is heading in the future. A disapproving figure might be hovering in the background, perhaps someone from your own tribe.

19. SUNDAY. Variable. The subdued morning gives way to an enjoyable social time with loved ones and friends. It can be a case of the more the merrier. Many cups are likely to be running over. The stars support a liaison with a delightful companion. A date with a special someone is foreseen, although you may end up among a crowd. Taurus singles are in for a stimulating experience and some quality interactions. The witty and the wise can be very entertaining, with long stories to relate. Penning a meaningful letter or e-mail that is full of good humor should be satisfying to you as well as the recipient.

20. MONDAY. Difficult. Today's astrological guidance warns of abrasive and confusing dynamics. Thoughtfulness and reflection are required before you react. This is particularly so when it comes to issues connected to your current and future security. Militant tendencies could leak to the fore with tolerance a little threadbare, which could strain patience. Battling the system is likely but ultimately useless. Rash actions and words are apt to prove destructive and unhelpful in any circumstance. Be alert for tactics of passive aggression and pettiness. Choosing to drop to a base level of expression equals giving way to your opponents.

21. TUESDAY. Unpredictable. Keeping everything on an even keel and avoiding rocking the boat should be an achievable aim, although fraught with testing situations. Conditions could be a little stormy at times, producing some big waves. It might be necessary to contain a burgeoning swell of emotions that can be unstoppable once released. It's one thing to be as stable as possible, but quite another to even dare to keep a lid on information trying to explode out and be expressed. In particular you may have to help another person who needs to let loose and vent. Straddling both sides of a debate within an association is difficult, especially if you try to maintain that position over the long run.

22. WEDNESDAY. Conclusive. Knowing when to pack up and move on can be a hard skill to master. Those in the fixed earth sign of Taurus prefer just keeping on. Some kind of ending is heralded by the stars. This might involve having a discussion, or even lead to putting your views in writing. Certain ties may have to be cut. A specific connection has lived out its time and purpose. This may relate to an individual, a group, or an affiliation. So rehearse your farewell statement. Stick to your truth and be honest. Closing with decisive and unambiguous clarity makes way for a refreshing new start.

23. THURSDAY. Stormy. Many situations may seem as if their foundation was originally built upon a fault line. The need for amendments and adjustments can persist. One thing that seems reliable is that nothing is set in stone, especially when it comes to your colleagues and associates. Someone might render you dumbfounded by a display of changeable and fickle tendencies. A certain person may make false promises, but only to thine own self can you be true. Keeping your own counsel is the best tactic. The words of others are surely colored by their personal agendas. Be wary of taking on any new commitments.

24. FRIDAY. Uplifting. Goodwill and appropriate praise for recent achievement are likely. You may have won the prize, or someone dear to your heart may make you proud. The dynamics of pride and personal validation can be put into action. A little positive reinforcement always goes a long way. An opportunity exists for the brightest and the cleverest to show off, particularly when it comes to a literary or artistic bent. Some great work can be produced right now. You may have a mentor or teacher to thank for contributing to your success. Be generous in sharing good feelings and good times.

25. SATURDAY. Rewarding. Productivity is foreseen if proactive initiative is put to good use. It's true that one man's trash is another's treasure. Consider gathering a collection of old belongings and attempting to turn a small profit by selling what you no longer want. Basically try to get rid of clutter. Getting into some kind of marketplace and setting up temporary shop can be the way to go. Or you might try selling on the Internet. People are likely to be helpful when you're out and about. Spontaneous encounters can be laced with sparkling conversation. New friendships might be seeded, to blossom forth in times to come. Even romance may result from casual meetings.

26. SUNDAY. Enlightening. Neptune, the glamour planet of poetic art and grand illusion, is being triggered in the Taurus horoscope today. Both words and movement can be effectively joined to create high-quality results. Taurus people whose bread and butter comes from entertaining others are likely to be on stage at present. Photography and filming could be a part of the picture. If not an entertainer yourself, you could be a part of the crowd enjoying an inspiring event. An international flavor is also signified by the heavens. Enlisting foreign elements as part of a project will be helpful to many aspects of the creative process.

27. MONDAY. Hopeful. Today's New Moon occurs in highly dynamic cosmic surrounds. Attention will begin to turn to a novel phase when it comes to formulating a future path. Take care with words delivered and heard. Many interactions are likely to prove strongly transformational in many ways. New perspectives can be taken on and reviewed. Confronting ideas may continue to resonate well after today. Someone might be quite disgruntled when you announce your most profound wishes, especially if money is involved. Don't buy into their pessimism and narrow view. Hope rules today and needs to be nurtured.

28. TUESDAY. Mixed. Taurus people who are engaged in long-term efforts might see results beginning to show. Your industry and action are supported by the heavens, as is stamina. If certain outcomes are still to come, the persistent will be able to keep forging ahead. This is particularly so if a real estate deal or improvements to the home are your primary goals. A partner will be helpful when it comes to negotiations with a power broker connected to where the bucks may be found. Secrets and the secretive are also signified. Although all things seem equal on the surface, some astute detective work might be needed.

MARCH

1. WEDNESDAY. Revealing. The beginnings of a process are taking form, involving unraveling a slippery web of deceit that has built up over time. There is no doubt that it will all be resolved eventually. The situation is not a matter of if, but when. If you have told one or more untruths, take some responsibility and go into damage control. If the sham is the work of other people, you're likely to be called upon to make a decision and to do something proactive. Quietly observing and noting what is going on within a social network might be a clever tactic, but care is required nonetheless. Strive to keep an objective check on your personal perceptions.

2. THURSDAY. Appraising. Planet Mercury, astrological lord of communications and the mind, turns retro in your solar sector of hopes and assistance for the future. It's not surprising if you now enter into a phase of reviewing the value of particular associations. Thoughts and discussions with friends are rehashed as well-known territory is reviewed once more. You may find that certain of your relationships soon undergo a metamorphosis. What has seemed like a casual connection might evolve into a more intimate exchange and understanding. This evening is ripe for a very private date and close interaction.

3. FRIDAY. Restrained. Good management will tend to rule over good luck. Practical dimensions have a way of sometimes trumping the pleasures of life. The necessity to pull in your belt and become a little more frugal is unavoidable. Besides counting the pennies, you might have to also count the calories and be a bit ruthless when it comes to overindulging in the good things of life. There seems great future benefit from restraint that you diligently apply now. A structural problem in a dwelling is likely, and whoever is in charge can prove hard to deal with. Phoning a higher-up could help. Distractions, probably from a friend, may spark the evening.

4. SATURDAY. Glamorous. An exciting newcomer can soon become your friend. A larger-than-life individual, oozing knowledge and charm, is apt to attract a lot of attention. This person may be a foreigner or a person you normally think of as way beyond your reach. Small seeds planted now in any alliance are set to grow over times. It's easy for you to get all revved up. However, a degree of confusion and misunderstanding is also in the ethers. This indicates that care is needed when it comes to jumping headlong into a situation. The person who is currently in charge may not be steering the ship very well. If you see the vessel being abandoned, you've been warned.

5. SUNDAY. Special. Venus moves into Aquarius, your horoscope sector of career. There is opportunity to get ahead in your vocational path by focusing on circumstances concerned with enjoyment rather than work. You might encounter a key person at a social or artistic event. After talking shop, they will like what they hear from you. Interactions of a magical, witty tone color a party atmosphere or any gathering. And the more exclusive, the better! Access might be granted to highly regarded locations and occasions. A new romantic connection is foreseen. Just keep in mind that it pays not to judge a book solely by its cover.

6. MONDAY. Problematic. Hints could begin to reverberate, indicating some type of disruption or discord to come. Tiny, even unconscious, barbs are capable of implanting emotional toxins that escalate and fester. These will need somewhere to go in the long run. If it's you dispensing these little poison arrows, realize what you are doing. Turn it around now or you will later have to pay the price for your contribution to this situation. If you are on the receiving end of another person's poison, it's up to you whether to become infected or not. Hate is a preventable disease. A carrot dangled by an inspiring superior could motivate you into chasing extra pay or a promotion.

7. TUESDAY. Sensitive. Brothers and sisters can be significant in your life today, or some other relatives. Family members could meet, possibly because of a formality or ritual. Family factions may become evident, perhaps concerning a legal hassle involving property distribution. Clear communication and really listening, not just hearing, will be crucial in order to achieve the best outcome. If power and money are facing off, and your own coffers are in the line of fire, choose your words with extra care. Some negotiations are likely to get tied into knots due to various agendas involving control. A void Moon cruises most of the day. Refusing to argue, at least for now, appears to be a wise choice.

8. WEDNESDAY. Bright. People you hardly know can make or break your day. According to the heavens, they're much more likely to help. Your vigor may be low, so someone else will have to get you motivated by giving decisive directions. You may prefer to just spend time lolling around, yet still be out and about. Enjoy solo time at a local café, reading a book or writing letters in the old-fashioned way. Spontaneous encounters with unusual individuals are in the cards, especially as the day goes on, although no one is likely to simply knock at your door. An exotic date among good company is just the ticket for Taurus lovers. This is a night to reach out.

9. THURSDAY. Expansive. Today the Sun is in excellent aspect to Jupiter. So the symbolic heart of all life and the luckiest planet are positively linking your horoscope sectors of partnership and friendship. That's good for you, and also for others in your life. Be open to all that is beyond your normal routine. Encountering a prospective new partner seems likely for Taurus singles. This person could be right around the corner or across the hall. Greetings, meetings, and interactions of all variety should be positive. Networkers and Taurus people logged onto the Web are in for uplifting, enjoyable contacts. An eclectic gathering with unusual, interesting discussions are bound to be fun. Writers and speakers can take effective creative gambles.

10. FRIDAY. Bumpy. Coming down to earth so firmly that you actually bump can be the effect of one of today's experiences. The heavens favor practicality and responsibility, ideal for the mechanics of getting real. Rebuffing the facts and passing the buck are not going to be tolerated, particularly by those in some form of senior position. Taurus nervous types, rare but not unknown, may be dealing with the stirrings of subtle anxieties. Inner tension can build if not given suitable attention. A massage or a beauty spa is an especially good antidote for the Venus-ruled. Even candles and aromatherapy, or indulging any of the senses, can help soothe your body and mind.

11. SATURDAY. Combustible. Even your best laid plans can tend to go awry. It's good to be flexible since scattered and shifting tendencies are unavoidable. Someone not keeping an appointment, or their propensity to keep changing their mind, is likely to irritate you. Your tolerance and temperament are being tested. People might have you tiptoeing through an emotional minefield that's their terrain, complete with emotional outbursts and mental mishaps. Sometimes it feels right to give as good as you get, particularly in defense. However, this is probably not one of those times. Let any emotional charge settle before attempting to talk. Nothing can be rationally sorted out while it's dominating your every thought.

12. SUNDAY. Tricky. Fools and their money could be easily parted, either willingly or unwillingly. This includes losing a special or prized possession, not to mention personal dignity. Lady Luck may sweep bounty from the gambler's hands and the indulgent. Scams, rip-offs, even thievery might get tangled in the process of simply seeking fun. This doesn't mean a good time is unachievable, just that you must remain aware. It's better to be safer than sorry at the best of moments. The current cosmos reflects quality experience with a loved one in an exclusive, private setting. Staying in bed all day, as a lifestyle, can become very appealing.

13. MONDAY. Variable. The hours initially cruise along in the same old everyday way, with nothing new or exciting on the horizon. This could be the calm before a storm. Expect the unexpected, or at least anticipate that the daily dynamics will suddenly accelerate at some point. Although the heavens are promoting physical activity, guard against pushing yourself too far or too fast. Accidents and injuries are possible unless you exercise caution. Of course, nothing ventured, nothing gained. Going beyond past limits and boundaries can result in breaking exhilarating new ground. A bit of extra force can achieve a lot, but too much would be sure to fracture a good alliance.

14. TUESDAY. Auspicious. Benefits of past negotiation could at last show results and returns. Now is the time to take plans one step further and build upon what was established earlier. You can grasp a bushel of opportunity if you're prepared to move quickly. However, hesitate and you are likely to miss well-deserved chances. Good times may burst into this day via good humor and good company. The Full Moon highlights the likelihood of a party or other celebration. Indulge in all pleasures of the heart. Children could figure prominently, interacting happily even in a grown-up setting. However, a lunar eclipse is also in the cosmos. Don't ignore an infant's health issue.

15. WEDNESDAY. Pressured. If you wake up angry and annoyed but don't know why, it could just be the wrong side of the bed. The morning ritual has a down tone, and all the coffee or vitamins in the world aren't likely to help. If this is becoming the norm, review certain habits and basic lifestyle factors such as diet and amount of sleep. Any challenges with vitality likely stem from a deeper and more fundamental source than a mere supplement can balance. Good star contacts are in play when it comes to connecting with the right specialist to aid in diagnosis and care. Hard workers are in for a rare opportunity. What goes around will come around.

16. THURSDAY. Visionary. Outcomes of a larger order than just the personal can manifest with ease. A project that is connected to a greater visionary aim or is built on the foundations of your imagination will flow and even receive a boost. Spiritual sensitivity leads to unconditional positive regard. Your altruistic and philanthropic ambitions may now find necessary support thanks to an increased public profile. Sacrifices, both small and large, should pay off as long as they're made with true integrity and lack a selfish agenda. Coworkers may form special ties, exchanging thoughts regarding bigger ambitions. You cannot be too compassionate or understanding.

17. FRIDAY. Significant. Your willpower is likely to be very strong and can be utilized for positive encouragement. Precision and incisiveness are also present, making for effective application of your energy. Work has the potential for significant achievement. Bosses should be pleased with the efficiency of employees, which probably rests on a deeply bonded team spirit. Interactions with people in high-up positions will flow. Taurus people who are seeking help around the office or house can locate the right one for a messy and long-overdue job. The only proviso is that the work should not be given to someone you already know. A neutral professional relationship will get things done in the best possible way.

18. SATURDAY. Tense. You may be angry and not even realize the vibes you're giving off. Arguments could ignite needlessly, as can the frustrating feeling of being damned if you do or don't. Starcrossed communication wires are probably the basis of these problems. Someone may not feel they are being heard or validated for what they need to get across. Usually if you feel this way, some part of you refuses to hear anyone else. Right now it's probably a lot to ask anyone to walk in your shoes. When it comes to your own actions, know the consequences unless you are willing to cooperate and compromise.

19. SUNDAY. Helpful. Someone urgently wants to connect with you. A call for assistance, possibly from a friend or partner, could lead to early rising. It's probably not a life-or-death emergency, but it might seem so as circumstances are distorted and overdramatized. You can assume the role of counselor when someone seeks to cry on your shoulder. As a Taurus you are known to have solid compassion and a willingness to take on burdens not your own. Offering a soft place to land is well and good, but personal boundaries may be tested in the process. Contemplative, soul-lifting stars are touching base today. Spiritual, generous atmospheres can form almost magically.

20. MONDAY. Refreshing. Happy astrological new year! Tonight marks the birth of spring as far as the heavens are concerned, a good excuse for a party. This tradition of celebrating is an oldie but a goody. Beginnings are blessed this evening, but only as long as real foundations have been put in place. Whatever's going on, low-key events are apt to be most satisfying. You may want to arrange a gathering at home connected with your friends as well as your family. The element of surprise, and even unruliness, is also present. High spirits may assert themselves. The waning Moon signifies that a certain situation will run out of steam sooner rather than later.

21. TUESDAY. Vexing. Someone who is sly and artful can run ragged rings around other people, and charmingly so. This person, especially if it is you, might as well have fun. Anyone with any smarts will get what's going on, responding with goodwill and reciprocal humor. However, not everyone possesses a healthy, flexible sense of enjoyment. Sometimes a square peg attempts to fit into a round hole. Restricted beliefs and dogmatic morals can lessen any fun. One person getting too serious, or on a high horse, is apt to make the others defiant or even more silly. Maintaining a sense of grace and graciousness among all the shenanigans is a class act for which you can strive.

22. WEDNESDAY. Intense. A Sagittarius Moon is making its monthly contact with deep and invisible Pluto, which continues its long transit of Sagittarius. If you have noticed a certain cycle of intensity, where you feel you could explode on the inside, you're probably tuned in to the rhythm of this cosmic pattern. Recognize and care for any emotional tension that may emerge. Something you haven't seen coming might otherwise blindside you. Themes are likely to relate to holding on versus letting go, or to destroying versus recycling. A bigger force, greater than you, can be holding the major control in a situation. Just keep in mind that this too will pass.

23. THURSDAY. Disconcerting. A diversity of different tasks to deal with could have you feeling like you're all over the place. Bills, budgeting, partnerships, competitors, career, and public obligations, plus more, are all clamoring for your attention. A general feeling of disarray, like a bomb has hit, may fill your psyche. The first thing to do is sit down, breathe, and stabilize. Panic is usually just a cop-out and a good way to waste energy. Later you can make a to-do list, check it thrice, and prioritize. This will likely show that everything doesn't have to be taken care of at once. Pace yourself, and live to search and destroy another day. Spend the evening enjoying your very favorite company.

24. FRIDAY. Positive. The cosmos appears to love the unassuming and humble. Even Taurus people who prefer to remain under the radar, or strive to be a little secretive, might find it's not easy at present. Working behind the scenes, especially for a greater cause, could lead to reaping rewards and attracting additional support. Quiet achievers are apt to be gifted with some kind of recognition and validation in an overt way. Creative endeavors should flow well, culminating when a long-term labor of love is finally unveiled. The familiar is an appealing environment at day's end. A favorite place in the garden, or a special room in the house, calls to you.

25. SATURDAY. Fascinating. Your vivid imagination takes center stage, shining with the brightness of charisma and glamour. Enchantment is in the ethers, lending a special something to the Venus-ruled personality. Artistic, poetic, and otherworldly talents are likely to be very inspired and expressive. If not, you could be in the wrong field, or perhaps just numb to the muses at the moment. Romance can somehow saturate your world. A good venue for a new liaison may be some kind of fantasy setting. Enjoy the escapist atmosphere of a theater, gallery, or bar, and be open to all possibilities.

26. SUNDAY. Linking. Venus and Mars are lining up today and tonight, a contact that won't happen again for a while. One planet is in your astrological house of getting ahead, the other is gallivanting around in the house of acquisition and security. This star pattern creates a feeling of wanting to make hay while the sun shines. Another individual or a partnership is apt to be a component of any deal. Actually, these two celestial bodies are a classic sensual combination. They are most ideal for making love and, in this case, also for making conversation. Any difficult negotiations should be successful today as rough edges are smoothed off.

27. MONDAY. Electrifying. Mercury has recently turned direct and is only just getting over being totally zapped by being conjunct with Uranus. However, bright sparks will still definitely fly, thanks to the Moon catching up with both planets. Ideally, necessary adjustments and delays will now be overcome and the processes in question can get moving. Intellectual breakthroughs and innovations might be exchanged. Less ideal with this astrology is the potential for scattering, splintering, and every person for himself or herself. All the word play and lip service in the universe may happen, but there's no follow-up in the future. Some ideas are apt to even cause shock.

28. TUESDAY. Troublesome. A dark tone is holding sway over the moods of many Taurus people at present. Although you know what they say about going to sleep without resolving an argument, last night may have contained abrasive tension making for sulking and brooding. Or you may experience some kind of headache, literally or figuratively. For an unfortunate few, the day might entail all of the above. Many issues are connected to money and a feeling of powerlessness, even if other people aren't directly involved. You may worry about the financial problems of your nearest and dearest. Not feeling safe should be talked out with someone you trust and respect.

29. WEDNESDAY. Cryptic. Today's solar eclipse in Aries impacts your twelfth house, a sector traditionally signifying the clandestine and self-undoings. This highlights a propensity for danger in accepting what's unclear, as well as the possibility of misplacing things or other types of losses. Someone you would never suspect could be hiding something. A person in a group of peers may be colluding with another who is related to your social circles. The kindness of an empathic individual in a higher position can prove very helpful when it comes to your reputation and professional or social standing. Your greatest ally is faith and trust in the greater meaning of life.

30. THURSDAY. Dynamic. Think about how much you are worth and really feel you deserve. Big business is in the ethers. Taurus people already holding a degree of status and clout can pull rank today. Strength and determination may be effectively asserted from behind the scenes. Taurus leaders, especially, can enlist the services of others when it comes to dealing with some type of power struggle. Even the average and placid Venus-ruled among you could feel like a demigod or goddess in your own backyard. A sense of fortitude and resilience can be called upon with ease. Iron fists within velvet gloves would probably be the best description of this approach.

31. FRIDAY. Fortunate. Accidents happen, and one today has the potential of producing something good. Mental dexterity and monitoring your attitude will aid in turning lemons into lemonade by just adding sugar. If feeling too fixed to take this sort of direction, or too lazy, it might be easier to choose a separate and more emotional course. However, you must decide if that would be better in the long term. Good friends are worth their weight in gold, helping you smooth over what's likely only a misunderstanding. Social activities are looking up, whether with old friends, workmates, or your significant other. Get out and about. This is not the night to be a shrinking violet.

APRIL

1. SATURDAY. Cautious. The addiction to indulging yourself isn't just about having in general. There can be something hypnotizing when it comes to a shopping mall or a for-sale sign. It may be that you don't want to miss the latest trend. April fools among you should take a good look in the mirror, and really ascertain what's driving a tendency to throw away good money. Superficial, compulsive attitudes to keep acquiring more and more can trip you up and negatively impact your credit rating. Honesty and self-integrity always are better than pretension. Spending, or more likely charging your purchases, could blow out of proportion and only add superficial effects to your image.

2. SUNDAY. Helpful. Other people are appreciative and apt to express their thanks to you in some fashion. Prior favors and goodwill are likely to be returned in kind. This especially relates to family members or to someone who is regarded as such, probably someone who stayed awhile in your home in the past. A gift may be given, or a debt finally repaid, putting cash in your wallet. If you are trying to get necessary aid, remember that blood is thicker than anything else. Disruption can manifest itself, possibly via a good buddy. The maxim that a friend in need is a friend indeed might prove true. When someone you know well is caught between a rock and a hard place, you will get the phone call.

3. MONDAY. Defensive. The average Taurus can become really courageous when it comes to getting a deal's value and worth. Security, both emotional and material, is at the forefront. A lot of energy will have to be spent for the sake of money, whether spending, saving, or trying to borrow some from the appropriate source. You may have to face off with a power broker, or institution, and hastily supply correct paperwork. Having an onsite temper tantrum will be like a flea trying to bite an elephant. However, any lack of calm assertion or initiative will go against your best interests. The family and friends of someone major in your life will be a vital part of today's dealings.

4. TUESDAY. Calm. Taurus people who truly enjoy their own company may be blessed at present. Heavenly activity takes a bit of time out until near the day's end. You may delight in cocooning into a private mood and being restful. Even in a crowd, a sense of disconnection can somehow comfort you while you engage in reflection. This could be one of those empty feeling times. Anyone you try to reach out to may not be around or be unavailable, which can be frustrating if you want to connect and talk. It's likely that you will have to leave messages. The latter hours can be just the opposite as people try without success to reach you.

5. WEDNESDAY. Unsettling. Certain people might be leeching your energy, probably without even realizing it. If you are hoping to keep new ideas or original commentary under wraps, extra care is required. You could worry about some manner of intellectual plagiarism, where an important personal thought might be spirited away to become someone else's. Walls can turn out to have ears if people speak too openly or neglect being choosy about who and where to relate. This could be a general problem with any kind of secret or news. The power of words can make or break a project. Gossip is in the air, along with distortion and exaggeration. Consider whether you really believe what you read and hear.

6. THURSDAY. Promising. Saturn has just left reverse motion and now gears up to retrace its steps. Hallmarks over time to come can be seen in certain turning points that are beginning to be revealed. Blocks and limitations on you should now be loosening up, and any past delays could finally be revealed as having greater reasons. Restructuring and the urge to repair or recycle are encouraged by the heavens. Constructive happenings can take place, especially if related to the domestic or career spheres of life. With your ruling planet, Venus, waltzing into Pisces, turn your attention toward dreams of future hopes, how they may be reached, and who might be of aid. Answers are likely to be close at hand.

7. FRIDAY. Enjoyable. Quality time with those who share your living space, or with other family members, is one of the potentials of this day. Housemates or neighbors could hang out together. Like-minded camaraderie is sure to be enjoyable as hours pass with natural entertainment among all. A romantic date may be delayed, or be given a rain check because of more pressing obligations. Watch for someone going over the top in reacting to a wish for more privacy or a preference to stay home. You may find yourself venturing out in order to care for someone who is ill, perhaps family. Visiting an institution is also foreseen for the caring Taurus.

8. SATURDAY. Challenging. Being fired up almost to a state of jittery restlessness can fuel many of your choices, actions, and consequences. A surplus of vigor and motivating inspiration might fill your spirit. A lot can get done if such hyped-up energy is channeled in productive directions, but thereby lies the challenge. The basic issue becomes one of choice and direction. If you aim at nothing in particular, then nothing can be hit. The stars are indicating that rationality and clarity could be rare. The best outcomes can be strived for later in the day. This morning a big distraction could put all goals out of your mind for a while.

9. SUNDAY. Pleasurable. Having to have, especially for sentimental or aesthetic reasons, is a Taurus instinct. That age-old syndrome of eyes connecting from far across the room might result as desire overtakes your heart. The allure of someone special, or at least something special, can be irresistible. What's deemed of beauty has a way of reaching through a crowd and over distance. It may be the love of your life, or simply a decorative object you admire above anything else in a store. Playing with scents and dressing up can be fun, especially before a special event. This could be indulged in solo, with a friend, or even with business associates.

10. MONDAY. Renewing. Youngsters are apt to be a delightful source of distraction, yet they might prove challenging with their constant interruptions. Taurus people who care for or work with children could have an action-packed time. Something new can be learned at any age. The speech and actions of those around you can awaken fresh points of view. In fact, the words of an acquaintance may turn out to be particularly significant, catalyzing an entire new way of perceiving what has been going on. You could feel as if you're either being taught or doing the tutoring, but both are likely the case. Differing beliefs tend to contribute to a healthy debate providing you keep an open mind.

11. TUESDAY. Positive. Medical and therapeutic themes are present, whether you are dealing with an ongoing concern or a new issue. If you have been saving vacation time and resources to finally see a specialist, this could be the day. Or at least this is the time to make the appropriate appointment, rather than procrastinating any longer. Be ignorant of your own body's messages at the peril of stable health. Proactive follow-through pays off, if you don't delay. Heavenly contacts support taking action with conviction. A focused and well-structured fitness routine is sure to prove a life-changing asset. Consider joining a health club or conferring with a personal trainer.

12. WEDNESDAY. Trying. Anyone who is supposed to be of service to you could seem not helpful at all. Even dealing with a waitress or store clerk could be a hassle, with the wrong order, bill, or just a negative attitude. A tradesperson might have to cancel an appointment due to their own misfortune, or the individual concerned may just be tardy and unreliable. Misunderstandings are waiting for a chance to crop up and annoy you. Make sure to get a clear and watertight price quote and description of any job that will be done for you. Check your appliances, car, and other gadgets to see if they need service. Preventive maintenance will pay off.

13. THURSDAY. Auspicious. Taurus animal lovers, especially anyone thinking of getting a pet, should carefully consider where to go. Rather than buy through a pedigree breeder or a pet store, it's more likely you'll find a perfect new best friend in an animal shelter. Taurus is an earthy Zodiac sign which adores and understands nature, or most aspects of it. There may be an opportunity for you to work with fauna or flora as some kind of vocational change. Or maybe you can take a course in horticulture, flower arranging, or cactus cultivation. Conversations might be loaded with transformational intensity, for ill or for good. Take care with flippant conversation that could hurt one listener in particular.

14. FRIDAY. Emotional. Mars, god of war, enters the emotional sign of Cancer in your sector of communications. In addition, the intensity of the Full Moon has just peaked. If you've been maintaining silence while someone has been stirring you up, this may be the day for that person to duck for cover. Still waters, actually full of deep activity, are apt to overflow with torrents of feelings that you need to get off your chest. Moody verbal clouds can have a silver lining, since emotional release is much more healing than building up layers of toxic implosion. Put your cards on the table by confronting the other person reasonably. Being candid doesn't mean getting in their face.

15. SATURDAY. Magical. Keeping company with someone very special to your heart guarantees an enjoyable time. Going somewhere together, invoking the experience of a whole different world, is sure to be well worth it. Why not visit a seaquarium, a theme park, or any fantasy-oriented setting including the movies? Wherever you go, the greatest delight can come when an intimate and rarefied atmosphere is created with someone. This vibe can echo into the evening, making it excellent for events such as a costume party. You will thrill to the glamour of a special occasion.

Someone significant at a gathering makes an instant connection with you.

16. SUNDAY. Tricky. Artful Mercury sidles into Aries, impacting the Taurus twelfth house of the hidden and the unseen. Mercury takes on a crafty astrological tone as it affects your basic possessions. So it's not surprising if you think the fairies have stolen something, or maybe some mysterious intruder took it. Whatever appears missing has probably been put in a new place, or is buried under a mass of other stuff. The cosmos reflects that any loss is only temporary, and reunion with the object concerned will happen. Fast, sly talkers may spin all kinds of creative raves. A spiritual group could offer enlightening information, but there's apt to be a catch.

17. MONDAY. Strategic. A fox seems to be in the henhouse, stirring trouble within a group. Or someone may be pulling the wool over your eyes at present. Either way, silence and quiet observation are better tactics than overt confrontation. Given enough rope, the perpetrator will soon be lassoed. Where your loyalties lie is sure to be tested, possibly through a forced choice. You may have to opt for taking the side of your usual cohorts or crossing over to an individual who is holding the reins of power. The ambitious can get ahead, but perhaps only by some type of soul-selling to the devil. An alliance might undergo ruthless refurbishing.

18. TUESDAY. Stormy. This is one of those days when you may confess that you just don't know what came over you. The cosmos is giving off signals indicating heavy intensity. The tiniest trigger can unwittingly set off a domino effect of escalating destructiveness. Words and information are the likely weapons of choice. In addition, an occasional punch could be thrown that's more than just verbal. The blame game needs to be halted in its tracks. A period of brooding may be in order. A neutral party is the best choice for any needed mediation, able to understand the larger picture and restore order. Don't make any new commitment.

19. WEDNESDAY. Enchanted. Past-lifers and new-age heads might feel validated today. Whatever your version of karma, it is likely to assert itself. Signals and symbols of guidance can appear in the surrounding everyday world. For those sensitive enough to tune in, a psychic reader and her crystal ball aren't needed. You will be your own best personal guide. If destiny places a lottery ticket in your path, especially via an acquaintance, grab it with both hands. Luck is afoot for Venus-ruled Taurus people. Connections belonging to family, friends, or a partner may help you attain your ambitions. Romance is also in the air, so Taurus singles should be on the lookout.

20. THURSDAY. Festive. The monthly period of solar returns now kicks in, as the Sun begins to light up your Zodiac sign. Happy birthday to all Taurus. Your ruling planet, Venus, is very well connected to Jupiter right now. Spring can feel like it's truly sprung, even if the weather doesn't match. Fortune and love are still in the air from yesterday, allowing Taurus romantics and risk-takers to strike while conditions remain favorable. The vibes are definitely set to diminish before the day is done. Limits may be hit, especially for anyone being greedy and irresponsible. After an auspicious entry into your sign, the Sun makes an adverse aspect to the Moon just before midnight. Time out!

21. FRIDAY. Busy. Get some solo space so that you can do your own thing. A case of cabin fever may have set in, leading to a yearning for escape from restraints on your personal freedom. Getting out of the house is apt to appeal, perhaps to create distance from a domestic responsibility that nevertheless must be dealt with sooner or later. The stars are smiling upon objectivity and practicality. You may now realize the true nature of a personal relationship. Consider whether it offers solid support or whether it is undermining and limiting a situation. It's likely that other people think they know your best interests. However, the problem is that they're not you and can't read your mind.

22. SATURDAY. Successful. If something is due for a complete makeover, the timing for it is excellent now. This is particularly true when the action relates to achieving your future ambitions and enhancing your public image. You don't have to be famous to be successful. Everyone has some kind of positive profile. Taurus people dreaming of becoming a household name can take a leap of faith with today's stars in play. Auditions or interviews for a position based on individual talent and creativity can succeed, with good opportunity to land the job. Grace and courage are in the air, but it's up to you when it comes to balancing the two. Give it your best shot.

23. SUNDAY. Active. One minute you could be sitting alone, the next going somewhere in special company. Lolling around is a great start to the day, but activity should be stepped up quickly. Friends are apt to come on the scene with plans that are a lot more active, even boisterous. Or you may opt to check out local stores or markets, with the possibility of a chance encounter exciting the day's tone. If your plans are open to modification and adjustment, it's likely that daily occurrences will be quite surprising. One party can follow another. Indulge your senses to top off this pleasant day.

24. MONDAY. Misleading. Big promises could turn out to be like overblown flowers, the type that can overwhelm the senses. What appears to be a great opportunity might just be a trap. This doesn't mean you should run in the opposite direction if you spot anything attractive, or if it spots you. But be discerning and cautious. You could be in for a favor from the gods right now. You may find you are magnetic to other people even though you can't put a finger on why. Just keep in mind that's there's ultimately no such thing as a free ride. Eventually you must pay for what you take, and the point becomes how and where and how much.

25. TUESDAY. Interesting. The sentimental and curious Taurus is likely to turn on to times past. A vibrant discussion, perhaps with a sibling, may bring up the subject of prior family history and pertinent historical events. Conferring with a parent or elderly relative can give you added insight into your genealogy. You may have to go far to do so, but there is definite value in what these individuals know. If you are examining your own psyche, you can come up with remarkable insights, shedding a bright light on matters once shrouded in mystery. Interesting reunions, sometimes touchy, are signified. If you hide something regarded as good as gold in a safe place, don't forget where you put it.

26. WEDNESDAY. Outstanding. The true nature of somebody can be brought out for all to see. This pertains especially to a person who has worked quietly behind the scenes, whether it's yourself or someone else. There could be astonishment at what's been achieved and produced while no one was looking. Servers and assistants are in line for some reward as the truth of their input is realized and acknowledged. If it's you, pat yourself on the back, and let others thank you, too. Or it may be the time to give kudos to a helper who has done a great deal on your behalf. Either way, what goes around will definitely come around to benefit you.

27. THURSDAY. Encouraging. A New Moon occurs in each Zodiac sign once a year. Today the New Moon takes place in your sign of Taurus. This lunar phase is an ideal time to begin anything. A new cycle of emotional biorhythms should be kicking in. Potentially a fresh point in life is marked, where steps may be taken toward greater internal growth and self-awareness. Setting all kinds of aims that are geared to improve anything about your identity and sense of self are blessed right now. Intellectual applications and endeavors should be charged up. These are excellent stars for activity related to writing, multimedia involvement, and expressive movement.

28. FRIDAY. Entrancing. There's a sucker's born every minute, as an observant soul once said. It's up to each of us to ensure that we're not one of them. Besides knowing yourself well and possessing emotional intelligence, you could opt to have your full personal astrological chart drawn up and interpreted by a competent, reputable practitioner. The time appears right for any Taurus who is self-interested enough to check this possibility out. Someone or something alluring this way comes, both for those who are looking and for those who do not realize they are looking. Confusing, disarming charm fills the ethers. Remember the story of the wolf in sheep's clothing!

29. SATURDAY. Edgy. The wisdom of experience and time is favored over taking off like a bull at a gate, bucking a reality check. If the opportunity occurs for someone senior to raise a more seasoned voice, listen! Patience is pertinent. Important foundational aspects must be in place to ensure desired outcomes. A vulnerable edge may disturb your psyche. Melancholy is indicated, but of the contemplative type and not the depressive version. Taurus individuals who love writing or reading can take advantage of such energy and get absorbed in the words, your own and those of others. Draw on the strength in tribal dynamics, whether from family, friends, or peers.

30. SUNDAY. Volatile. Social strings can be pulled and certain corners cut in deciding to move a deal or job along. But haste not only makes waste, it could jeopardize your reputation. Changing a goal in order to increase the speed of accomplishment over its quality would display a cheapening integrity. Going over the heads of underlings to someone in charge may be the right tactic in a large organization. Superiors are apt to offer more productive suggestions than would any of the middle management. Nevertheless, the cosmos leans toward the control freaks today. Err on the side of diplomacy.

MAY

1. MONDAY. Sensitive. The Moon returning to her own sign of Cancer for the next few days is usually an endearing and nurturing experience. Recent spats of jealousy and intemperate control dramas of love and desire can be smoothed over today. Douse the fires of any still-burning emotions through sensitive and caring communication. Be especially thoughtful of those from whom you seek enduring closeness and respect. Hold down any consuming obsession for purchases that are too expensive and sure to plunge you into anxious debt. Appreciate the simple joys of conversation with neighbors, colleagues, or fellow commuters. A swim or a walk can refresh.

2. TUESDAY. Fertile. This promises to be an active, refreshing day of social contact. A lively gathering with new faces will remind Taurus singles that there are plenty of fish in the sea. Intriguing company should not be hard to come by as long as you get up and moving. Remaining sedentary is unlikely, unless you are practically cemented in place. Embarking on studying a technical subject is favored, particularly if a great teacher is available, willing, and able. Hooking up to a new network or video conferencing should be considered for effective communication and more convenient information gathering. Jump in the car with a friend and head somewhere strange or unknown.

3. WEDNESDAY. Tricky. The great mysteries of life often seem elusive and just too hard to fathom. Straining conscious understanding of the infinite and eternal will lead to burnout rather than breakthrough. Anyone who promises to reveal the secrets of the cosmos is a dubious character, to say the least. Come back home to your local environment and daily life, where you're comfortably in familiar territory. Work with what is known. Pretense will be quickly and embarrassingly unmasked by someone who is more genuinely knowledgeable. If you are in possession of confidential information, think twice before casually disclosing details or inadvertently blurting them out.

4. THURSDAY. Exacting. The healthiest outcome will emerge from honest effort and keeping your feet firmly planted on the ground. Normally this wouldn't present problems to you, a practical Taurus, but lately it's been all too easy for fantasies to distract you and for wishful thinking to send you off on tangents. Be tough on yourself about real needs and practical goals. Keep in mind that you must help yourself, and that charity begins at home. If you offer a fine example of self-discipline and dedication to those with whom you live, the expectations and demands you make of them will be taken in the right spirit. Consolidate family security and living environment to support and stabilize your career ambitions.

5. FRIDAY. Restrained. Simply because you're loved and approved of doesn't mean you'll always get your way. Friction is likely when you proceed like a bull at a gate. If irritation and tension arise, exercise restraint and give way with compassionate understanding. Forgiveness may be the highest form of love. Expressions of grace and tenderness win support, affection, and respect. Whether it's an argument at home or a struggle in the workplace, you'll feel foolish later if you blow small issues out of proportion. Winning at the expense of other people could result in the loss of what was precious. Endings are the natural order of things and must be accepted as inevitable.

6. SATURDAY. Expressive. Mercury, planet of commerce, crossroads, and thieves, is back in your sign. This gives you a glib tongue, and you're likely to have plenty to say for yourself. Proceed slowly and surely. Concrete thinking trumps abstract conceptualizing during this period. It's a time to put up or shut up. Expressive youngsters will be great company, giving voice to what lies deep in the human spirit. Learners want to listen to your experience and ideas, especially involving arts and crafts. Hobbyists can take deep pleasure in a favorite pursuit and pastime, such as gardening, quilting, painting, woodwork, or sculpture. A love affair that has been a secret until now may be revealed.

7. SUNDAY. Exuberant. Make this a dynamic, exhilarating day of self-expression. Spontaneity of thought and the music of chance lead in the perfectly right direction, so surrender yourself for the ride. Of course you're not just a passenger on the wheel of fate, you're in the driver's seat. Keep your eyes on the road and your hands on the wheel. This sort of cavalier style is sure to attract individuals who are on your wavelength, as if you were all in a secret club, intent on enjoying each other's pleasurable company. All of your plans won't work out, but magic doorways can open nevertheless. A free-spirited potential lover could be introduced, leading to a joyful relationship, however short-lived.

8. MONDAY. Cautious. Keeping conversation light is your best approach to the day, although the intensity of a particular person could make that impossible. Confronting encounters may force you to take a stand and communicate your intentions and views. Manipulative tactics and power plays can temporarily sour any partnership. Be vigilant in detecting unconscious behavior that could abort any new friendship or companionship. Customers and clients can be difficult to satisfy and impervious to attempts at humor or playfulness. Anyone with authority is likely to pull rank, even over the smallest matters. Risking resources that aren't yours, or reckless use of credit, can be a serious mistake.

9. TUESDAY. Demanding. Petty annoyances could spoil the day if allowed to get under your skin. Even loved ones can infuriate you by forgetting important details or behaving inconsiderately. Try to maintain dignity and politeness in the face of rude responses and abrasive characters. An angry exchange is possible with an unsavory neighbor or a seedy local character. Dress codes need to be observed in certain contexts, especially where uniforms and safety clothing are required. Health treatments, or visiting someone who is receiving care, can be squeezed into your daily schedule. If concerned with your physical appearance you might embark on a program of cosmetic treatments to enhance your looks.

10. WEDNESDAY. Outstanding. The application of imaginative ideas at work requires boldness and confidence. You and several associates may have been working away in the background on a potential design, concept, or project. This will need to be promoted vigorously if it is ever to see the light of day. Trust in the integrity, quality, and beauty of whatever is most important to you. Talking and writing is one thing, but actually displaying it can be entirely different and far more persuasive. Stay alert for sales of designer clothing and luxury items that were too expensive originally but are now worth considering.

11. THURSDAY. Divisive. Your current friends and companions may not be to your partner's taste and style. Do not make matters worse by bringing together people who are naturally unsuited or antagonistic. Separate conflicted and warring parties for the sake of peace and harmony. A jealous lover could be taunted and slowly enraged if you choose to flaunt a potential rival in their face. Playing one off against another is an unseemly and hurtful game. Be clear with everyone as to where your allegiance lies, and settle insecurity with an act of public loyalty. Parental disapproval of a spouse or date needs to be faced head-on but could test the bonds of love.

12. FRIDAY. Favorable. In a period where casual and surprise encounters can lead to valuable relationships, this is a special day for joyful meetings and happy outcomes. An interview situation offers the opportunity for making an excellent impression. You will be viewed favorably. Schedule professional consultations now, especially if technical or complex matters need problem solving by knowledgeable experts. Good advice and timely wisdom are available for the taking. Grasp it quickly and don't look back. Return a partner's generosity with plans for an exciting evening out in an unfamiliar social context. This will provide stimulating entertainment and a memorable experience that enhances your relationship.

13. SATURDAY. Leisurely. A restless evening or late night is likely during this Full Moon period. Strange dreams can linger into the daylight hours, causing you to seek interpretations and oracles. Before reading too much into a dream, remember that this unconscious processing allows for conscious sanity. You might be a little hung over from too much of a good thing. Indulgent lazing in bed could be hard to resist, and you may not emerge until almost lunchtime. A lingering chat with a neighbor or family member is another relaxing option. The day becomes progressively more social, possibly culminating in an invitation to an exclusive party. Dress to impress if you go out tonight.

14. SUNDAY. Delightful. You'll be in the mood for company, but not just anybody will do. Taurus singles may have targeted a particular individual with whom to develop a closer rapport. You may have spotted this person in church, at work, or while roaming the aisles of a supermarket. To make more personal contact might require the help and introduction of someone who happens to know you both. Couples can make this a passionate day of intoxicating sights, tastes, smells, and touch. A partner who has recently received a raise or generous paycheck might want to splurge on a gift or other treat for you. Together you can plan your future.

15. MONDAY. Upsetting. Workplace rivalry could erupt. Be aware that the force may be with someone else. You can play the role of idea person, and you're sure to have a say. Nevertheless, your suggestions may not be heeded, let alone understood, by the boss or someone else in power. It might be a better strategy to wait for another time to offer your best thoughts. If the household purse strings have slipped from your grasp, no amount of practical pleading on your part is likely to stop a determined mate's extravagant purchase. Suspicious behavior by a family member won't be unmasked or explained to you simply because you ask.

16. TUESDAY. Fair. Turn your attention to family members and other loved ones who are currently far from home. Give them a sense of roots by updating them on all the local news. Whether you connect via the Internet or send them a personal letter in the mail, offer your best thoughts on whatever is important to them. Studies require full attention, with significant lessons or assignments coming due soon. Armchair travel might grab your imagination, perhaps leading to peruse world maps or go one step further and start planning a trip. International work commitments could mean packing and preparing to leave home for at least one member of the household.

17. WEDNESDAY. Bumpy. Overconfidence and impatience are traps for the unwary. With bad timing, these negative traits could undo the best laid plans. On the other hand, by maintaining dignity and patiently implementing thorough strategies, there's every chance of success in a variety of personal goals. Suggesting proposals to officials, especially those connected to property, is timely. However, there could be hidden resistance to your ideas from neighbors. Handling legal issues involving family affairs might arouse old resentments and unresolved enmity. Elders could be called upon to resolve disputes. In all matters, the law of the land and the letter of the law should prevail.

18. THURSDAY. Challenging. Playing it safe and straight is best today. Any public role will benefit from professionalism and experience. Express mastery of your chosen career and you'll gain added respect. This should also generate loyalty among clients and customers, or win them over from the competition. Taurus people who are aware of inherited talents and abilities can make the most of them now. Weighty concerns in your personal life may preoccupy you, making it hard to concentrate on work. Or you may be so busy that overtime keeps you on the job way past quitting time. Treat every challenge and obstacle as a learning experience. Don't forget to share what you've learned so far with those who can benefit from the knowledge.

19. FRIDAY. Good. Falling in love or developing a crush could strike the romantically inclined, probably in a group environment. Someone who has been invisible until now might boldly make their desires known with a tempting invitation to a secret rendezvous. Fairy-tale prospects can have surprises and twists, which may require more social flexibility than you're prepared to give. Promoting your enterprise with elegant design elements should have the desired effect. Shop for the right fashion for street wear and work. This may be bought with less effort and less cash than usual. An enchanting movie, musical performance, or gallery viewing would suit your mood later in the day.

20. SATURDAY. Pleasant. Having fun with friends, entertaining at home, or doing both separately and together can be an expensive proposition. However you'll probably plunge ahead, only to count the cost later. It's wise to recognize that fun will inevitably be costly and can be justified as long as it doesn't become an obsession. Paying for the pleasure of other people, or just spending along with them, is good to do with your money. Be wary, however, of being overcharged in the flurry of transactions, whether mistakenly or knowingly. Approaches by a friend to borrow for a good cause could become annoying. Quickly yet politely refuse rather than stringing this person along simply to be nice.

21. SUNDAY. Enjoyable. Fresh possibilities for both business and pleasure are apt to be aroused through meeting friends of friends and making new acquaintances. Networking electronically as well as in groups can enhance your career prospects and expand potential growth for current enterprises. You're most likely to spend time in stimulating, exuberant company, bumping into some weird and wonderful characters. A community event or a gathering of your extended family can be a whirlpool of activity. Time flies by while you enjoy the passing parade of assorted individuals. Your social world has more than enough variety now.

22. MONDAY. Productive. It is important that you attend a special and somewhat secretive meeting. This could be anything from a critical forward-planning team at work to the latest local gossip relayed by phone. Whatever the subject or context, become informed and stay in the loop. Guard against burying your head in the sand, trying to ignore problems and pitfalls. Contribute ideas and opinions even if they are not popular, but then step back to avoid getting in too deep. Conspiratorial and clandestine involvements could leave some people embarrassed; make sure it's not you. A background briefing regarding a commercial proposition or the private assessment of personal finances would be worthwhile signaling the way ahead.

23. TUESDAY. Variable. Tension can develop when your attention is distracted from business by irritating calls and annoying conversations. This stress could even escalate to become a major headache or some uncomfortable muscular pain. Make yourself temporarily unavailable so that you can work quietly on problems at hand. Whether that means turning off the phone, locking the door, or hanging a busy sign on the instant messaging software, it must be done when uninterrupted focus becomes necessary. Take the time to look at worries in a positive light, then move toward resolute action that will make a difference. After a hard day, relaxation and confidence will well up from within.

24. WEDNESDAY. Opportune. It's a fresh start for Taurus people as the Moon returns to your sign once again. However, it's also the last dark days of the lunar month, which cautions against taking on the world or embarking in new directions. Current conditions offer a chance to pause and digest recent events. Take particular note of your own responses. Consider personal care such as a haircut or body treatment, or the removal of physical blemishes. It is becoming clear that you are your own person, individually distinct from family members and friends. Happiness and fulfillment lie within you. Act in your own best interests, since no one else can better understand what you want and need.

25. THURSDAY. Lackluster. Drifting along and dreaming can become a pastime, possibly at the expense of your work and career advancement. Not listening to instructions and behaving forgetfully only lead to taking longer to get anything done. Do not take on anything requiring sharp attention and precision performance. Spontaneous gestures of camaraderie over a casual drink or two could turn into much more. Nevertheless, even the most sincere, dedicated workers need downtime now and again, so don't feel guilty or be evasive about relaxing when the opportunity comes along. Some tall stories might circulate within your circle and be blown out of proportion, gaining false currency and putting you in a negative light.

26. FRIDAY. Steady. Unless pressing matters demand direct personal attention, make this a leisurely morning. Finish up any loose ends from the past few days. Outstanding correspondence and phone calls can be handled with ease. A lunchtime stroll in the park or a regular gym session should blow away the cobwebs, letting you turn your mind with a fresh eye to plans for the month ahead. A chat with a brother or sister can put certain financial matters into perspective, but keep things confidential and under wraps. A New Moon overnight is a great opportunity for good sleep. However, the temptation to burn the midnight oil with someone special could be too strong for some Taurus people.

27. SATURDAY. Dynamic. Good ideas are coming thick and fast, but don't try to explain yourself or expect other people to quickly understand. Some financial matter that needs quick action must rely on intuition rather rather than many external opinions. Taurus people who are employed on an as-needed casual basis might be able to supplement the feast-and-famine cycle with a more personal enterprise. Appreciation of cutting-edge style in business may be a winner for those who back their own ideas in the face of herd mentality. When chaos breaks out around you at some point during the day, rise above the confusion and focus on the big picture. This higher ground can surely be turned to your advantage.

28. SUNDAY. Starred. Decide if you can afford to finance plans and projects or if you need backing from someone else to get an idea off the drawing board. Perhaps a partner is needed for a business, or a loan application might need to be prepared for an investment proposal. A relative could leave you a sizable inheritance, some generous blessing that you were not expecting. Any money that is borrowed or comes to you from another source can be made to multiply and build wealth for you. Shopping is a priority today. You can use credit cards for several costly purchases. A beautiful item that's been on your priority wish list for some time might finally go on sale and be irresistible.

29. MONDAY. Comforting. There's strength and sustenance in staying on local ground with at least one familiar face for company. A whole range of characters can be waiting in the wings to populate your day with many human interest stories. Making presentations to strangers and unknown groups might require the help of someone who is very genial and outgoing. Taurus students with questions can get answers from a helpful teacher or more advanced member of the class. A chance drive with a friend is likely to surprise you both when uncanny similarities are revealed between you. Traffic should be brisk and taxis available if you must buzz around town or pleasure.

30. TUESDAY. Frustrating. Just getting around in your world could be more rough and tumble than usual, making yesterday's smooth passages all the more remarkable by comparison. Once you arrive at your first destination, it might already feel like the wrong move. It could be a battle to complete the usual shopping circuit, leaving you frazzled and irritable. Parking is apt to be another headache. Try to work out this stress on a physical level by going to a gym session or yoga class. The weather may even permit swimming, as summer makes its presence felt. Whatever you do, don't take tension back home to an unsympathetic household. Loved ones are likely to have little tolerance for emotional outbursts and a bad mood.

31. WEDNESDAY. Guarded. The security of your home and loved ones can be a priority as the cold, hard facts of survival present themselves clearly. Take pride in being self-responsible and self-sufficient, however tough it becomes sometimes. Parents and older relatives are supportive, if a little distant or judgmental. Make it clear that you want to stand on your own two feet. Refuse any offer of assistance that is humiliating or has strings attached. Equipping, furnishing, or redecorating a living space can be a costly yet unavoidable expense. Be practical in your choices. Search for secondhand goods and timely bargains that will do the job just as well as brand-new equivalents.

JUNE

1. THURSDAY. Constructive. Escaping from oppressive responsibilities and the endless round of duties is apt to be uppermost in your mind. Whether intelligent insight or pragmatic rationality gets the upper hand, it will remind you that material dreams can only become a reality with effort and money. In the good old tradition of the carrot and the stick, you may need to first mentally imagine and design outcomes before laboring toward their realization. Softening an approach to competition can bring to light other ways of interacting beyond struggle and one-sided outcomes. Welcome theatrical creativity and dramatic expression into your own living room.

2. FRIDAY. Rewarding. Taking the time for deep sharing with your mate, partner, or another member of the household is a great way to start the day, almost guaranteed to put a spring in your step and a smile on your face. Intimate caring and a sense of belonging are an ideal platform for taking on the world. Finish dealing with outstanding bills and any overdue payment before another batch of invoices inevitably arrives to cause the next flurry of anxiety. By getting a lot done before lunch, there might be a chance of going home early or at least taking some time out. Recreational interests gradually gain the upper hand, with gardening, crafts, and writing likely to appeal. The evening is ripe for love.

3. SATURDAY. Diverse. Now that Mercury has moved along to the lunar world of Cancer, tall tales and legendary stories will enter into many conversations. Try to discern the difference between fact and fiction or you could be taken for a ride in more ways than one. Early risers should be rewarded for the effort with all the beauty of a spring's day. Spending special time with your mate or partner this morning will enhance the whole day. Games and sports of all kinds, even those strange or unknown to you, can be enjoyable. New friends are sure to come along if you stretch out a little. Gambling and impulse shopping can leave your wallet and bank account forlorn.

4. SUNDAY. Touchy. If caring for kids this weekend you can have a lot of fun. Just don't overdo the force or insensitivity that adults sometimes display without meaning to do. If this happens, expect hurt feelings and tears as youngsters deal with their sense of powerlessness in a world that's always bigger than they are. If you are not in the mood for childish demands, invite your own friends over to play. Displaying overt interest in a good-looking neighbor is guaranteed to arouse jealousy, which may be good or bad depending on what you want. Freedom-oriented Taurus individuals could experience a sense of being trapped with anyone from a spouse to last night's fling.

5. MONDAY. Disquieting. Running into a former workmate may not be pleasant, especially if you never had much in common. Neither of you may be able to resist firing a volley or two over matters left unsettled from the past. Employing a home repairman could turn into some sort of cosmic payback, when a seemingly small job becomes an extravagant production due to incompetence or carelessness. This could be the time to schedule a thorough medical checkup, paying special attention to a potential hereditary condition that might benefit from careful analysis. At the very least, check your family medical history. Sweet-toothed Taurus people should restrict sugar intake.

6. TUESDAY. Fulfilling. Make this a day of truly enjoying whatever you do, from housework to the profession or job that you've mastered. Vocational satisfaction is a special blessing, so express this at every opportunity. You reputation, whether with clientele or superiors, is escalating. Use this profile to enhance your earnings and to further your ambitions for more career fulfillment. If experiencing unprecedented success, treat yourself to an elegant wardrobe addition for a special occasion or a better look in public. Or you may opt to buy luxury models of tools of the trade. Suggest dinner and a drink with a fellow worker. Celebrating is well-earned and affordable.

7. WEDNESDAY. Mixed. Coordinated precision activity is favored, if it must be done at all. Joining your skills with another person's experience allows personal goals to readily be achieved. Get menial work out of the way before lunch, so that you can give people your best attention for the rest of the day. However, don't expect all of your encounters to be relaxed, friendly, or even respectful. Running into trouble as you walk through the door at home is a likely scenario. Territorial disputes can erupt in private interpersonal contexts. Somebody's not happy with their current living arrangements. The resolution of friction will come with certainty in a week or so, but not today.

8. THURSDAY. Stormy. Today might bring the mother of all battles to your doorstep. Any dispute or difference that has been waiting for a showdown is likely to flare up now. There can also be positive connections coming home to roost, perhaps concerning money negotiations or legal documents. Any agreement signed today will have serious consequences and binding expectations. Mediation by a person who can be objective will assist in resolving a deadlock. Group processes add an overlay of chaotic intelligence for problem solving, but outcomes are likely to be unpredictable and systems may be out of equilibrium. If you can't stand the heat, get out of the kitchen.

9. FRIDAY. Risky. Don't believe everything you hear, especially early in the day. Friends are a likely source of the latest speculations and hearsay circulating as gossip. Pay careful attention to anyone relying on your skill. Be wary of negligent distraction. Tumultuous feelings may still be swirling, but your furtive imagination can blow things out of proportion. People engaged on your behalf, professionally or technically, may prove to be incompetent or fraudulent. Don't be put off with half-truths and quasi-facts if your intuition says that something is wrong. Understandings in extended and blended families could be stretched if trust is lacking. Covering up for superiors will be seen as misguided before long.

10. SATURDAY. Cooperative. Wisdom suggests that order must prevail for the well-being and security of both your public and private life. Grudges and strategies of revenge only poison chances of genuine agreement and fair compromise. There's a need to forgive and to cooperate for the good of all. Family togetherness can lead to bonding truths being openly shared. Negotiating arrangements and signing a property deal could be on your agenda. Or a domestic settlement such as alimony and child custody might reach the stage of mutual acceptance. Organize the affairs of the sick and elderly, assuring that a legal will is current and appropriately reflects the person's wishes.

11. SUNDAY. Auspicious. An extreme magnetic attraction or repulsion could grip you at this Full Moon phase. It may be bigger than both of you. There can be an unmistakable charge in any encounter. This could mark the turning point of passionate commitment in a relationship, either because you and your partner want it so much or perhaps because you're already in too deep. In any event, there are no half measures in dealing with people at close quarters. A career dream may come true when you get an offer from a large corporation or finally land a lucrative contract with an influential customer. Have faith that fate is sweeping you onward and upward to ever greater fulfillment.

12. MONDAY. Expansive. With deals in the pipeline, projects on the boil, and numerous external responsibilities, you could be boarding a flight or out on the road first thing this morning. While escaping the hothouse environment at home might be welcome, you may find the separation hard, especially if it happens on a regular basis. For those already away from home, maybe visiting distant relatives, setting up a business, or exploring the possibility of relocation, foreign customs and climates might be hard to comprehend. Put duty and security first in everything you undertake. Be extra cautious in action and decision. Hidden antagonists can be lurking, ready to launch criticism and attack you at the first stumble.

13. TUESDAY. Satisfying. Travel for pleasure, particularly a family vacation, can be booked and then embarked upon with confidence. Even a short trip to visit relatives or former neighbors will be pleasant, with news to share and stories to tell. Dealing with officials and legal affairs should proceed smoothly and effectively, with any questionable or disputed matters going in your favor. Making a speech or other presentation will be received positively by your target audience. This is sure to be a relief to those who must deliver a hard message as sensitively as possible. Workplace training can be a successful exercise. New employees needed for business expansion can be found by advertising widely.

14. WEDNESDAY. Progressive. Strategic meetings of a project team can set the stage for beginning a major effort. Spend today making the planning clear so that everyone knows exactly what their role is and how it fits within the overall scheme. Whatever your work, constructive teamwork and a sense of belonging to an effective organization will be a source of well-deserved pride. Protect and maintain your valuable reputation by maintaining high standards of service and quality. It's possible now to strike a functional balance between career commitments and domestic needs, allowing at least some time on a regular basis for socializing privately with friends and family.

15. THURSDAY. Hopeful. Heady romance is in the air. You might imagine yourself taking the leading role in a fantasy of choice. Despite how the situation looks now, it's unlikely to prove true or reliable. The mistake could lie in believing projections as if they were real or reciprocal. In contrast, attempts at promoting events as larger than life can be disarmingly successful. This is a fine time for bringing attention to your unique talents and qualities, to who you are and what you can do. Taurus entrepreneurs and artists should succeed well with public efforts. Don't hide your light under a bushel. Let it shine, however different it might be from current styles and standards.

16. FRIDAY. Lucrative. Business is apt to be brisk and profitable early on, which will be a boon for those who get off to a flying start. Immediately focus on completing current work satisfactorily, including collecting wages, fees, and proceeds from a sale. Requesting a bonus or higher salary is also timely in this important financial period of the year. Career success has social implications. There may be an introduction to old, established families of the district. Expect more doors to open for networking and patronage, which can only be good for your earning potential. Companionship with someone from childhood could be fortunate for both of you.

17. SATURDAY. Unstable. A spontaneous good time with friends would be a welcome relief from the pressure at home or the emotional demands of those closest to you. Take a chance to get away from routines and needy people. The farther you plunge into uncharted social terrain, the more you will realize that most people do want something. Someone around you is lucky, so tune in and encourage their daring as you ride their wave. Freewheeling independent characters who are answerable to no one but themselves might be thought-provoking if you feel stuck in a dead-end job or relationship. If there are communication problems with your partner, get a friend to deliver a message, or write a letter.

18. SUNDAY. Trying. The cost of socializing and simultaneously maintaining a household might be catching up with you, resulting in bills taking longer to pay than normal. It's time to cut down on expensive outings, or learn to mix with pals and relatives without overspending. Hosting members of a club or group at your place is sure to cost more than anticipated, so consider asking for financial contributions. Following the trends and styles of people around you won't be personally satisfying. When it comes to spending money, make your own choices about what you want. Membership fees and annual contributions can fall due shortly.

19. MONDAY. Manageable. Visiting an elderly relative shows respect and support so that the person feels secure and appreciated. Anyone responsible for the sick and frail is in for a busy yet satisfying day. Those suffering an illness or having medical treatment are likely to make a full recovery, given enough time off and plenty of rest and individual attention. This is the time for arranging your private life and bringing order to your own backyard. Having the house to yourself might be a blessing. Much can be accomplished alone. Physical disciplines with a spiritual philosophy, including martial arts and yoga, will reward steady practice. Or perhaps dancing will be more exhilarating and arousing.

20. TUESDAY. Demanding. Maintaining silence in the face of provocative words will be far more effective than reacting foolishly and taking the bait. Control yourself and avoid the embarrassment of an outright confrontation. A youngster can be provocative, and may require stern discipline rather than reasoning or words of wisdom. Tough love might be the order of the day. Feisty conversations could be masking real intentions that are inscrutable but genuine. The evening should be more to your taste. With the summer solstice almost here, marking the longest day of the year, this is an appropriate ritual juncture to celebrate the natural world in all its beauty and bounty.

21. WEDNESDAY. Hectic. Suddenly becoming the center of attraction could put you uncomfortably in the hot seat. It's imperative to please yourself, but this may not please other people or even suit them a little. Be ready to explain, defend, and justify personal decisions and attitudes. However, rather than being aggressive or righteous, display good humor and your more likeable qualities to smooth the waters and ruffled feathers. You are apt to feel torn in several different directions at once, trying to cover all the essential bases such as relationships, family, and career simultaneously. Seek an intelligent outcome to this dilemma which also leaves time to have a life of your own.

22. THURSDAY. Pleasurable. In contrast to yesterday's feelings of being between a rock and a hard place, a generous and inclusive social tone sweeps you up today. The Moon and Venus together in your sign, oriental and beautifully visible in the predawn sky, herald love and pleasure for Taurus people. Anyone formerly upset by your style, or dubious of your intentions, will now see the light and warm to you. The retrograde passage of the Moon's Node into Pisces marks the start of a gregarious and interactive period. This will bring you a passing parade of entertaining characters. Making intuitive choices among this human mix will brighten your days.

23. FRIDAY. Problematic. Security and income stability should be a priority. Figure out a realistic household budget, then decide how it will be funded. Practical necessities must be included, so luxuries and indulgences are likely to be omitted for now. Don't forget less glamorous essentials such as health care, home insurance and maintenance, equipment or machinery service, and the needs of dependents such as children or aging parents. When you add it all up, there will be a number of good reasons for continuing to work hard and earn enough. Taurus people who are temporarily unemployed and are being supported by family should make a determined effort to achieve financial self-sufficiency.

24. SATURDAY. Positive. Whatever you say today will be well received. Make a particular effort to listen attentively to younger people, who have much intelligent insight to offer in their own way. At least you'll understand where they're at and what's on their mind. Lovers can be particularly sweet with each other. For the astute there may be conversational clues about little gifts of affection longed for by that special person. Taurus artists, advertisers, promoters, and teachers could exhibit special style and grace. Intelligence and vision can be expressed with clarity and aesthetic delicacy. Paying for training close to your heart might be one of your best expenditures ever.

25. SUNDAY. Enjoyable. The New Moon in Cancer is an opportunity for quiet thinking. If certain people come to mind, give them a call or drop by for a visit. Joking and telling stories with friends can flavor the day with enjoyment. Cruising the street, window-shopping, and hanging out at the mall will allow Taurus singles a chance to meet someone special, if on the lookout. If you already have a sweetheart, you might choose to study something that brings joy to your partner. A massage course, learning to prepare homely cuisine from the old country, or taking up a certain craft can be pleasing.

26. MONDAY. Easygoing. Shooting the breeze with friends at lunch will be more to your taste than sacrificing personal pleasure for the boss's expectations. A sudden urge to get out of the house or office and connect, even with total strangers, should be followed rather than doubted. The magical mystery tour is a preferable option to boring yourself with routine predictability. Exploring a different park or garden, strange store, or unfamiliar neighborhood can give you an enhanced awareness of local territory. There's always someone new to meet, even around the corner. Classes and seminars will stimulate Taurus students who listen and actively participate.

27. TUESDAY. Relaxing. Host a low-key party or other celebration at your house for a shy friend, neighbor, or relative. You don't really need any excuse to invite people over for a get-together, sharing food, drink, and good company. It might be something as small as dinner with household members, or a broader invite to the whole clan. Breaking bread together amidst laughter and conversation puts the heart in any home. Expressing yourself openly and truthfully with those who share your living space will produce a special bonding. These connections can go farther to embrace extended family, friends of friends, and fellow workers, all tuned to the same frequency.

28. WEDNESDAY. Bright. Before settling in for the summer season, make a last push to carry out whatever short trips are important, especially those that involve the expectations of people near and dear to you. While it might be hard to get motivated and moving, there may be lingering regrets if you don't go. Visiting someone who is immobilized, institutionalized, or significantly out of the loop for some other reason will earn their undying gratitude and loyalty. Cooperative and communal living ventures can be discussed, with advantages and disadvantages being raised honestly and openly. Interviews for a person to share an apartment or to rent a property can lead to the right person.

29. THURSDAY. Good. A bird in the hand is worth more to you now than wishful thinking of what might be. Don't be led astray by false promises and alluring fantasies. This is particularly relevant when it comes to getting the balance right between your work and personal life. Show genuine appreciation to family members and the solid support you get on the domestic front. Being seduced by a glamorous career dream will only leave you flat if it doesn't materialize. Fulfilling happiness is there for the taking with a passionate lover, spouse, or partner. Romantic graces should be accompanied by attentive sensuality. A natural momentum should take care of things once you get started.

30. FRIDAY. Variable. Enlist the support of your mate or partner to draw the line with kids who demand material gratification with no end in sight. This could be crucial if the budget is tight and getting tighter. Even the best advisers are fallible, and their suggestions might cost you. Gambling and stock tips are unlikely to make money for you, even if the person you hear from is normally lucky. You're more in the mood for fun than work, and spending will be easier than earning. Leave work early, and remember that the best things in life can be free. The fragrance and delicacy of nature, even your own garden, and the company of a caring person, even a regular friend, will be best.

JULY

1. SATURDAY. Challenging. A certain group could become newly important somehow. Rivalry is a part of many scenarios, either arising naturally or in the context of a special event. Either way, this is within an atmosphere of camaraderie and like-minded spirit. If you're a member of a team involved in a competition, work hard to counter the unexpected which may plague a match. Athletic or cerebral challenges can be highly stimulating. Novel strategies, game plans, and even new suggestions on rules and techniques are also likely. For the classic Taurus couch potato, keep in mind that spectators are also important.

2. SUNDAY. Tempering. You may be feeling a bit under the weather, or perhaps just burnt out after some kind of excess. Too much of a good thing can lead to a required period of recovery and rebalancing the body-mind connection. It's best not to fall into the temptation of taking part in more of whatever the culprit was. At least call time out for now. The choice is your responsibility. Substituting one activity for a more constructive one is a good tactic when it comes to dealing with delay of gratification. There's also the reward system to consider. Treating yourself after a goal is achieved is more the Venusian way.

3. MONDAY. Useful. Joy is to be found in the most ordinary of activities and in the everydayness of the world. You have the capacity to focus on the journey, rather than simply rushing toward the prize. People should work well together today, especially as part of an established group. You may actually prefer to be grounded to a task rather than out running around, frittering away your time. The streets can even feel a bit abrasive. Remaining in a contained space or getting on with whatever you have to do is sure to be productive and satisfying in the long run. Taurus people who are involved in family business or a home-based industry are likely to be pleased with today's results.

4. TUESDAY. Fair. The heavens have lately been focusing on the practicality and security of work, and this vibe still remains. In addition, a more fiery tone is beginning to prevail. Although the tangible routine of life can still rule, a lot more action and interaction are now foreseen. A formal meeting with professional colleagues might take place out of necessity on this holiday. In some cases this could prove perturbing, but such an encounter should go well. A self-gratifying, even hedonistic tone comes into play later in the day. Then you can enjoy a party or drinks at the preferred restaurant or bar. Let someone new on the scene know exactly where you stand.

5. WEDNESDAY. Restless. Gremlins have been around since Mercury went into retro-gear yesterday. The normal symptoms might begin to show in problems with communications, gadgets, and anything tricky, plus items becoming irritatingly lost. These types of dynamics, and then some, may be most notable within your own home environment, or as part of family affairs. A phase is commencing in which you are likely to revisit and reconsider prior decisions and thoughts. Opinions can be revised and changed, from the warmest mutating into cold withdrawal. Moving because of a career dream is an idea worth mulling over.

6. THURSDAY. Volatile. Jangled nerves might have you thinking you better lay off coffee or other beverages. That's not a bad idea, but it's not necessarily the source of an urge to keep constantly on the move. Agitation that sparked the atmosphere earlier in the year can now make you seem very itchy for change. Only the comfortably numb could be immune to any indications of restlessness. The need for change, or the absolute desire for it, is the current theme. Major areas of life, possibly more than one at the same time, hold the potential of notable shifts and modifications, especially of relationships and your vocation. This shift may be your choice or not at all what you now want.

7. FRIDAY. Guarded. Talk covers many subjects today. Keep in mind the possible consequences, even if it's only over coffee with a friend. Sensitivity to respectful expression is needed when it comes to communicating and trading thoughts. Intimate discussions and high-impact conversations may be increased in intensity or personal meaning simply by one word. Any Taurus engaged in counseling, or in the counseling process, might reach remarkable depths and discover new awareness. Negotiations and paperwork connected with an institution cannot be put off, particularly if related to financial deals like loans and home repairs.

8. SATURDAY. Fulfilling. The heavens are packed with a virtual scramble of star contacts. There's a selection of vibes to choose from at present, depending on exactly what type of Taurus you are. Energy can be directed toward and around your own private nest. Or any practical duty might be dropped for a complete change of activity proposed by a group of friends. Or it could be a special date with someone you have idealized for a long time. An event that's been on hold for a while might finally be happening. A valued new possession may be acquired, but only after an objective inquiry to compare prices and guarantees.

9. SUNDAY. Surprising. The company of beautiful people and objects is always beneficial to a Venusian soul. Cruising around the mall, or the markets, or even a gallery or garden is likely. Your hard-earned money can be spent on more baubles, bangles, and beads, or whatever else grips your fancy. Recycled objects, antiques, and resurrected styles can all be sources of satisfaction, even if you are only browsing. Cosmetics and hair styling may become a priority, whether you are actually using them or are just seeing what's available and what's new. A spontaneous trip to the appropriate parlor may lead to a surprising transformation.

10. MONDAY. Active. Travel and moving around in general are indicated by patterns related to today's Full Moon. You might be on the way to foreign places, possibly as part of a group. Or perhaps you are taking someone to a station or airport to see them off. An international aspect also is present and may lead to someone coming right to, or through, your front door. A visitor from out of town may appear unexpectedly, or at least send you an e-mail or a letter indicating a desire to stay with you for a short while. Roll out the welcome mat. A notable event is possible in the immediate neighborhood. Taurus students cramming for a test may be up all night.

11. TUESDAY. Trying. A proposed deal with an organization or a hierarchy of control might have to be negotiated. This is apt to involve rehashing a familiar issue from times before. Defense and offense may be so ingrained in a certain standoff that the differences are irreconcilable, and even mediation will be to no avail. Waiting a little while more, in any process, is advisable now. A sticking point could occur when personal opinion tests the limits of a well-accepted rule or law or tradition. A dispute is capable of splitting a group into two and polarizing many people. This may involve a spiritual or philosophical difference that is suddenly out in the open and attracting attention.

12. WEDNESDAY. Demanding. It's not about you at present. The requirements of other people are likely to hold greater sway most of the day. A parent or other elder might require extra time and attention. Or it could be that you need to adhere to a long-term accepted tradition such as a regular gathering of relatives or a community group. Partners may need extra energy to focus on the other half in the relationship. This would not be unpleasant, but the required emotional intensity will take up more of your personal space and energy. Creative dreamers may see their imaginative capacity reach for the stars, with some highly inspired perceptions. This is a starred night for fantasy pursuits, or plain deep sleep.

13. THURSDAY. Persuasive. There is the possibility of a gift in the mail or to be delivered in person. Flowers and candy might be likely offerings. Or the present may take the form of words, spoken or written. Either way, you can look forward to receiving a message of endearment or gratitude. A fervent and fiery cosmic ambience is set to enter the ethers, potentially making for passionate times. This general intensity will hold sway over most of the day and dominate the tone tomorrow as well. Staying power can be fortunately displayed by the strong-willed Taurus. On the downside, be alert for obsession and brooding. Major emotional blocks can be removed with discreet determination.

14. FRIDAY. Dynamic. An astrological headline for Taurus would read today: Big cosmic happenings, as your planet Venus plugs into Pluto and Mars. Powerful magnetism and strong charisma can be the gift signified by such an astro contact. Highly attuned instincts and a sensual type of intuition will allow you to attract whatever it is you want. Just keep in mind about being careful what you ask for because you may get it. Face-offs concerned with power and money are a challenging potential. Who's in control and what are they worthy of are central questions that need to be asked. Sudden events may surround a colleague and draw you into their sphere.

15. SATURDAY. Tactful. Something needs to be said, words that incorporate a degree of sentimentality or emotional investment. A normally receptive friend or family member may not have really listened the first time around. The proviso is that anything can be discussed now as long as it's not related to money. Steer well clear of talk about a loan, or some important material object, which of course is probably exactly the subject you want to raise. There's more value in listening with an open mind and heart rather than sounding off unthinkingly, turning into a mere noisemaker. Take the time to analyze a situation fully, and don't let impatience lead to an attempt to cut corners.

16. SUNDAY. Quiet. It's tempting to communicate nothing at the present time. Cosmically not much is occurring, and what is happening has a minimal, reserved flavor. Energy is generally low. This is not a problem unless you're trying to organize a dynamic event or want the world to stimulate and amuse you. You can succeed in being the host with the most in your own backyard if plans have been made in advance. The Sun today may as well be hiding behind huge dark clouds. It's up to you to take notice or not of today's external forces. Trying to swim against this astro tide is apt to leave you exhausted and bound by duties, rather than having some degree of fun.

17. MONDAY. Stimulating. Positive vibes and the potential for satisfying outcomes and achievements punctuate this day. Sparks of opportunity and generally free-flowing dynamics are the tone of many interactions. Brainstorming is sure to be on fire, intuitive, fast, but very subjective. All good intentions aside, a lot of lip service is also in the air, and misunderstandings can still pepper your experiences. The communication planet, currently retro-Mercury, is getting heated up and frazzled by keeping too close company with the Sun. This augurs possible emotional or mental burnout for a few Taurus people. It's okay to use your energy powerfully and effectively, but don't go overboard.

18. TUESDAY. Sensitive. Lovely Venus tiptoes into the liquid sign of Cancer, taking her mind off the material and turning attention more inward, toward a softening phase. With the Moon also in your sign now, it's no surprise if you, too, become softer and less intently rigid. As a Taurus you are likely to be hypersensitive to the rhythm of the lunar cycle. If currently in a relationship you may feel highly sensitized toward your loved one, as even deeper understanding develops. You could note increased vulnerability to even slightly negative words, plus an increased tendency to care too much about what is said by those on the outside. Be gentle with yourself.

19. WEDNESDAY. Complex. Attention turns to you and your own thoughts. Many Taurus people have been in a fairly long-term process of attempting to define a clearer sense of direction and purpose in the world. The future is apt to still feel undefined and hazy. The big question is where you are going with your life. Feeling that you are able to communicate and really be heard is important. A conversation with the right ally can help you gain clarity with any perplexing problem. Belief in yourself is what really must be addressed. Look deep into your own heart for the answer.

20. THURSDAY. Frustrating. If attempting to structure something really sound you have a challenge on your hands. All the will in the universe can be present, along with the drive to go. However, it's probable that the timing is not quite right for embarking on the pursuit of a certain desire. If rushing to nail this aim, frustration can stare you in the face as your actions are thwarted, delayed, or twisted. A major trigger for flying off the handle could be aggravation connected to security and income. A good physical workout is an excellent method for sublimating negative angst, as long as you don't push it.

21. FRIDAY. Opportune. No guts, no glory! You can muster plenty of fortitude and courage at present. Rebound into this day, inspired with a vengeance to focus on getting results. Be sure to perform suitable follow-through. Big decisions can be made, fueled by a flame you have kept burning with inspired foresight. Resources can be poured into acquisition of a major long-term investment. Taking a risk and a leap of faith might be the choice that confronts you. Individuals in higher positions are capable of showing their generosity, which may in turn instill the extra confidence you need to believe in taking a well-calculated gamble. Trust in your ability to recognize opportunity and turn it to your advantage.

22. SATURDAY. Lively. Dynamic shifts are foreseen as the Sun happily enters fiery Leo. At the same time, feisty Mars shifts into an earthy chart sector concerned with pleasure and procreative fun. In a nutshell, your vibes are heating up, especially when it comes to pursuing good times and amusements. People of the heart who light up your world and self are positive magnets for you to hang out with. A courtship may be ignited spontaneously. Love can be just around the corner in any environment that you regularly frequent. This evening, a cool waning Moon joins with Venus in chill Cancer, promising a sliver of serenity. Find a person and place for a quiet conversation.

23. SUNDAY. Auspicious. Change and expansion come from those with whom you've chosen to associate. You might find that a discussion with your mate or partner leads to planning an exotic trip. Or it could be that variations in the life of a family member encourage decisions to modify your own life. A connection with a teacher or leader within a spiritual group is apt to grow. In addition, look forward to goodwill and bonding with a new significant friend or to an alliance with an organization. Both are likely in a similar context. Anybody and any cause that's purposeful, related to lofty ideals, and a little off center will surely appeal as you stretch yourself.

24. MONDAY. Wistful. As sunny and friendly as your environment will be, a strong subjective mood may saturate your psyche. A tendency to internalize and dwell on various woes and worries might occur no matter where you are. You will probably prefer a familiar environment and opt for restful, reflective times. This day marks the darkening closing phase of the previous lunar cycle, making it ideal for being but not for doing. A New Moon in Leo is just coming to bud, shining a point of focus into the home and domestic sector of your natural horoscope. In certain instances the front door, or even the bedroom door, might not be crossed except in case of real necessity.

25. TUESDAY. Favorable. Look forward to a new addition to the family, or to a group who you consider like kin. A birth, or the announcement of a baby on the way, could be a classic manifestation. However, not all news about little ones will involve infants. Conditions now augur well for beginnings in general, especially those related to any aspect of the foundation of your life. Focus on getting the primary stages of any project up and standing on their own two feet. Either way, something notable and probably pristine is sure to enter your home environment, at least over the next month. An increase in responsibility will add aspects of struggle, with significant adaptation required on your part.

26. WEDNESDAY. Interesting. Important messages and contacts require attention. Networking, getting on with current business, and at least one noteworthy negotiation are indicated. Encounters are likely to be pleasant, with a civil, even refined tone prevailing in the atmosphere. Professionals are apt to be very organized and helpful. If you are a professional, or desire to meet with one, this is a positive time to pursue an introduction or make an appointment. An individual from overseas, or someone away on a trip right now, is apt to make some type of connection with you. You will receive good news, or even a meaningful token, from this person. After all, little things, sweet things, mean a lot.

27. THURSDAY. Sparkling. The waxing Moon triggers Mars, going on to meet with Jupiter. For Taurus folk, all this cosmic sparking takes place in areas of your natural horoscope concerned with significant others and sex. Some kind of bumpy ride is foreseen, but it's indicated to be fun and not at all boring. You may be strongly attracted to a newcomer, offering pert remarks and flirtatious play. Star patterns are perfectly aligned for fresh connections. For Taurus people who are already committed, here's a chance to spice up the same old, same old. Any new alliance formed today could build into a meaningful relationship, even if it's ultimately a case of just becoming the best of friends.

28. FRIDAY. Supportive. If you feel void of romance and not ready for love, you definitely have a problem because the heavens do not agree. The cosmos is literally shoving Taurus singles into some kind of notable liaison. If you're sitting alone and separate as the world goes by, wake up and perk up. If no one seems that interested in you, they have probably given up trying to scale your self-imposed ivory tower. Venus people are magnetic to other people, but it's all about personal worth and perceived personal value. Encouragement and validation remain in the ethers nevertheless. It's your decision when it comes to new involvement.

29. SATURDAY. Positive. All of your recent obsessive tinkering, or time invested in getting a new pastime off the ground, can show promise now. It might just be the early stages, but it's enough to keep your faith and interest on high. Tricky Mercury is finally out of retro-gear and is now beginning to move in the right direction. Communications are about to improve as gremlins that have been in the works get exterminated. Serious consideration can be given to taking on some kind of apprenticeship, probably related to an aesthetic trade or the arts. Deeper interest and clearer ambition could be identified by doing a bit of detective work. Research what is of concern to you, looking at it from all angles.

30. SUNDAY. Eventful. The heavens are active and energetic, and ideally you are as well. You may be up for doing something different, whether you are planning on getting out today or not. It might be a case of rearranging all the furniture in the fun of a redecorating frenzy. It it's not your own house, friends and neighbors may offer spontaneous doings and a rapid turn of events. A group of them could invite you to join them somewhere far from your usual stomping grounds. Like-minded associates meeting at a convention suits today's tone. Civil discussions and activities are likely. This is also a good day for mediation and equalizing anything that's out of balance.

31. MONDAY. Beneficial. Slow and steady is the classically touted speed for those born in the sign of the Bull, and it's probably your style today. In some instances this may make you feel a little directionless and even slightly disillusioned, perhaps due to recalling an earlier conversation that still echoes deep. Intense thought in attempting to comprehensively analyze a dream could distract you. Use quiet moments, if possible, to ponder in silence and alone. These are the kind of thoughts that should not be voiced or spoken of just yet. Go about your everyday job wrapped in the buffer of inspired concentration. It is too soon to divulge a new plan or idea.

AUGUST

1. TUESDAY. Favorable. It could be a case of two heads and bodies being better than one, also two hearts and souls. Physical and creative activities can be very enjoyable, especially if you are working with a partner. Put a lot of energy and drive into a heartfelt effort perfecting a special project. Improvements are easily made today. You are apt to be unusually responsive to constructive criticism. Companionship stimulates your ideas and actions. Exploring a recreational interest with a friend may lead to a whole new social network and view of the world. One-on-one games as well as expressions such as dance, again with a cohort, are interesting possibilities.

2. WEDNESDAY. Happy. This can be a highly significant day when it comes to a special relationship. The cosmos indicates that now is the time for an established connection to evolve to a different level that is for the better. Parents, family, and friends might all be interwoven in the experience. For some Taurus singles marriage could be in the air. Or you may be ready to at least recognize and display a deeper romantic commitment. Feelings and personal rituals can be shared with ease among your nearest and dearest. A celebration or other gathering should go well, although probably better if outside your own home space.

3. THURSDAY. Active. All variety of communications and messages are filling your head with much information, although this shouldn't be overwhelming. Mercury tries to be your friend, unfurling all sorts of positive networking for social or business purposes. Friends have connections, and connections have friends, leading to deals and trade-offs. An heirloom, inheritance, or legal payout might unexpectedly come your way. If you have been waiting for the approval for financing or some kind of loan, it can come through now. However, the day is not all smooth. Some hopes and wishes may still have to be modified.

4. FRIDAY. Stabilizing. Earth signs are connected to the worlds of acquisition and the building of solid structures. If you are in such a game on any level you can anticipate a lot of movement within your chosen sphere of operation. The present is generally good for laying a strong foundation from which long-lasting benefits grow over time. These could be early assets in a portfolio, the base for a residence, or initial steps toward future security with the first deposit in a new account. Handling possessions and money is often a Taurus hobby, and the only stress is when you do not have enough to feel safe. An irritating disagreement with an institution needs to be sorted out now before it escalates.

5. SATURDAY. Cautious. Worldwide events are capable of knocking at the door of your personal consciousness. Perceptions can be changed and lenses of global understanding can be better focused. A lesson in holding on versus letting go can be enforced. An event might prove that some processes or forces are more awesome than any one individual could ever be. The stimulus is apt to be outside your home or city or even state, most likely international. A universalizing experience might relate to being in a public environment, seeing a TV show, or reading the media news. Make sure you're not just buying hype.

6. SUNDAY. Excellent. Highly pleasant astrological patterns are at your beck and call. Social events appear eclectic and unusual, so you will not become bored. Spontaneous partying and quirky celebrating are foreseen, even among strangers in a public venue. Any recreational time with youngsters is sure to be entertaining and engaging. The inner child within you may be awakened, leading to rediscovering the essence of real fun. Play is a priority with virtually all Taurus, adults included. Wonderful times are augured for lovers, whether long-term or in the earliest days of togetherness. Even lone Taurus folk are in for a stimulating time. Just get out and maintain your good sense of humor.

7. MONDAY. Promising. Elders, especially along your father's family line or possibly your own direct parent, can play a special role in your life. If you haven't connected for a long time, this is a very appropriate day to do so. A significant relative could drop by, although likely only for a short visit. Or you may receive an invitation to a get-together, likely a reunion of those who were close to each other in the past. Taurus students and groups of learners are also prominent in the stars. If involved in study or in objective discussion and research, you will be well able to achieve your aims. Publishing opportunities are available for writers and pundits.

8. TUESDAY. Affirmative. A positive attitude infuses your heart. Regardless of everything or anything else on the schedule, put fun at the top of the list. Giving and receiving should be on your agenda, as bounty is shared among many. Interesting connections and events are likely, particularly if there's a special occasion coming up for a family member or friend. Treating a beloved to their favorite indulgence cannot help but bring joy to all involved. A role reversal is possible when somebody who holds you in high regard treats you generously. Win-win dynamics appear unexpectedly. A gamble taken with a partner will probably reap beneficial results.

9. WEDNESDAY. Reflecting. The Full Moon peaks in the Taurus sector concerned with life's direction and potential achievements. This celestial event illuminates your ambitions. Turn your thoughts to where you're heading, how you intend to get there, and, most importantly, why. This phase incorporates contact with misty, dreamy Neptune. Basically two possible results about certain aims are in the cards. Shades of confusion and doubt can enter in, as can a visionary breath of uplifting reinspiration. Take stock of how life's garden has grown so far. A reality check could have you seeing only a bunch of weeds, but try to also notice the beauty that is there.

10. THURSDAY. Hectic. Expect busy comings and goings throughout the day. Mail and messages flood in, and at least one can be very notable. Any past negotiations revisited now are sure to prove quite different in tone. There's a lot more heartfelt animation, although people will be sticking to individual opinions with stronger resolve. Higher-ups are capable of overinvesting in their own stubborn pride and holding control. Try simply separating from the pack and walking away. People who consider themselves above the rest in some fashion may decide to pull their illusionary rank and lord it over others. In this case your detachment is likely to prove a virtue.

11. FRIDAY. Challenging. Loyalties and liaisons may undergo testing incidents which appear out of the blue. Unstable, inconsistent vibes fill the air. You get to know who your friends truly are when hitting challenging times. A good buddy is likely to be going through a tumultuous period and be in need of real understanding and support. It's not that you must come to the rescue and fix a situation, since the circumstances are probably beyond that point. However, offering a receptive ear to listen, and real validation for the feelings of the other person, are the most important aspects. Just being there and letting the person know of your good regard gives an advantage.

12. SATURDAY. Easygoing. Quiet time is likely to hold the greatest pleasure for you. The focus turns to simply being home alone. However, as your guardian planet Venus goes into the vibrant sign of Leo, you can anticipate more social activity in general. Don't be surprised if your solo space is broken by the warming energy of another person, maybe even a crowd, creating a more interactive turn of events. Taurus people with a strong creative leaning could see this energy blossom into pleasing results. There might be talk of changing your residence in some manner. This may entail moving out and away, someone moving in, or at least a spate of redecoration.

13. SUNDAY. Enjoyable. The general tone of this day appears flowing and primed for all versions of time-out activity. Public and private happenings appeal, especially if related to a special occasion. Although amusement and entertainment are present, this is also an excellent time for a gathering concerned with practical matters. Get to work organizing some kind of group effort. A lot could be enjoyably accomplished, and quicker than expected. People are apt to be excited, quite happy to add their ideas and efforts to any endeavor that you propose. However, at times there might be too much goofing off and horseplay within the ranks. Be tolerant but goal-oriented.

14. MONDAY. Renewing. Taurus is a sensual zodiacal indicator, often loving both quality and quantity. Self-interested goals and events can dominate your mind. This especially pertains to your appearance and fitness. The vain, or just beauty-conscious, know what needs to be done. You might decide that it's finally time to get your hair cut or colored or have some kind of spa experience. Fashion followers, from the tasteful to the victims, might be acquiring more baubles and beads. It's best to get your whole wardrobe out of the closet for a review. Mull over different ways of combining the same old things with a few new purchases to get different looks.

15. TUESDAY. Intense. Magnetic attraction can be magical as some intimate cosmic interactions play in the heavens. This vibe may have come on strong last night, leaving you with not much sleep since then. More than usual, Taurus lovers are apt to desire remaining together all day, putting energy into being part of a pair. There are great stars offering you a tide, so take advantage if you can. If unattached but not wanting to be, you could be smitten by the development of a sudden crush. This may be even more astonishing because the person in question is almost completely removed from the normal pattern of your life. Be open to all possibilities.

16. WEDNESDAY. Exciting. Yesterday had a fair amount of sizzle, but present cosmic offerings hold the potential of busting off the passion scale. Heights and depths of mood can feel downright bipolar. There's apt to be an extreme edge to proceedings and interactions, so be prepared as fiery and forceful dynamics fill the atmosphere. Your single-minded focus can hone in on anyone or anything with precise intention. When it comes to close relationships, especially if recent, tricky psychological territory may have to be traversed. The possessive green-eyed monster of fear, insecurity, and jealousy is in the wings, ready to pounce on the unwary.

17. THURSDAY. Positive. The heavens are jam-packed with all sorts of cosmic triggers, and overall they're positive. However, you are apt to be set back by the words or actions of a youngster. Children are unpredictable at the best of times, but today they could be especially disruptive or experience their own upsets, requiring grown-up intervention. Remain objective. Try to see through youthful goggles. Home decorators and garden designers are likely to be engaging in favorite pastimes. This is a starred day for picking

blooms, pruning, weeding, or simply enjoying a beautiful environment. Bringing a bunch of flowers or a new aesthetic touch into
your home fills your Taurus spirit.

18. FRIDAY. Unstable. Legalities and arguments are highlighted.
Having to make a choice, probably a major one, is today's essential
theme. Make-or-break could easily be the title of today's dramas. It
seems that a situation has to be handled with objectivity and compromise, somehow finalized completely. Avoid fence-sitting and in-
decisiveness, which will not prove helpful in maintaining any
position of security. If a decisive call isn't made by you, it's possible
that greater powers will demand their way, and it will be irre-
versible. Define your values clearly and precisely, then don't back
down.

19. SATURDAY. Buoyant. An outgoing mood laced with good humor and open curiosity is literally just around the corner. Stimulating interactions are foreseen with people in the neighborhood. It
could be that new people are moving in nearby, or you finally meet
those who have been right across the street for a while. A little hospitality shared now will go a very long way in the future. Have fun
with foreigners and with learning about their cultures. There could
be a discussion with a group of close friends about the likelihood of
traveling overseas together. Some Taurus people may see their
partner having to go on a trip, possibly with coworkers or to visit a
distant family member.

20. SUNDAY. Easy. This biblical seventh day is perfect for rest and
relaxation. Mercury and Saturn are on top of each other in the
chart sector of the familiar, along with the Sun and basically much
of the solar system. The waning Moon, void but homey in Cancer, is
heading toward the same place. This is enough to make many Taurus people stay at home. Indulge in some serious reading and reflection. Even television offers worthwhile programs. Study and
practical domestic chores are industrious exercises especially if
you're left to yourself for part or all of the day. Prepare a to-do list
and stick to it.

21. MONDAY. Uneasy. Unclear mixed messages may be emanat-
ing from a person in charge or from someone to whom you have to
answer. What's unfolding, and how it affects your personal standing
and security, might be uppermost in your mind. The threat of a lay-
off from work is probably the worst case scenario and the greatest
worry. It's best not to dissipate mental clarity by cultivating unsub-

stantiated fears. Nothing's sure at this stage, so do not even attempt to confront a situation now. It's better to wait a couple of days before boldly going where you have never been before. Prudence is the better part of valor, but the time is coming for direct action.

22. TUESDAY. Taxing. The daily grind may have you feeling ground down. Someone could offer the temptation to shirk your duties in favor of a more amusing invitation. With responsibilities hard to ignore, necessity must hold precedence over frivolity. Self-employed Taurus people may have to be especially hardworking. This is not the time to take your finger off the pulse of a visionary project. Being present and hands-on makes you most productive today. Problems, if any, can be solved rapidly, particularly if egos are checked at the door before sitting down to a powwow. Keep the big picture in mind.

23. WEDNESDAY. Starred. Willful energy at the start of the day fires you up for an early chance at seizing the reins of power. Whether at work, home, or out and about, many tasks can be ticked off your to-do list. If you fall into the category of having to take care of someone besides yourself, take advantage of the current vibes and get moving. Couriers, go-fors, and assistants are sure to attract favorable attention. A very empowered and fresh new Moon is forming as both Moon and Sun join in the fellow earth sign of Virgo, a generally auspicious event for Taurus. You are entering a novel monthly phase of parties and pleasures and diminished worries.

24. THURSDAY. Opportune. One word in the right place can get a long-stuck state of affairs moving rapidly for the most positive of reasons and results. Perceptions and comments can become incisive and frank in nature. Someone in the family may disclose information that could totally change a situation. Youthful individuals may shift your own perceptions and that of others, helping you see a difficult scenario in a whole new way. The worldly-wise awareness of your mate or partner might inspire respect, whether through conversation or reading. Look to a friend for the encouragement you are seeking.

25. FRIDAY. Unsettling. This can be one of those milestone days, for very personal reasons. The day's significance will be even more intense when looking back upon it in the future. For those whose life may have recently changed irrevocably, a chapter is now closing, permitting a new phase of experience to being. The announcement of a birth or a pregnancy should be celebrated. This is also a time when a relationship might falter and cease. Lovers' tiffs and verbal altercations can tend to get out of hand. Trouble and dark warnings may become a part of the proceedings. However, even an event such as an affair coming to an end is very likely to turn out to be a blessing in disguise.

26. SATURDAY. Inspiring. Taurus and its planet Venus are about refining the senses and perceiving essential beauty. Inspiration can channel your soul into being in accord with current star patterns. The really intuitive might even hear the harmony of the cosmos and be able to put this into some kind of creative expression. There's an ideal energy available for Taurus artists, designers, and craftspeople. The musically inclined are likely to be singled out, whether playing, composing, or just being a dedicated listener. The right sounds could be therapeutic if explored today. Check out your music collection, or perhaps even go to a concert under the stars.

27. SUNDAY. Transcending. Spiritual and mystical energy maintains and increases, ideal for utilizing this day in ritual or worship. The artistic and creative can feel and display even more inspiration, leading to wonderful results. Taurus people seeking to turn this kind of production into a career path could meet with the right opportunity and contacts, at least to establish an imaginative craft as a solid secondary income. Some form of recognition is a definite potential. A star may even be born or discovered, if only within the scope of your own arena. For most people, it could be more about enjoying the accomplishments of someone already famous.

28. MONDAY. Significant. The power of one idea, one word, or one person can show itself. From something small, awesome things could grow. Be mindful, though, because this kind of evolution might be positive or negative, depending on the underlying intent. Clarity and mental precision will help you. Intellectual potential can be acknowledged and empowered, especially when the right trigger is supplied through the thoughts of someone else. Taurus engaged in research, study, or just trying to get to the bottom of a mystery might find the key that unlocks realization. Good astro contacts are abroad for the romantically inclined, offering delightful insights.

29. TUESDAY. Revealing. Interest from other people, and interest in them, is apt to be amplified. There's a lot of general curiosity of a romantic flavor, whether conscious or not. Posing, preening, and flirting can all color your body language when in the presence of a special someone. Falling in love or lust is also likely today. The arrows of Eros are flying around, and passions rule. Be aware of who's targeting you, or of which person you choose to court attention from. Sugary compliments, manipulation, possessiveness, and envy are all part of the atmosphere.

30. WEDNESDAY. Uncertain. Reality checks versus imaginative hopes could have you on a psychological seesaw. Outside input can also contribute to distortions and indecisive wavering. How to get a new plan off to the best start is the sticking point. Dreams and ambitions may be out of kilter with what you need to move ahead. Perhaps the truth is that you don't want to head in a direction already decided upon. A detailed review is necessary before launching into a commitment. A new relationship can become a concern if none of your family finds it has much value or chance of future success.

31. THURSDAY. Pleasant. A loved one can shine brightly for being especially clever. This person, likely a youngster, may be recognized or receive a prize. For parents who have been noticing something remarkable about a child, it might pay to explore their talent further. That doesn't mean that you've got a genius or a child prodigy on your hands, but be observant. Engage in shared games and activities. If specialized talent isn't really showing, there's still major value in emotional bonding and mental stimulation. The important thing is to validate uniqueness. Don't take loved ones of any age for granted. Rough-and-tumble fun makes this evening special.

SEPTEMBER

1. FRIDAY. Accomplished. More power comes to you as your guardian planet Venus makes positive and strengthening contact with Pluto. You may be able to move mountains and assert yourself with great impact. You might even feel imbued by a quality that you can't quite identify but certainly welcome. Controlling a situation, organizing, and delegating come naturally to you now. Taurus leaders and managers are very efficient, able to accomplish any job thoroughly. Change and renovation are very much in the air, although unsettling. However, you can take it in stride. Your supercool handling of any potential crisis gives you an enhanced reputation and added respect.

2. SATURDAY. Intense. Despite many good things, you may have noticed an underlying intensity in the atmosphere over the past few days. You have reached a point where evidence of this mood asserts itself. When it comes to bottling things up, it's better out than in so that the pressure doesn't become unsafe. Unresolved issues can burst forth. The degree to which a problem has remained unaddressed will be matched by the degree of destructive venom with which emotions are vented. The cosmic charge peters out as the day draws to a close, leaving you drained and exhausted. Expressing rage cleans the slate. Letting go but remaining in control is always good therapy.

3. SUNDAY. Sparkling. No matter what the weather, today can feel like the calm after a storm. Clouds clear away and the sunlight emerges once again. Communication lines should be open and flowing, with social interaction in the cards. The camaraderie you long for can now come to the fore. Self-esteem may grow through the auspices of a mutual admiration club. Mixing with like-minded friends and being in jovial company will be sure to restore your faith in human nature. Positive individuals can be like natural coaches while also bolstering a sense of faith in yourself. The unconditional company of loved ones, especially children and your partner, will prove worth its weight in gold.

4. MONDAY. Starred. If you've been pleasantly sailing along in a liaison for a while, now it could get even better. Synergy demonstrates its presence with an uncanny and compelling edge. Motivation is on the increase when it comes to wanting to grow closer. A sincere chat is capable of identifying a newcomer as more deeply simpatico than first perceived. Conversations might enter into personal experience, dwelling upon such subjects as religion, philosophy, or the nature of being. Information traded is sure to be fascinating, and probably will lead to a lot of growth if followed through with initiative.

5. TUESDAY. Surprising. Present astrology indicates that brilliant, even shocking awakenings are possible. Increased consciousness and greater comprehension are yours, but with differing degrees of impact. A flood of realization could get volatile Taurus people riled up with excitement or with plain agitation. Long-term sacred cows can now be confronted, prompting the necessity for you to change radically. The key is how you are prepared to shift and on what level. You may make changes that are tangible and outer, or inner and more attitudinal. Excess and electricity are in the air, leading to either static misfiring or a sparkling atmosphere.

Someone you respect could appear like an emperor in new clothes when reality hits.

6. WEDNESDAY. Magical. Many Venus types may feel like calling this day a twenty-four–hour vacation. It could even be like Valentine's Day as far as some are concerned. You may be smitten by a newcomer or at least drawn deeper into an ongoing relationship. Those already in committed partnerships can see the connection swing either way. In certain cases there may be wandering eyes and inappropriate observations, symptoms of waning interest. Conversely, many pairings can expect deeper emotional communication. A strong, magical charge is signified by the heavenly patterns. Sensual and escapist indulgences might become a siren call to the addictive.

7. THURSDAY. Good. Tonight's Full Moon is capable of bringing with it the unexpected, especially when it comes to other people chopping and changing like the wind. Nonetheless, pleasant interactions should be the norm. One meeting in particular is apt to be of quite notable importance. Open people and open doors present greater vistas of worldview and meaning. An organization or group that may have held a fascination for you for a while now offers the chance for an even greater encounter. Taurus students are sure to have beneficial interactions with teachers or others whose knowledge is valued. Questioning a mirror's reflection might hold the seeds of a future cosmetic makeover for you.

8. FRIDAY. Cautious. A friend or a business associate may be harboring a self-centered agenda, belied by their apparent generosity in sharing resources. It is crucial to watch out for someone with the gift of gab. Do not be snagged on any prominent hooks. Miss the fine print of anything and you are at peril to the best outcome. A large public gathering where you are a participant in the crowd is a strong possibility. There could be a political or other meaningful tone to a group event. A major convention of like-minded specialists is another possibility. Revolutionary new ideas could be unveiled. An animated, critical debate will get minds and mouths moving.

9. SATURDAY. Sensitive. Messengers are likely to be ignored. Do not accept a request to speak to someone on behalf of someone else. Outrage and betrayal of privacy are sure to fuel continued fireworks. A friend might ask you to transmit information to their nearest and dearest because they can't face doing so. However, it usually never pays to take on the responsibility of conveying feelings and opinions which aren't really yours. Caring and listening may come naturally, but fixing and rescuing are often just glorified meddling. Review your real role and position in order to ultimately decide what your own agenda really is and how you will carry it out.

10. SUNDAY. Easygoing. Taurus, as stoic and enduring as can be, is still one of the Zodiac types that needs consistent periods of time out. Expect a profound sense of just wanting to be still and on your own. The cosmos is fairly sedate right now, although a powerhouse of energy is available to be drawn on in the earlier half of the day. However, an insular, even reticent vibe may overtake you later, continuing well into tomorrow morning. Whatever meditation, reflection, and respite you favor, take advantage of current conditions to create it. Intimacy and privacy can be accompanying themes woven into the hours after dark. Love is waiting in the wings.

11. MONDAY. Uplifting. Concern about personal appearance could become apparent, whether it's your wardrobe, physical condition, hair, face, or the whole package. It could be the excitement caused by a newcomer that motivates this urge. Sincerely wanting to overhaul an old image may possibly be due to a desire to impress a friend or a prospective lover. Applying for a new position, or preparing for a public appearance, are other potential reasons for a change over. Discrimination is necessary to select between impressing with the right professional image or spoiling your chance due to overinvesting in mainly the glamour aspects of your presentation.

12. TUESDAY. Energetic. Mercury, patron planet of communication, goes into mutual reception to Venus, which is great for Taurus people. Those who use words, thinking, and communicating in general to earn a buck are in for all sorts of breaks today. The heavens are favoring the artistic touch, whether the context is an everyday duty or a more specialized application. Rapid and refined creative processes can enhance many tasks. More astrological reception also turns on the symbolic force of the Sun and Mars. Warmth, efficiency, and pleasantries may all enhance your experience. You have great energy to utilize for diplomatic networking, trade, and dealing with work as a mediator.

13. WEDNESDAY. Comfortable. Retail therapy can strike your wallet and probably via your credit card. Fortunately you are used to coping with bills once the dust of any shopping frenzy finally settles. Acquisitiveness will beckon many, whether it's something ritzy or purely utilitarian. However, once you get the object of desire in your possession, you may wonder what was so attractive about it in the first place. If nothing else, you have acquired a future surprise present for a friend. Home, and a good meal, are the most compelling activities tonight.

14. THURSDAY. Expansive. Loved ones might want to share your resources and are apt to ask frankly for support they need. You may be perfectly willing to give, but the issue is not a lack of generous regard but the lack of funds when it comes to sharing. Delays and adjustments are foreseen concerning a prior promise. Taurus parents are apt to find that a child's demands require more expense than first figured. Delayed gratification, in general, needs to be a common lesson for the impatient. Too much talk and a tendency to overanalyze or overjustify are usually just avoidance. Rely on your heart and feelings rather than your head. Intuition will not let you down.

15. FRIDAY. Hectic. Dynamically charged and very active star patterns are coming and going. Busy busy rush rush is the dominant theme of the day. Danger lies in being some kind of jack-of-all-trades and master of none, as your energy scatters and fragments quite easily. Your attention span is sure to be low just as activity accelerates. Irritating little accidents may plague you. Nonetheless, Taurus folk addicted to excitement might be motivated by the idea of going to more extremes, and really pushing their luck. Ironically, the capacity to concentrate and coordinate reflexes is also intensified, as is the uncertainty principle.

16. SATURDAY. Pressured. Fixed earthy Taurus is not known for flamboyance and drama, unless there's something special in the circumstances. However, the song and dance within your love life might seem to put you in a standard soap opera. You may create an admirable award-winning performance stemming mostly from interaction with your significant other. It ultimately takes two to contribute to any war of words. You may be forced to stop in your tracks and get real. Something has to change or your relationship is apt to fizzle. A wiser individual, with insightful depth, can aid in clarifying what you want and what you can expect to get.

17. SUNDAY. Good. Sleep late this morning if possible. Slow and easy suits the start of the day. Puttering around and allowing distractions may be the preferred pastime. Maintenance and kind of handiwork should be a job well done. The beauty of nature's wonders could lure you into a park or to bask in the pleasure of your own yard. The company of a pet is marked by the heavens. This can be a delightful day with animals in general. Being active and more interactive increases as the day unfurls. You might become unexpectedly but pleasantly social. Enjoy giving service and hospitality to a variety of visitors, including neighbors you hardly know.

18. MONDAY. Problematic. A strong capacity for stubbornness laces together the astrology of today, as if it's the cosmic glue of the universe. It's probably not only you who has a good amount of stick-with-it-ness, but seemingly everyone else who you encounter. Whatever direction you turn, you'll tend to come up against firmness exerted by other people. Digging in the heels will produce little or no movement at any of the places where it's really needed. With battles of wills so likely to form, be aware and strive not to contribute to any petulant games. You can waste your energy by resisting what you know cannot be stopped or derailed.

19. TUESDAY. Pleasant. Two of the most benefic planets flowingly connected in the cosmos has to be good, even when it's apparently not. Beautiful Venus and expansive Jupiter are aligned today and tonight. To the Taurus this offers opportunity, which always carries the catch of having to be spotted at the right time. At present, the best part of the day involves romance and fun. Money gains and gain in general are also indicated, particularly coming from outer resources and via the values of other people. If gambling you might encounter a fortunate streak, or at least have a good time losing. Keep all of your options open wide.

20. WEDNESDAY. Bumpy. Easy come, easy go is a mantra you might have to chant. Erratic energy can come in spurts and flashes, as if there's a switch between full speed ahead and full stop. A brief but highly exciting encounter is apt to shatter any monotony this day holds. Your heart may flutter when a certain eye contact is achieved and expectations swell markedly. However, the heavens are fickle at the moment, and a brief affair is prone to pop like a balloon when it's out of sight and out of mind. Lessons in attachment, and the nature of what's really special, underlie many of life's most meaningful experiences.

21. THURSDAY. Agreeable. The depths of the dark of the Moon increasingly enfold the tone of the hours as this day passes. It should come as no surprise if everything feels fairly wound down by nightfall. However, you might not guess it, especially earlier in the day when shades of previous fun and good times provoke more of the same. A small celebration is possible with a familiar group, possibly related to the announcement of a greater event to come. Something pleasing or at least of note connected to a youngster is also foreseen. A significant culmination or turning point is likely when it comes to a creative project.

22. FRIDAY. Renewing. This is a time when everyone should be a skilled astrologer, as the heavenly action makes such an interesting dance. A New Moon and solar eclipse occur in Virgo in the morning. Then the Moon enters Libra, and just before midnight the Sun enters Libra. Libra is the sign in the Taurus solar chart that is related to health, daily habits, and the principles of serving and being served. Focus turns to everyday routine, even more so than usual. This is a great time for beginnings, however tentative due to a fair amount of vulnerability being present. Embarking on any improvement should pay off big time.

23. SATURDAY. Imaginative. Trading, dealing, networking, and industry all have greater momentum. A cooperative gathering where wares and ideas are offered and shared is sure to prove informative and uplifting. Taurus people involved in weekend business will see time fly by quickly, with much traffic coming and going. A job on the side has the potential to take over your entire life in time. Apprentices and craft lovers are sure to be blessed with satisfying results, leading to even greater visions and goals. The imaginative Taurus, whether hobbyist or professional, could have to be pried away when it comes to taking a break from the work at hand.

24. SUNDAY. Significant. Boundaries between social classes and cultures are likely to be porous or to completely dissolve. This could involve an event that concerns a subject capable of enmeshing everyone in a melting pot of experience. Exploring the foreign and the exotic in many fashions is certain to widen your worldview and introduce inspiring new perceptions. Photography and filming are worthwhile pursuits. Individuals and occasions where the camera is important, or even central, could dominate the day. Taurus people with an eye for a special moment and the means to capture it creatively will find the environment full of images of an artistic nature.

25. MONDAY. Productive. This is a good day for fixing long-standing problems concerning matters of a domestic nature, including the house itself. This also pertains to the personal section of your work environment. Putting everything in its place, from filing to furnishings, could involve a total cleaning and weeding out in some cases. Of course, the same could also be more lip service than action. Pore over renovation and decorating information in a magazine, probably with a friend. You've got to plan before taking any action, but plan to act soon. Actually, the prodding of a close associate will produce some practical action sooner rather than later.

26. TUESDAY. Peaceful. The waxing Moon is in the seventh house, and Jupiter's aligned with it. Peace rules the planets, with love in the stars, because the Taurus goddess Venus is also present in the pattern. Relationships and affairs of the heart are in focus as these cosmic offerings support a special date and the pursuit of any type of fun with a preferred companion. These are also sensual stars, and the sign of Scorpio is highlighted. Only you know what this can really mean, so enjoy. If single and loving it, be ready to ward off potential mates. This is not the time to make a definite commitment.

27. WEDNESDAY. Beneficial. Health and its maintenance are highlighted. This doesn't mean Taurus people are going to have a physical problem, but the body is the primary messenger of well-being. Anyone who belongs to one of the earth signs should not ignore any signals of aches and pains. The stars aren't reflecting anything wrong, just that benefit of some sort is the real potential. This is a point where if you are determined you can finally see that a health program is starting to reap results. Those on a healing path may now make the right connections or note significant progress.

28. THURSDAY. Rewarding. The dexterous, agile, and quick are most likely to make the grade and still be standing at the end of any race. This is not usual for Venus-ruled Taurus. Rivalry and competition are in the atmosphere, possibly from unexpected quarters. At the same time, there's likely to be an acceptance that the spoils will deservedly go to the victor, whatever the outcome. The aim is contesting for a special position or dream achievement. Success is relative. It can stem from getting the right seat next to the right someone at a gathering, scoring a pursued prize, or being promoted to the alpha place in any group endeavor.

29. FRIDAY. Uncertain. Not everyone can be happy and full of joy twenty-four seven. As a Taurus you know what goes up will always have to come down, just to retain equilibrium. Serious vibes have a way of infiltrating your psyche today, and as soon as you wake up. Be wary of the force of changeable moods, and grasp the opportunity to understand them better. You could discover that a hindrance to happiness is rooted within self-perpetuating negative beliefs. The filter with which you perceive the world is up for grabs. Questions, new and more profound, are likely to be too compelling to ignore. Talk over the future with your best friend.

30. SATURDAY. Steadying. Consider entering into a part-time course of learning. The skills pursued are likely to involve a creative or decorative subject. Working together in a group, but on individual projects, is sure to be stimulating. Enjoyable new associates are likely. Volunteering to help an organization as a result of your belief in its ethics and mandates might be an attractive idea. However, you could be expected to devote more energy and time than you have to give. Perhaps on second thought it's more realistic to show support in some other fashion.

OCTOBER

1. SUNDAY. Productive. Socializing and meetings with friends can bring a sparkle to the day, resulting in informal networking. Positive communication sees you getting to the heart of a matter under discussion. Creating beauty becomes a focus, either in interior decorating or updating your environment. Your partner may shed a new light on relationships with a progressive group. A choice must be made between a solidly practical approach and one with more feeling and creativity. Give yourself plenty of time and you'll make the correct decision. Devotion to studying a practical subject will make the week ahead easier once you put in the preliminary research.

2. MONDAY. Harmonious. Relationships are a source of harmony in groups and associations. You could meet a valuable new acquaintance or a potential creative colleague. Intense emotional interchanges are possible. There's a feeling of getting to the heart of a pending matter. Don't be afraid to hash out an issue in order to clear the air. Socializing at work, combining business with pleasure, sees bright ideas being hatched. Developing a business idea with a friend can be the seed of success. Check details of life such as your car, and nurture bodily needs with proper checkups and caring maintenance. It's a good time to gird yourself for health and productivity.

3. TUESDAY. Buoyant. An energetic atmosphere pervades the day. There's potential for optimistic go-getting that leads to acting assertively on your latest creative intuition. An urge for transcendence can see you being drawn to music, dance, or theatrical pursuits. Give yourself time to regenerate quietly, letting yourself tune into subtle natural realms. Sensitive Taurus nervous systems should avoid alcohol at this time. Be careful of anyone offering a too-good-to-be true angle on a spiritual or civic matter. Unless a practical plan is in place to back it up, it could be pie-in-the-sky. Getting to the bottom of a mystery in a partnership, or indulging in deep discussions, can give a satisfying depth to the day.

4. WEDNESDAY. Stimulating. Prepare for an exciting day. Plans can change at a moment's notice. Radical leading-edge feelings and concepts emerge. Enter into discussions about free energy, freedom, and innovative approaches to society. Even mainstream conservatives could consider downsizing or even a total change in personal values. If events seem surprising or disjointed, try to take a progressive angle while cultivating a flexible attitude. Being open to what's new and untried can make for an interesting day as you shift out of any rut you may have been in. Teams following an untried path can have positive breakthroughs in inventions, with the courage and idealism to take events to the next level.

5. THURSDAY. Cloistered. Hidden emotions unfold and draw focus away from purely practical concerns. Swimming in the tide of old memories of love can be therapeutic, nurturing you before you begin another cycle of outer world achievement. Take time to replenish your feeling side with a visit to nature, somewhere out of the public eye. Working alone or immersing yourself in a project linked to emerging trends of art, fashion, or fantasy can help your vision soar with practical idealism. Give your soul free rein to set the pace, letting expenses catch up with you later. An energy boost via your mate or partner can give you added fuel to achieve your goals.

6. FRIDAY. Disconcerting. Polarized opinions at work may be at odds with your sensitive Taurus nature. It is best not to jump to conclusions or react too hastily. Instead, take time to evaluate all the facts. Putting personal desires on hold to accommodate the demands of work meetings and other pressures could see you giving more than you want to these situations. Go a step further to ensure the success of projects. Don't leave anything to chance. A new emotional cycle is promoting fresh, imaginative feelings and a desire for change. Use diplomacy and tact throughout this busy, people-filled day. Avoid being hard to please. Focus on turning negatives to positives.

7. SATURDAY. Passionate. Feelings are ramping up as hot tempers and ardor characterize this all-or-nothing day. Wild emotional weather encourages you to be careful of trading insults or accusations. Use the fiery atmosphere to assertively forge ahead in challenging activities, dance, or physical activity. Begin new projects, independent action, and imaginative creativity. Nurture your own desires. Socialize in a refined group, with music and pleasing surroundings enhancing a few spirited arguments during the day. Reading a good mystery or researching a topic thoroughly can add excitement and intrigue to the day.

8. SUNDAY. Innovative. Putting your own interests first suits you as solid earthy interests demand attention. Friends may drop by, and the focus on gracious living makes this a harmonious day. Consider updating the interior of your house or planning a more nurturing work environment. Fresh new fabrics and a style makeover can have you feeling lushly secure, bathed in new colors and inviting textures. Romance beckons as someone cultured and aesthetic organizes a rendezvous with intimate overtones. A lover or partner from a distance could challenge your certainty about many aspects of life. Ground yourself in your values and act from a secure center.

9. MONDAY. Inspiring. Vibrant new people are replacing some of the players on your stage of life, but there's a potential for emotional contraction. Sort out issues head-on, remembering to view the glass as half full rather than half empty. Take a long, hard look at what you lack. A partner could become an enthusiastic mentor, inspiring you to intensify your studies and create a permanent bond with the subject. Take advantage of your ability to be usually open to fresh ways of thinking. Networking with other people can enrich life and diminish feelings of doing it alone. There's strong physical energy to assertively move ahead in a fiery spirit of determination. Center yourself, then get going.

10. TUESDAY. Fulfilling. Concentrating on areas of value to you, such as linking a talent to a second income, can boost your finances. A job requiring a pleasant manner in dealing with the public will be part of this busy day. Follow flashes of inspiration that occur like lightning. Be sure to write down ideas before developing a definite game plan. Ideals are strongly linked to nurturing the greater good in areas of art and music. Work containing a design element in creating a harmonious impression will be high on the list today. Take advantage of pleasant relationships with colleagues to network ideas thoroughly and develop new ones.

11. WEDNESDAY. Successful. Anticipate a variety of experiences on this day which is good for energetic tasks. Success in completing challenging physical jobs at work or feats of incredible endurance are possible. A victory at work is likely, either with a cooperative team effort or as an individual success. Your dynamic leadership skills will be tested due to a need to outwit the opposition or a worthy rival. It could be crunch time for a financial or property matter, so be prepared to let go of something old to make way for the new. If it feels like someone is sitting on your shoulder and whispering a sweet message, take notice; it's the real thing.

12. THURSDAY. Caring. This busy communicative day centers around family and friends, who take the edge off a purely work-driven schedule. Getting to the bottom of a disagreeable subject with a lover or partner becomes easier. Good health and a feeling of fortitude help you rise to the occasion, even in difficult matters. Short journeys to visit relatives or neighbors, and activities with children, can sap much of the day's energy. Let elders assist or come along for the ride. Allowing yourself a slower pace will suit you best. Take advantage of the harmonious air of possible cuddles and compassion. You're due for a break from relentless hard work and the drive for survival.

13. FRIDAY. Exuberant. A happy feeling of warmth and expansion pervades relationships with your partner, family, and friends. Even work has the air of a happy family, allowing you to accomplish goals in a caring, cooperative manner. This is an ideal time to treat yourself to a day at a spa, to gather the clan together for a fun family dinner, or to cozy by the fire for a snuggling session with that special someone. Expressing yourself should come easily, whether in writing, acting, or dancing. Be open to a special new friend who might be introduced by a family member. Be alert for a feeling of positive, immediate resonance with this person, who could be a soul mate ready to bring happiness to both of you.

14. SATURDAY. Sensitive. Be careful of a touchy family member's feelings. This is a priority. Directing family members into productive channels can be a task you'd rather avoid, but duty calls. Try to get out of any rut of repetitive behavior. Develop new strategies for dealing with problems around the home. Building up your energy for a few moments, then acting with concentration, can help you achieve more than you think possible. Joint resources will get a boost from a benefactor, thanks to your willingness to give more of yourself and expand beyond narrow boundaries. Socializing should be full of beautiful characters, connected to you and to each other in a sharing of feasting and great music.

15. SUNDAY. Dreamy. Enjoy the day's drifting ambience, but check that communications with your mate or partner are truthful and clear. Conversations could become dishonest or deceptive. It's best to wait until another time for discussions needing concrete facts. Go where truth and fiction don't have to be so carefully sorted out, such as a compelling movie or book discussion. A project requiring writing or research can be fascinating, even as a hobby, and a mystery could be solved. Broad-minded subjects hold your interest as your work involves playing detective. Take time out to regenerate, perhaps by reading a great detective story. An inner-world journey can be potent.

16. MONDAY. Fortunate. Taking a calculated risk could pay off as your heightened charisma mixes with increased willingness to be diplomatic. A mature, hardworking approach is a must. Be careful not to cut corners. Authority figures could be putting a foot down and requesting heightened productivity, but your inspired approach will pay off. A lover could give a serious ultimatum, and romance will be earnestly intense. Try to rise above fearful emotions regarding financial limitations. Savor the moment, not the bank balance. Although you're yearning for solidity in a changing world, work may not provide a secure feeling. Gardening and a favorite craft can produce tranquil peace.

17. TUESDAY. Expansive. Investigating and broadening your mind in areas you usually consider too expansive can delight you. Foreign languages, psychology, and subjects containing a mysterious, intriguing quality are calling. Be careful not to charge from extreme skepticism to blind faith without checking the background of teachers or mentors. You might be a babe in the woods when it comes to a new interest. Be careful of outrageous prices or of someone promising the moon. Aim at building something of worth that's a testament to the future. Many people dream, but you've got the fortitude to achieve. Find security in the capital assets of classically successful ideas.

18. WEDNESDAY. Exciting. Shock and surprises characterize today. Meeting with a workplace group will include some unsettling and possibly disruptive characters who want to overthrow the established order. Prepare to be adaptable, being careful of making hasty emotional decisions or saying anything you would find hard to take back. You're in the mood to say more than you possibly should. Your body needs tender loving care to avoid frying or frazzling nerves. Try a therapeutic massage rather than bingeing on junk food. Enjoy new religious and philosophical interests, but avoid getting into any dogmatic arguments. Taurus students will relish research and can make exciting progress.

19. THURSDAY. Tricky. Navigating around other people's hidden agendas or jealousies requires that you be careful who you lock horns with. Aim to maintain harmony as much as possible. Channel your amazing talents and energy into work. Physical health is positive, giving you plenty of stamina. It's mental health that you need to take care of, keeping things simple and avoiding overexaggerating any current problems. A situation with a partner or close friend could seem vague and hard to pin down. If someone isn't giving attention equal to your own, perhaps it's best to let go. Keep away from anything underhanded. In romance you need someone to give you a straight reality check.

20. FRIDAY. Beneficial. A change in values is broadening your horizons. By putting more love into what you do you will reap the rewards that come from a feeling of abundance. There are fears to contend with. However, rather than worry or feel you're not smart enough, concentrate on what you really are good at. This will eventually bring definite rewards. An older person could be disapproving in their attitude. If you feel misunderstood, turn to those who are already part of your soul group. Others must earn your trust. Focus on work and on broadening your network of supportive colleagues and friends. Design, fashion, publishing, and art offer success for you at this time if you just keep it real.

21. SATURDAY. Explorative. Getting away to explore the great outdoors could lead to an amazing adventure. Staying at a cabin in the mountains with friends, autumn leaves, and extreme sports could see you enjoying much more than a plodding weekend. Being out in the open, exploring the new and untried, can bring more adventure to life than you've had for some time. The inner adventure may call some Taurus people. An out-of-body experience or incredible lecture can reveal new aspects of a deeply interesting world. Energetic self-assertion will get you out of a rut in a happy, nonthreatening way. Associates could be surprised by what you do, being used to a more predictable and sedate you.

22. SUNDAY. Extraordinary. You could encounter your muse in a sea of artistic inspiration as you deal with deep, passionate emotions. Setting up a studio or taking on a combative stranger might not seem hard with the intense strength of your feelings. Try not to waste a valuable opportunity. Center yourself to avoid being competitive. With your romantic partner there is so much to share and create. Hidden, dark, or unrelenting emotions could surge to the surface of your awareness, requiring you to deal with anger and to be honest instead of keeping a lid on your feelings. Relish the positive mood of life becoming more interesting if you try new activities and encounter fresh people and places.

23. MONDAY. Intense. Ambition and a strong desire to move forward to achieve your goals can give you instant progress. You won't let anything stand in your way, whether at work or romantically. In pursuing what you want, just be careful not to impose your will on other people. Even if they're attracted to you, make sure you're honoring their own more subdued style of life. Enjoy the extreme emotions that might be generated, but be careful of any sort of violent outburst. There's a tendency to go overboard. Giving yourself an intense challenge is likely as you open up to innovative feelings. You're updating the ability to communicate emotionally, in contrast to maintaining a cautionary silence. People will be celebrating with you.

24. TUESDAY. Significant. Love and passion combine so that you can stretch yourself in developing talents in areas you love. Take advantage of your own additional drive and determination. Time spent counseling other people or dealing positively with legal matters can provide a sense of satisfaction at the end of the day. You may need to reel yourself in after the big events or feelings of previous days. Apply positive caution, which hopefully you won't translate into unnecessary worry. You are apt to be impatient with restrictions after tasting freedom. Maintain a solid work ethic even as you teach your spirit to soar.

25. WEDNESDAY. Intriguing. Having to deal with hidden emotions or secretive feelings is likely. Relationships and money issues are intertwined. You might be tempted to stray from the straight and narrow. Try not to use sexuality to get where you want to go in life. Manipulating other people will only backfire. Cultivate your relationship with life and work, and limit the distractions that can complicate things. Incredible passion is available with a soul mate. Personal relationships are still high on the list of what's taking up your attention. Someone sensuous and serious has your name and number, but you'll have to be on the same wavelength to find each other.

26. THURSDAY. Variable. Clarity of thought could see you clearing the decks and arranging an overseas trip to expand your options. Making sound judgments and mature, sober decisions gives you a rational edge over strong emotion. Being in nature would suit your mood. Traveling for business should work out harmoniously. There's definitely a trend for endings and beginnings in your studies. This may involve graduation into a higher class. You may be gathering information behind the scenes while your life soars to an overwhelmingly obvious set of new circumstances. An erotic experience could be incredibly fulfilling on an emotional level, a reward for all your hard work.

27. FRIDAY. Dynamic. The necessary physical energy to attain your goals and move toward more freedom is yours today. Galvanizing yourself, warrior-like, to achieve a large scale goal with a partner could bring a sense of ultimate accomplishment. You're being drawn away from protected security and into larger issues of your world. There are tough things to face, but you're not alone. Martial arts or a positive transformation of violence in your everyday world sees you being a rock of Gibraltar on behalf of other people, with bravery being rewarded later. A teacher or mentor you meet at this time can give you a profound sense of nobility and influence your transformation. Do not take refuge in the superficial.

28. SATURDAY. Steadying. Attending to down-to-earth tasks, including tidying up paperwork and arranging a social occasion linked to work, can ground you and bring a sense of normality. Outdoors activities, such as hiking or challenging team sports, could lead to victory and even a trophy for the athletically minded. Use your heightened physical energy to charge ahead with physical tasks involving a partner or close friend. Overseas influences are strong, and you could hear from a distant friend with a suggestion for changing your life. Collaborating together on an entrepreneurial project could be successful. Romantic influences are strong. You and your lover could have a beautiful time in nature getting away from it all.

29. SUNDAY. Spirited. Getting used to a radical character recently introduced to the family could be a bit of a stretch. If this person challenges your values, there may be arguments to contend with. It might be wise to take the path of least resistance if you can't really communicate with each other. Some areas of life could be all or nothing, with one or two extremely wonderful events as well as coping with sadness when a loved one leaves. Throughout the day there is a profound spirit of love that takes you out of the ordinary. Children could share some intriguing messages that you're starting to understand. The challenge of not understanding someone you love may lead to educating yourself further.

30. MONDAY. Challenging. Keeping a flexible yet strong ego is important in today's climate. There's a longing to be swept away in fantasy or illusion, yet a quick reckoning with reality is sure to catch up. Avoid anyone promising a quick fix. Also avoid escaping into alcohol or pills. If life is getting too much, spend the day nurturing your mental health. On the positive side, music, movies, and the arts give you a feeling of wonder. Taking a fresh angle or altering a fixed position will bring you rewards and extra energy. A group meeting can be full of pleasure and interest, so enjoy the feeling. Make up for lost time by pleasing yourself.

31. TUESDAY. Energetic. Make sure to line up plenty of physical tasks since you are ready to power on, letting nothing stand in your way. Fighting for a cause like a noble warrior can see you leaping into the fray to help people who are less fortunate. A new physical regimen would be great, increasing your fitness level with a positive and radical makeover. A partner may come along for the ride, as you inspire this person and others toward victory. Just make sure that power doesn't go to your head. People are looking to you for guidance, and you may be getting used to the role of adviser. If you don't know how to respond, send them to someone who does.

NOVEMBER

1. WEDNESDAY. Mixed. Concentrate on maximizing expansive opportunities to meet new people who excite your world. Emotional surprises give an eccentric edge to the day. Colorful characters fill your world, time plays tricks, and normal is just a memory. To achieve victory, concentrate on your purpose, finding new paths rather than those already tried and tested. Relax control a little and link up with supportive friends. Relationships and romance are up for grabs, with sudden attractions and possible changes of direction from a partner. Computers or electrical items could be untrustworthy. Make sure batteries and solar power are handy as you navigate your way.

2. THURSDAY. Intuitive. Computers or telepathy could play a large role in your dealings with other people. Meditation is vital in order to harness a golden opportunity to achieve penetrating understanding in research, developing technology, or with people who require the skill of a detective to understand. Going out on a limb and taking a calculated risk can result in unusual success. This is a day for being progressive and future-oriented. Relate to those on the leading edge. Make sure you can pick up the pace and chat casually about all manner of unusual subjects. Be careful not to go overboard in commitments by promising more than you can deliver, since your enthusiasm is high at this time.

3. FRIDAY. Revitalizing. The things you love doing with partners are being upgraded in surprising ways. Planning interesting new activities suits your relationships, injecting fun and lightheartedness into your life. Worry needs to be avoided or soothed. Don't overlook or strangle the positive solution waiting in the wings to assist in expanding your life. Idealistic secret feelings containing fascinating new imaginings hold the seeds of a practical new beginning. You may feel you've got more than enough emotional energy to fight the good fight. Your courage conveys an element of the knight on a charger contesting a noble cause and eventually prevailing.

4. SATURDAY. Productive. Today's new emotional cycle could see you craving time to become absorbed in your own activities. Spending time in nature, singing favorite songs, gardening, or indulging in life away from the demands of other people is important at least for part of the day. A small emotional sacrifice might have to made, whether attending to a sick relative, listening to the urgent worries of a friend, or giving time to a charity. You've got the strength other people desperately need at the moment. Show them how to do the simple things in life that keep a person grounded during challenging times. This evening favors quiet time with a loved one, perhaps enjoying an intimate dinner for two.

5. SUNDAY. Frustrating. It may not be you, but someone in the environment will probably be expressing disharmony. Lack of proper communication leads to frustration. The best you can do is encourage people to speak up and be heard, in an attempt to tone down a potentially volatile day. Lack of realism or outright dishonesty is possible. Be aware of various perspectives in a realistic way, sorting fact from fantasy. Children especially could tell tall stories. Being a good listener may be the last thing you're in the mood for but try to promote tolerance if you can. On the positive side, this is a good day to curl up with a book or watch a movie, letting the characters in fantasy land thrash it out.

6. MONDAY. Renewing. Although already stretching yourself and your resources, you may now be asked to pull a rabbit out of a hat. If you go the extra mile in advising or helping someone achieve, you might be surprised just what you wind up with. You may generate a great amount of creativity under sometimes trying circumstances. Partnerships can be a cause of confusion or be hard to pin down. Be wary of acting the savior in a relationship that needs professional assistance to get through an addictive drama. If you're feeling restricted, speak to an optimistic friend who can give you a pep talk, a hug, and tell you how wonderful you are.

7. TUESDAY. Erratic. Be cautious of making major purchases or expecting too much from persons or objects you rely on for security. A change of heart may see you lose interest in something you once held dear. Values and tastes are being upgraded and sorted through. A decision to let go and downsize may leave you in a temporary vacuum. Going off the beaten path can reveal challenging and interesting ways to redirect your life away from purely materialistic concerns. An exciting person could enter the scene, stimulating a change in design, thought, or philosophy. However, remember to come to your own conclusions, and make newcomers earn your trust and your devotion.

8. WEDNESDAY. Unsteady. Although you may long for your home environment to settle down, be careful of settling for second best. Be truthful with yourself. Look for facts in a situation which at best may be hard to determine accurately. A change in your immediate environment or family can see you letting go and eliminating something you thought you had to have, but something that just isn't working. Something new and better is sure to come if you meditate and fulfill your life as best you can. Try not to indulge in too much escapism when there is so much potential to bring beauty into your life and that of others. A boost from someone unexpected could balance the scales to make you feel life is truly worth the price you have to pay.

9. THURSDAY. Disquieting. Letters, e-mails, and faxes from family members and friends on emotional topics can require you to deal with other people's strong feelings. Tender loving care is needed. Try to pour oil on troubled waters if you can. Visions of love ever after could see a need to refrain from family feuding. Be mature, setting a good example for younger ones who benefit from demonstrations of loyalty without constant arguing. People around you could be expressing themselves in over-the-top ways. If you're in the mood for theater, opera, or the mingling of truth and fiction, turn to writers and those in the arts. Fertile new ground is up for grabs.

10. FRIDAY. Intense. A desire to be at home could induce cabin fever unless you plan carefully. Some aggression in communication needs to be channeled into vigorous debate or wrestling with the tension of a game of chess. Work could be filled with challenges to produce under difficult circumstances, yet there's support when you come back from the battle. Extreme sports, flirting with danger, and walking on the wild side of the thunderstorm are all possible. Romance tonight could include a power play and secret flirting, with aspirations to heaven thrown in. Remember you always must pay sometime. Take a deep breath and seize the day.

11. SATURDAY. Volatile. Wires could get crossed unless you shine the light of love and clarity on a few people who want events to be tangled. Aim to keep things simple even though delays in transportation, abrupt changes of plan, and refusals to talk things over calmly could be the order of the day. Tune into harmony. Tread carefully to keep out of danger when those around you might be losing it. Playing sports is sure to result in a feisty all-or-nothing game. Avoid being sarcastic with loved ones. Don't demand too much off anyone. They're probably not in the mood to give very much. If you enjoy being argumentative, this could be your day to enter into a formal debate.

12. SUNDAY. Restrained. Duty comes before pleasure in a romantic scenario. You need to preserve dignity even in the wild dreaming of it all, between the dark and the light. Try to strike a balance between preserving your reputation and fulfilling yourself. Solitude, or time spent finishing work on projects and preparing for the week ahead, could assuage guilt for taking time out for yourself. A shortage of resources is temporary, so get together with friends who can brainstorm toward the possible and positive. You're operating under foggy conditions that haven't yet settled. For someone who likes firm ground, this could be a bit frustrating unless you cultivate patience.

13. MONDAY. Jovial. Breaking out of inhibiting limitations and envisioning new solutions to challenges can fire you up in a positive way. Suddenly remembering your sense of humor, you become open to more progressive ways rather than being stuck in a rut. Inventing, playing music, counseling others with a tough love attitude, and whistling a happy tune as you work make you a favorite among colleagues. Be willing to go out of your way for others. You could even don the hero's costume for a while. Work hard and you'll have the satisfaction of succeeding despite laboring against the tide.

14. TUESDAY. Constructive. Attend to practical tasks such as organizing the office and cleaning up in general. This is a good day for rescuing your work from the overly emotional dramas of past days. Checking health and taking care of a burnt out nervous system, whether yours or someone else's, could see you generously being of service. You're likely to get things done in an assertive way, confirming as you go. Just watch out for the agendas of a couple of negative characters who might aim to confuse you or at least be hard to pin down. If they don't want to positively contribute, let them go their own way. Your pet might need some extra attention or vitamins plus a thorough checkup.

15. WEDNESDAY. Expansive. While being generous with your love and time, you need to strike a balance dealing with a power struggle in the environment. Taurus entrepreneurs will enjoy taking a gamble. Pit your wits against the odds and sail with the tide of trends and fashion. Being around the beautiful people, especially artists, musicians, and fashion designers, can make you feel like part of the action. Your world is opening up, with new people and interesting invitations. You will take to this like a duck to water. Just be alert for jealousy from those who are used to you playing the humble rock of strength. It's time you had a bit of attention as a reward for all that hard work.

16. THURSDAY. Enthusiastic. A willingness to try new activities can see you being more generous and open-hearted in relationships with other people. Insights into work habits will help you get to the bottom of restrictive problems in a harmonious way. Try refining your approach to office systems and workplace surroundings. Taurus teachers and students can expand their in-depth learning thanks to a lucky break or chance meeting. Taking a well-calculated risk may pay off if you've done your research thoroughly enough. A controlled, disciplined approach to work will see you come out on top. Let down your hair tonight when free-spirited friends beckon.

17. FRIDAY. Tricky. Enjoy a diplomatic and sociable day, but just be aware of any underhanded or dishonest tactics from recent associates. You need to keep your wits about you, as you divine whether the motives of some people are sincere. This is a progressive time combined with a hint of danger, providing some thrills. However, stay safe and explore mysteries from the comfort of home. There will be plenty of choices to choose from. Challenges and extreme situations could lead you to embrace life passionately. A romantic connection will be felt instantaneously yet with depth. Check out your new love's background carefully, then follow the magnetic attraction.

18. SATURDAY. Demanding. Duties and responsibilities demand much time and energy. A budget or schedule must be worked out, leaving less time for socializing. Refusing to be dominated by the clock, and giving yourself enough space and time to help family and friends, can make you ultimately more productive. Feelings are deep and intense. Enjoy an outing in nature with friends. Sharing yourself deeply will bring more contentment than any frothy partying. Someone may unburden their fears to you, and your loving reassurance could mean more than you know. Relationships are warming up and could become passionate.

19. SUNDAY. Eventful. Trusting what intuition and instincts tell you can be vital and fulfilling. A challenging environment may somehow bring out your best qualities. A win of some kind is sure to be satisfying. Try not to be overly sensitive if someone picks an argument. Tensions reflect what's going on with the elements in the outer world. Cultivate adaptability. Go easy on yourself so you don't burn out. A sense of adventure in relationships can lead to traveling on an intriguing outing with a special person. Venturing far from home territory will blow the cobwebs away. Meet a few colorful characters, talk, and ease the built-up tension.

20. MONDAY. Focused. Your good intentions come together in laser-like focus as you accomplish tasks with clarity and concentration. No one can stop your drive and determination. Just be sure to spare a little compassion for those around you who are not feeling so feisty. Legal matters could be all-or-nothing events. Challenges and obstacles can be overcome with a failure-is-not-an-option style. Take a few deep breaths today as you go about the battlefield, and remember there are gentler pastures ahead. Secrets within relationships or issues of joint resources could demand attention. Be as honest as you can, even though the world seems to reward a stealthy attitude.

21. TUESDAY. Cautious. Hidden feelings and a determination to win at all costs advise against throwing yourself into battle without first doing your homework. Try to curb sarcasm and general hostility. Get out and exercise to harmonize your emotions, in order to act calmly when other people may lose their cool. Sudden changes in a relationship, and unspoken undercurrents, suggest withdrawing. Build up your energy. Only confide in people who have earned your trust. Conquering mountains and other such feats of physical endurance are a positive result of today's all-or-nothing atmosphere. Competitive sports could be on your mind for the weekend as an outlet for your emotions.

22. WEDNESDAY. Transformative. Positive restructuring of joint resources, or a deep shift in feelings toward finances and managing physical assets, could result in profound changes. You're in the process of appreciating more intangible values. Material goods aren't bringing as much satisfaction as they once did. Consider speaking to a trusted friend about your strong feelings. Look into ethical investment, perhaps contributing to your community by building positive projects with like-hearted companions. Relationships have an unconventional quality. See what you can learn, but don't be judgmental about individual characters you come across. It takes all types to make a world.

23. THURSDAY. Rewarding. Long-distance travel for business is harmonious, and a partner or friend joining you could sweeten the trip. Positive, unusual experiences can happen if you retain an open mind. Your world is expanding thanks to dynamic experiences, forcing you out of cubbyholes or ruts. Researching a new course of study, visiting a college or other learning institution, and better organizing yourself can bring powerful satisfaction even on this Thanksgiving holiday. Being around well-known public figures sees you making a contribution to the political world and gaining a reputation for constructive action. Being called on as a troubleshooter can lead to added respect.

24. FRIDAY. Successful. Promoting yourself and becoming well-known via the media for your work can take time. Concentrate on your professional reputation. An award or recognition for work well done could come your way. Putting in extra effort in a project is certain to pay off with a positive result, providing you can spare the extra time now. Give partners space to themselves, and don't stress out if you sense a withdrawal on their part. There could be excitement in your love life due to a third party. A sudden attraction could ignite, but make sure the person is free to be with you. Otherwise complexity will soon squash the relationship. Friendship and love will blend in some unusual experiences that suggest just enjoying the ride.

25. SATURDAY. Progressive. A feeling of wanting to expand can ripen into an eager willingness to learn more about a subject. Meeting an intriguing teacher while attending a lecture, updating your ideas at a favorite bookshop, or mixing with educated people can inspire a broad-minded interest. Unusual experiences could put you on edge if you're not adaptable. Having to understand people who are culturally different from you is important. A party finds you mixing business with pleasure. Business networking opportunities could arise, leading to positive developments. Romance suggests dressing up this evening in a classical way, then emerging into a refined environment of theater or music.

26. SUNDAY. Revealing. Experiencing hidden and mystical sides of your emotional nature takes priority. Search for a gentle softness that might not be reflected in the outside world. You may take refuge in dreams, novels, music, and otherworldly experiences. Take the armor off while you embrace your lover and the call of the mystical. Down-to-earth family members may wonder at your new interests and question why you're not doing the usual. Seek your sense of finding the exquisite in each and every day. There could be frustration trying to communicate feelings to your significant other. If the empathy of a soul mate isn't there, be silent and conserve your energy until you get back on track.

27. MONDAY. Sensitive. A need to get back to some sense of normalcy could nevertheless be emotionally restrictive. Group endeavors demand a lot of attention and time, forcing you to put your personal desires on the back burner. Positively dealing with financial issues can mix high ideals with the practical. A lending institution may inform you of positive news about a loan. Keep certain aspects of your life to yourself while you accomplish mundane tasks. You can escape restraints later. Put aside time for yourself when the mood turns ethereal. Beautiful moments in a relationship provide a natural high later in the day, when you break out of self-imposed limitations.

28. TUESDAY. Unsettled. Be prepared for sudden illuminations that change your feelings. A need to stay positively on guard and ready for anything mixes with carefully sorting truth from fiction. Adapt yourself to the state of the world and be receptive to what's going on, rather than charging through with your own agenda. Check transactions carefully. Ask people to say what they really mean if they're being indirect. For the artistic, breakthroughs can occur with flashes of brilliance, along with a need to dive deeply into the subject and feel the experience. A positive lightning bolt can clear the air, propelling you into a new aspect of a project.

29. WEDNESDAY. Tense. A need to channel aggressive energy assertively means you must be clear in communicating. Just don't expect much support from those in official positions. Be on your own, or at least with some privacy, as you work your way through a backlog of tasks that need straightening out. A sick relative could require extra attention and care. Dealing with who and what are most needy now is the best that can be expected. Navigate in the moment, trusting your judgment and that you can overcome negativity by staying in harmony with the light. Take a few deep breaths to fill up your reservoir of emotional sustenance, then press on.

30. THURSDAY. Inspiring. After yesterday's tension the sun is shining, suggesting that good fortune and emotional fulfillment are available. There's a need to be sure people are speaking truthfully about their relationships. This expansive day of moving forward suggests strong progress in behind-the-scenes developments. A new chapter brings fresh people into your sphere. Your inner warrior is ready to take on the world. New attitudes now being assimilated have the potential to bring happiness, prosperity, and success, as you eliminate negative or stagnant situations. A windfall could light up your day, with a grant application being approved or a prosperous backer appreciating your new project.

DECEMBER

1. FRIDAY. Stable. Time spent working behind the scenes on new projects can be productive, producing feelings of great satisfaction. You can fulfill an urge for creative challenge with strong support from financial backers or those in a position to contribute to joint resources. Develop definite goals and aims. Visualize what is possible. Act on a feeling of being able to take on the world and fight the good fight. See old friends and enjoy people you've known for a long time. As you enter a new era, it's grounding to be among friends who are also at a crossroads. A romantic attraction could lead to a deep, naturally sustaining commitment.

2. SATURDAY. Edgy. There is an unpredictable element to this day, with an urge for freedom leading to behavior that is out of character from yourself or those around you. Colorful characters can interrupt your world, bringing excitement but also a need to adapt. Avoid rigid approaches to finances. Bring hidden issues to light. Get away to a place where you can enjoy the simple life, leading you out of a self-contained box and helping you tune into the bigger picture in a balanced way. Challenging physical exercise could complete the picture, as you point yourself toward harmony and health. Communication with partners can contain some otherworldly subjects. Focus on what you know to be the truth.

3. SUNDAY. Difficult. Build up your energy reserves as you avoid taking on confused or troublesome people or situations. Lack of confidence could prevail, sending out an unsettling ripple of worry and concern. Try to maintain equilibrium. Channel feisty energy into breaking out of a pattern of self-imposed loneliness or isolation. This is a day to nurture yourself and others instead of merely responding to the conflicted attitudes of certain people in your life. An older relative or neighbor may need more than the usual amount of attention, cutting short time spent on your own interests. Go the extra mile and summon generosity of spirit. Gardening could be a productive refuge from stressful situations.

4. MONDAY. Mixed. Demands from a teacher or other higher-up could take you away from your own activities. In trying to complete assignments you are apt to be running against the clock. Slow down and try to enjoy the process of learning. Free up your mind. Personal relationships and esoteric subjects are calling. There's an odd mood to the day, with a need to be flexible. Strive to adapt to situations outside the norm. Conversations can be feisty. Although you're in the mood to take on someone in a verbal debate, know your own strengths and weaknesses. You might accidentally overpower a gentle soul or be fooled yourself. This stable time in a personal relationship brings a deep contentment and feeling of continuity.

5. TUESDAY. Profitable. A house or other property could at last be sold. Something of value, most likely a job or other source of income, is changing your world. Finances linked to a relationship need to be clarified so both parties can move on. This will be a positive development, with more freedom yet the security of knowing where you stand. Get to the bottom of a mystery involving a long-standing relationship. There's incredible depth of commitment to be explored almost effortlessly with a soul mate. However, a relationship for safety alone may have to be transmuted into friendship. Anxious thoughts about a personal situation, and black-and-white attitudes in regard to coping with a new relationship, could benefit from some timely counseling.

6. WEDNESDAY. Hopeful. A conflict over a hidden relationship could turn into a positive commitment after a period of conflicted feelings. Realizing there are presences in the background of your life who support your unusual personal situation or lifestyle should give you hope. It's usually a Taurus who maintains a conservative stance, but now it's your turn to experiment. A busy day full of relatives, neighbors, and family members includes going on short journeys to catch up with these people and to run family errands. Staying close to home suits you, with plenty going on to keep you interested and involved. If you're asked to mediate in a dramatic situation, stay as objective as possible and do not take sides.

7. THURSDAY. Comforting. Thoughts turn to home and hearth. Workmates could be working as a close-knit group in an emotive way. Be compassionate and sensitive in responding to today's softer mood. You may meet an irresistibly magnetic individual. It could be a case of fated attraction almost impossible to resist. Before you get swept away, however, ask a friend to do a background check on this person on your behalf. If the relationship is the real thing, it will survive objective scrutiny. Death and taxes could be on your mind. The potential exists for both a sacrifice and a positive gain. Keep the day harmonious by employing a strong constructive work ethic. Make the most of current passionate intensity.

8. FRIDAY. Eventful. A desire to get things done can see you successfully aiming for the top and achieving your goals. A note of successful optimism infuses today's proceedings. Finances are looking up. Meetings to discuss a project in the arts and with entrepreneurial people should culminate in you being given a green light to proceed. Holding on despite the odds, with faith in your abilities, brings ultimate success. If you have been fighting to hang in there in a situation but are beginning to give up, dare to walk on the creative edge. You may find yourself socializing in fine style at the best restaurant in town. A romantic moment could make you sigh with the cinematic quality of it all.

9. SATURDAY. Inspiring. A challenge combines with your tendency to be drawn into a web of escapism. Cultivate clarity under pressure. Refuse to take part in a drama unless the people involved are really aiming for a constructive outcome. A long-distance trip can be planned or taken. You may find a travel special that nips the budget significantly. Getting away for a long weekend is favorable, especially a journey to the mountains or the ocean. Take time out this evening to float in a healing bubble bath, relax with a few good movies, and enjoy an intimate fireside chat. A candlelit evening calls you away from the stresses of the day. Reinspire yourself with idealism as you continue to dream.

10. SUNDAY. Variable. Ideas of freedom and expansion can be at odds with your lonely or serious mood. Try not to be too hard on yourself. A desire to dedicate yourself in a responsible way might encourage you to promise more than you can deliver. Break away from superficial people and seek the higher mind in order to focus on philosophical teachings. Shades of the monk or nun can emerge, leading you toward a pure environment where you can contemplate life's mysteries. At least find a little time alone, even if children and other family responsibilities call. Getting out in the fresh air or playing some gentle sport can increase your feelings of happiness and connection. Review your pleasure-seeking activities and enlarge your options.

11. MONDAY. Revealing. Take care of your nerves. Surprising challenges demand an agile response to ever-changing situations. Craving freedom from financial obligations can move you to organize a less challenging repayment plan that offers more leverage. The positive development of being backed by more than enough financial resources can widen your capacity to serve the greater good while also meeting your own needs. Focus on abundance and magnetize it to you. A life-changing journey can be planned or actually undertaken. Transformation on a pilgrimage suggests that you won't return the same as when you depart. You can be incredibly enriched by the experience despite facing a challenge to your sense of security.

12. TUESDAY. Suspenseful. Attend to hidden issues, power plays, and behind-the-scenes aspects of your life. Be wary of any dishonest or underhanded dealings. Working hard in a spirit of discretion could be the best option. Colleagues may be stressed. Taurus owners of a business might need to have a meeting to clear the air and lay all the cards on the table. Extra rest will refuel your nerves, helping you avoid unnecessary arguments and disputes. People want to speak the truth as they see it, but you may not agree. Be on the lookout for a lucky break or a fortunate opportunity, with the possibility of a financial win of some kind. A surprise call from a distant friend could bring exciting news.

13. WEDNESDAY. Beneficial. Socializing for business purposes can be a positive experience. Introduce new clients at a successful luncheon or other function. Big changes are being made in your environment. Be ready for significant life events that demand strength of character from you. Diplomacy and social attentiveness are called for, as many people in your environment need attention. An idealistic group has a good chance of securing financial resources from a generous benefactor. Philanthropic projects thrive with a passion to better situations in a spirit of cooperation. A deep realization of life's possibilities can be channeled into art or a poignant encounter with a newcomer.

14. THURSDAY. Idealistic. Work should be pleasant as you act on your dreams in an artistic way. Happy harmony puts you in a good mood to celebrate the small details of life and the subtle beauty of food, decor, and nature. Passion to be original in your efforts can put you on the leading edge, daring to be different. Try to stay ahead of the pack. This sense of daring is mixing with the desire to move forward positively, away from restrictions. No limitations should be your motto. Traveling for business can be exciting, bringing learning and adventure. A romantic streak can lead to celebrating with your lover. Do not limit yourself.

15. FRIDAY. Positive. A luscious, beauty-filled day awaits you. Food, passion, and art take precedence. You're ripe to escape into a world that is a little bizarre and eccentric. Upgrading your work environment can be achieved effortlessly, transforming decor and systems to run more smoothly. Just be careful of taking on more than you can accomplish if given extra work to do. Promising too much and not delivering needs to be avoided. This evening enjoy a cultural extravaganza, perhaps a musical feast and a dance to be learned. Friends from other cultures have a lot to teach you as you emerge from your small world. A timely book can take you on a magical journey.

16. SATURDAY. Fulfilling. Having an intense time with your mate or partner can be full of all-or-nothing feelings. New experiences give an exciting boost to a partnership. Developing an ability to handle power could see you leading the troops or the family into a new arrangement containing greater stability. Take the reins. Your calm capability will be greatly appreciated by those around you. Remaining quiet and authoritative suits you. Other people will rely on your expertise in a developing situation. Being appraised for your strength earns you admiration from those closest to you. Sports can play an exciting part in your day, with a team going all-out for a stunning victory.

17. SUNDAY. Fruitful. Follow your heart where relationships are concerned, but look out for your own best interests. Powerful times are leading to a freer approach to your place in the universe. This will take you from coziness to adventure. You may end a long-term association and then have to sort through issues of joint ownership. A feeling of being able to start over encourages you to look forward to an exciting new chapter in life, living more by faith. Try not to focus on material possessions. Aim for a fuller relationship with nature. Exploring wide-open spaces can lead to sacred places and fulfilling times. If life seems to be going too fast, seek a peaceful place where you can simplify and slow down to compensate.

18. MONDAY. Expansive. An urge to follow your dream and break free of restrictions is strong. You may think about leaving a job to travel and find more fulfilling pastures. Be careful to stay sensitive to those around you as you consider any adventurous mission. Attend to details. An all-or-nothing expansiveness can land you in trouble. Knights on a mission would carefully prepare before galloping off, and it would be wise if you did the same. A free-spirited sense of humor can light the path for friends or family members who may be having problems at this time. Archaeology and ancient history meet in today's fascinating world of past and present. Continue to learn even as you teach.

19. TUESDAY. Stimulating. Even though you're reaching for an ideal, adapting to unusual characters or changes to your routine is important. Intense conversations need to be toned down in the interests of peace. Religious and political conflict may see you attempting to draw a sword, but remember that those who live by the sword suffer the same fate. Positive use of your talents helps you contribute to the whole wide world. Publishing and teaching are high on the agenda. Imagination and mental endeavors, after recent physical work, can be a refreshing change. Wisely channel your enormous willpower thanks to your passionate nature. Avoid burnout by varying your routine.

20. WEDNESDAY. Intense. Building something of worth and devoting yourself to activities which promise stability lend dignity to the day. Reel yourself in to be more productive. It's possible to achieve goals, climb mountains, and attain a consistently high standard. Your own slightly radical way of proceeding can cause a few raised eyebrows. However, your need to pioneer or get off the beaten path in some way has you forging full-steam ahead. Enjoy the day's stability. Believe in yourself and what you can achieve despite working under constantly changing conditions. Contacts with colleges, schools, and overseas connections are a strong theme. Today's learning curve will have long-lasting effects.

21. THURSDAY. Opportune. Shining your own light and continuing down your chosen path without distraction send you on a personal crusade. Taking aim, and diligently defining your goals in a philosophical manner, can produce excellent results by the end of the day. Working with a lot of personal space, and without anyone overseeing you too tightly, suits the mood. Your mental abilities are on track thanks to your sober, mature judgment. There's a price to pay for what you wish to achieve, but you're putting in the energy to assure success. Pay homage to the forces of love and order. Stay away from a group of radical people who lack compassion.

22. FRIDAY. Constructive. Focusing on how you appear in public and present yourself could result in a day of concentrated community work. Down-to-earth physical tasks could in order. Escaping will have to wait. You have the ability to be inspired yet make rational and sound judgments based on the facts. This could lead to helping people out of confused situations which to you seem obvious. Lending a helping hand to get a younger person started out in the world and setting a good example of behavior would be energy well spent. For Taurus people who have been working behind the scenes, public acknowledgment for a job well done could be forthcoming. A long-distance trip is harmoniously aspected.

23. SATURDAY. Energetic. A forward-thinking approach can get you away from familiar haunts and off on another adventure. Family will just have to catch up or come with you. A need to retreat after the hectic last few days can see you boating, canoeing, or indulging in a relaxed water sport. You are in the mood for a challenge. Your mind is able to penetrate mysteries as you concentrate on a good novel or perhaps write one yourself. Either you or someone close to you may have an adventure the world will want to read about. Document your feelings also. Enjoy the idealism of the day combined with your ability to deeply experience life.

24. SUNDAY. Demanding. Arranging and organizing this festive season may contain elements of duty before pleasure. A long to-do list sees you looking forward to a rest. An intense mental mood suggests doing some deep breathing. Cultivate a sense of humor if you can while conserving energy for the long haul. A group gathering could contain an element of worry, which you should be able to soothe if you remain calm. Technological glitches can get you off the grid, forcing you to make do with solar power and warm hearts. Being part of a large team doing their best in a spiritual sense will make you feel worthy to contribute. Work well done won't go unnoticed.

25. MONDAY. Merry Christmas! This unusual Christmas finds you adapting and holding to ideals of peace. There is the possibility of arguments or a sudden change of plan in a group situation. Take time to sit quietly and know you're not alone. Tests of patience and character can happen when you least expect it. Being kind to those on the fringes of society can lead to an eccentric friendship, where before you might have been judgmental. Putting yourself in other people's shoes and cultivating compassion can bring surprising richness and hidden gifts of the spirit. People will listen intently to any speech you make, viewing you as a calm and charismatic head of the table.

26. TUESDAY. Challenging. Spend some time alone once family obligations are met. A little space can be good for you. A feeling of being on shifting sands could be disturbing. Retreating into your spiritual life can help restore you after the recent big expenditure of energy. Focus on the positives and don't let temporary conflict get you down. It's easier to cope in the center of a storm rather than be worrying but powerless on the sidelines. Your guiding words for someone else, despite your own doubts, will help them more than you might guess. Trust your instincts and mental abilities. You're on track but a close friend may be caught in a fantasy world.

27. WEDNESDAY. Daring. Being assertive could lead to accessing your warrior spirit. New adventures are calling, and an urge to take risks has returned. Being behind the scenes tuning into imaginative pioneering can bring positive fun into your world. A drive for freedom could be at odds with structuring yourself. It is important to first get the hard work done, then you do not have to be dominated by any restrictive expectations. A new love could put a bounce in your step, tempting you to run off suddenly due to the passion of it all. Free-spiritedness and acceptance of responsibility could happily merge.

28. THURSDAY. Progressive. All systems are go for moving forward into an exciting time. With your energetic sense of possibility, this may feel like the position you've wanted to be in for some time. Security and adventure are combining in the galactic realm of private dreams, giving you a feeling of being able to successfully cope with change. Communicate your deepest feelings via art, music, or learning a new skill. A young person can come into your life, teaching you things about the new world and adding to your fascination and gratitude for life. If someone asks you to try something unknown, the adventure of learning and mastering it could bring special joy.

29. FRIDAY. Happy. A harmony of emotions and mind gives you a sense of contentment. This is a time for being aware of yourself as the Moon moves into your sign. Going about any job in your own time and working on your own projects will suit you. Blend personal interests with the feeling of getting things done. Enjoy slowing the pace a bit after recent epic times. Cultivate a sense of normality. Gardening, a sculptural project, cooking, and any type of learning are all favored. A special book with a hidden adventure calls for your attention. An overseas friend could arrive, prompting you to take care of them in fine old-fashioned style, with feasts and fresh linens.

30. SATURDAY. Uncertain. Try not to worry too much. Give yourself plenty of room to move. Keep things simple. There might be some confusion in the mix. A bill to be paid may give you an uncomfortable sense of going overboard. Maintain harmony, do your duty, and it will soon pass. Feeling you have to sacrifice yourself for someone else takes energy, but attempting to be generous will make you feel better. What you do will all come back to you in the future. Enjoy a social evening with people who are on your wavelength; otherwise you may feel lonely. A soul mate is out there for Taurus singles. Stay on your path, be true to your interests, and you'll meet up with just the right person.

31. SUNDAY. Bright. An exuberant gathering, plus the chance to have time alone, suggests a day of balancing celebration with introspection. Remain optimistic about possibilities of perfection. This busy day demands communication and an ongoing sense of humor, despite occasional difficulties. Being at home in an atmosphere of truth will welcome in the new year with idealism. Poetry and innovative plans blend with deep devotion. The magnificent drama of good versus evil continues, with more mystery, adventure, and security ahead. Tuning in to love, order, and peace will show the way. Romance descends like a dove for those feeling they've been alone for far too long. Take heart and gear up to have a happy new year.

TAURUS
NOVEMBER–DECEMBER 2005

November 2005

1. TUESDAY. Intense. Today's New Moon in Scorpio, your seventh house, is a focal point for decisions involving significant relationships. Some of you may be proposing marriage or making a commitment to your lover. Others, already in long-term relationships, might have reached the end of the road with each other, and need to look at separating. Either way, it is a big move, requiring the most serious consideration. Taurus people are currently coming to grips with a need for both intimacy and solitude. Those of you still unattached could find yourselves intrigued by a potential partner, despite your habituation to the single life.

2. WEDNESDAY. Deceptive. Secrets and lies might insinuate themselves into interactions with people today. Take what you hear with a grain of salt, and be careful with whom you share confidences and discreet information. Stories have a way of taking on a life of their own in the retelling, and, like whispers on the wind, can end up as a gross distortion of the original message. Your natural Taurus directness could confront less honest and forthright characters, and you can expect strange and shifty reactions. Interviews and consultations could be confused, inept, and less than successful.

3. THURSDAY. Misleading. Honesty may be the best policy. But despite good intentions, it can be tricky to get a straight story sometimes. A business partner might request a sudden meeting, and alert you to budgetary or taxation issues that need immediate attention. Somebody close to you may have a gambling problem, and ask you for a loan. Do not give them anything more than you are prepared to forfeit. You could get a sudden urge to secure your household and possessions against theft, loss, and damage. Get a valuation and arrange the right insurance to be comfortable.

231

4. FRIDAY. Helpful. Sometimes you have just got to trust people because they are in the driver's seat, even though you would like to be there. Physical and intuitive responses can clue you in, helping you decide who is genuine. In a whole range of matters, you may require the assistance of those with more experience, authority, and expertise. Schedule an appointment with your accountant, doctor, lawyer, or therapist, then address whatever your need or concern may be. Fall back on your mate as a source of wise comfort and reliable strength. Turn up the volume on romance this evening.

5. SATURDAY. Problematic. If you feel unfairly dealt with, look into your legal rights and consider taking official action. Trying to resolve it on a personal level may not work, but stay open to a fair resolution of differences. Before you can be happy in yourself and with your lifestyle, you may need to address outstanding problems and difficulties. It would be ill-advised to sweep them under the carpet, or pretend to yourself that all is okay. A proposed journey or career move, although attractive, could upset the status quo and create disquiet in your household and primary relationship.

6. SUNDAY. Comforting. You have probably got plenty on your plate now. So devotional services could focus and calm you through prayer and contemplation. Alternately, getting away from it all in nature can put things in perspective. Either way, you would do well to steer away from crowds and social formality. Only keep company with a close, understanding companion. There is an important opportunity now to use maturity, patience, and experience to address underlying tensions before they become explosive. Do not leave it up to others, or take your lead from current fads and fashions.

7. MONDAY. Positive. Stay focused on public and career responsibilities, despite whatever else is going on. You will be expected to behave appropriately and fulfill your duty, as people are relying on you. Set a good example and make your family proud. Presentations to higher-ups or officials can be well-received if you are thoroughly prepared. Do not be lazy by relying on another's efforts or input, as it will not cut the mustard. Students can succeed by studying hard at home and completing all necessary assignments. Some of you may need to make arrangements for an aging parent.

8. TUESDAY. Sensitive. With Mars going retrograde in your sign of Taurus for the last month, it has been a period of slowly building pressure. The point is to come clean with whatever is worrying you, then get on track with the life that you want. But that is easier said than done, especially because other people and situations are affected by your decisions. Reflect on the big picture today before taking any impulsive action. Wrong moves will only find you backtracking during the next several weeks. Take things one at a time, starting with career issues now. Are you in the right company, industry, and occupational niche yet?

9. WEDNESDAY. Mixed. The mood is not so charged today, and you are likely to feel mentally prepared to take on worldly tasks. Dealing with the public is always tricky, but you can stay calm when customers seem annoying and hard to please. Interacting personally with fellow workers might be irritating and uninteresting. However, working to solve technical problems through the application of experience and knowledge can grab your undivided attention and prove satisfying. The lines of power and authority are clearly drawn in the workplace, so respect them to avoid unnecessary hassles.

10. THURSDAY. Jumbled. Organizing or coordinating gatherings and meetings can be a handful, possibly making you feel like tearing your hair out. It may well seem like the tower of Babel, with everyone talking at once and nobody being heard or listening. Whether or not you are in charge, show the way by taking action in an effort to get something done. Always trying to understand those closest to us can be at times mysterious and elusive, even unnecessary and ill-conceived. Take a break from intense and claustrophobic intimacies. Mix and mingle with a different and unfamiliar social set.

11. FRIDAY. Pressured. Whether you are at home or in the workplace, try to find any excuse, good or bad, to get out and about. Being part of a group learning experience will be useful and instructive, giving you a chance to share what you know with others and receive their input. If your private life is drab, or your primary relationship consuming, planning a great escape to foreign shores could ease the pressure. Extreme demands on you from partner and family might predispose you to stay out and party this evening rather than going straight home. But you will have to face the music when you get in.

12. SATURDAY. Subdued. Maintaining a low profile and keeping to yourself could be a wise move. You are looking for something passionate and meaningful to grab you, and you will have to dig deep to find it. However, you are not alone in this quest, and it is likely that you know people who can offer clues and encouragement. Practicing and training in martial arts with other committed seekers could be a perfect mix of dynamic physicality, competitive contest, philosophy, and tradition. Quiet sharing within your domestic circle can get things off your chest, and strengthen a sense of purpose.

13. SUNDAY. Renewing. Nesting cozily with your lover, allowing the space and time for passionate embrace, would be a tonic for body and soul. Any marriage or intimate relationship can only flourish when nurtured appropriately with private sharing and unguarded moments. Show your affection physically, leaving explanation and complication for another day. Visiting someone dear to you at their sickbed will speed their recovery and demonstrate your deep care. Thinking about finances will make your head sore, and preparing work ahead would only muddle you. Take a needed break!

14. MONDAY. Constructive. Get off to an early start and out of the house, single-mindedly pursuing personal interests and individual tasks. If you are not looking after number one, then who else will? In any event, you are likely to be feeling more positive and confident. You are ready, willing, and able to activate and enthuse others as well. Schedule and attend meetings, events, and gatherings where your individuality and presence can shine. Taurus presenters and performers could entertain and create a profile for yourselves. Love is in the air for singles, and a chance encounter might linger longer.

15. TUESDAY. Strategic. The Full Moon in your sign of Taurus illumines some conflicts between private life and public life. While it may be a to-and-fro seesawing experience, make your best attempts at bringing personal and relationship needs into balance. Selfishness and self-centeredness are unlikely to help, but it would be foolish to lose yourself. A dose of enlightened self-interest is always essential. Experiencing cultural commentary, through movies, music, books, and art, can help you understand this all too human dilemma. Love your partner, but love yourself as well. Let them know who they are dealing with and what you want. Then you can make it work together.

16. WEDNESDAY. Demanding. Opportunities for growth and profit probably mean getting involved with people. But before you jump in, get your own house in order. Potential business partners will want to know what talents and resources you bring to the enterprise, and are likely to question you deeply about your motivations, goals, and objectives. Lenders and bank managers will want to see your books and tax statements before backing you. Even a lover could ask how much you earn and where you are going in life. Avoid entangling alliances before you are ready and know yourself!

17. THURSDAY. Diverse. It is possible to go backward financially unless you are vigilant and imaginative. If you are not earning enough, you may be heading for debt. Even those of you with a good cash flow might be suffering from certain poor investments. Plug the leaks in your budget, whatever the cause. You can be polite about quizzing your kids and mate concerning their spending habits. Explain the situation, and they are sure to cooperate. Have faith in a capacity to generate more wealth, and model yourself on successful friends and acquaintances who know how to play the game.

18. FRIDAY. Tricky. Doing sloppy work only means repeating it or rectifying errors, so leave things if you are not prepared to be thorough and effective. Unfortunately, you might be under client and customer pressure to deliver yesterday. If so, do your best, but do not expect too much of yourself or stake your reputation on it. Refuse to be pushed into purchases or expenditures, as you are not likely to be thinking clearly enough for small decisions, let alone big ones. Your spouse or lover may be getting suspicious of your secret life, and you could carelessly give yourself away.

19. SATURDAY. Lively. You and a living partner may be at cross-purposes about what to do. Compromise is not the best option, since neither of you will be satisfied. Why not suggest to each other what activities you prefer, and then take turns in doing them together? You will probably both end up enjoying it all anyway. But do get out around the neighborhood and in the streets. There is bound to be dancing, music, art, and theater to appreciate. And there is also the food and drink to accompany it. Have a jog or bike ride rather than taking out your moodiness on inappropriate targets.

20. SUNDAY. Nurturing. Getting involved with the bickering and the boasting of self-important friends and neighbors will surely waste time. Intended gatherings for whatever purpose could be ill-timed. Your presence is unlikely to be missed or make any noticeable difference to the chaotic experiences and scrambled outcomes. Stay close to home with your partner or a family member. Take your time to pick up the pieces and put things gently in order. But most of all, enjoy each other's company. Visiting nearby parents can be pleasant for all, as long as it is uncomplicated and excludes outsiders.

21. MONDAY. Opportune. Taurus in business could check inventory and cash flow, preparing for the holiday season's sales. A line of credit might be available, allowing the purchase of extra stock. An effective and solid marketing campaign can definitely attract more customers. You and your lover may be talking through the pros and cons of moving in together. Be thorough in your consideration of all the angles. If you have a family, the opportunity to purchase your own home could be tempting. However, it would probably require a second income, putting more pressure on you.

22. TUESDAY. Variable. At times you seem to be swinging from realism and responsibility to fantasy and escapism. And too much of one mode or the other is bound to frustrate you and exasperate anyone tied into your life. Finding the middle ground may take discipline and faith. But a good starting point is to appreciate what you already have achieved, making the roots of your security firm and solid. From that basis, you can then aspire to more fulfilling success and accomplishment. Be a star in your private world. Realize you probably have the good life already.

23. WEDNESDAY. Chancy. Speculative investments, such as stocks and bonds, might be a headache causing you anxiety. You may be regretting the control others, such as brokers and funds managers, have over your money. Perhaps it is time to renegotiate the situation, but do not panic and abandon ship just yet. Gamblers are advised to hold back and wait for more fortunate timing. Your partner could feel that your attitude toward them is too flippant and careless, and they might demand more conscious attention. As you are in a playful though reckless mood, you will not want to listen.

24. THURSDAY. Hopeful. The creative efforts that you are making in your job are possibly going unappreciated or being blocked by someone who is opposed to you. Do not waste your energy unnecessarily, but also do not give up hope altogether. Keep envisioning a more ideal circumstances, which could eventuate because of the appreciation of clients and customers or the support of a powerful person. Meanwhile, take clues from loved ones this. Thanksgiving holiday. Have fun at sports and games, and include your children. They will enjoy learning the playing skills from you, and your health could do with a vital workout.

25. FRIDAY. Troublesome. The pressure is on today, and you are probably in no mood to deal with it. Everywhere you turn, you are likely to find problems, delays, mistakes, and misinformation. Determination and a push on your part to make things happen will probably be fruitless. Even worse, it could turn people against you, making them more determined to stifle your initiatives. There is really no room to cut deals and no leverage to make demands. Accept the inevitable, leave things pending, and just go home. But be sure not to take out these frustrations on your partner, kids, and pets!

26. SATURDAY. Pleasant. Dividing time between weekend domestic chores and scattered social experiences could make you feel spread too thin. Neither activity is satisfying or complete, and matters may just end up being half done. A better alternative could be to explore the cultural landscape of your town or city, whether it is museums and art galleries, or parks and gardens. A public talk on a subject that attracts you could be vocationally inspiring. A wonderful vacation destination might grab you, but it could take a second job to pay for it. Everything you do today will be sweeter with a companion.

27. SUNDAY. Fair. Spend the early part of the day lazing around in relaxation mode. Small romantic touches for the edification of your lover would not go astray. Even routine activities can be soothing in the right frame of mind. It is likely that you have some formal event or social gathering to attend. Choosing something to wear could put you in a dither, and you may just not want to go. But if you are ultimately committed, double-check the time and venue, as plans might have changed or you could lose your way. For the sake of everyone else involved, be sure to grin and bear it.

28. MONDAY. Favorable. Meetings and interviews with influential characters can go in your favor. Being too feisty, pushy, or direct might put them off. Instead, be alert and receptive, allowing the person you are engaging with to take the lead and express themselves fully. Taurus in sales and service jobs will go a long way by remembering that the customer is always right. A checkup with your health practitioner could be timely or necessary. Your partner's strong emotional responses can be both a turn-on and overwhelming. Single Taurus people could be most attractive and sexually alluring.

29. TUESDAY. Deceptive. You may have to deal with some shady and unlikable people, and you probably have little choice in the matter. So keep your eye on the ball at all times, do not let them pull the wool over your eyes, and effectively transact whatever business it is that is relevant. If someone makes you suspicious, you are probably right about them. How much you get involved is up to you. But if you give them enough rope to hang themselves, they probably will. A certain decision could make you feel like you're damned if you do and damned if you don't. Wait until you are clearer.

30. WEDNESDAY. Eventful. A negotiation or deal that has been under way for weeks, or even months, could be nearing settlement and completion. Either that, or you will realize that it is doomed and walk away. Before signing off, meet with lawyers and relevant officials to assure yourself that everything is in place. Check with your accountant and bankers that all financial aspects are accurate and appropriate. Whatever you do, do not make this decision in response to rivalrous colleagues, or based on the opinions of outsiders. Have a heart-to-heart discussion with a lover about your true feelings.

December 2005

1. THURSDAY. Active. Today's New Moon, the first of two this month, highlights assets you share with others. A family matter is likely to come to a head and demand that the whole family get together for a powwow. It will work out much better in the long run if everyone is allowed a say in the decision making. But scheduling a time for you all to get together could be the hard part. Regardless, do not let this put you off. Home improvements may get the go-ahead when the bank approves your loan application. Avoid the direct debit option on your business account if possible. Making the repayments personally gives you the control over when and what you pay out.

2. FRIDAY. Sensitive. The power of love is a formidable force. But if it is abused and used to hurt in a lover's quarrel, it can be crippling. Do not let a jealous lover lay power trips on you if you know you have done nothing wrong. Let any cutting remarks run off you, like water off a duck's back. If you are arranging to have a surgical procedure done, you should find out which surgeon is the best in the relevant field and secure their services first. A relative or family friend could be a pillar of strength for you now, and renew your sense of belonging in your clan.

3. SATURDAY. Beneficial. A group or club to which you belong may be organizing a weekend away. Make sure you put your name down early, so that you do not miss out. It looks like it will be lots of fun, and singles might spark up a new and exciting relationship while away. In-laws could be a great help to you today. Call on them if you need the children minded, while you slip away and start organizing their holiday presents to avoid the last-minute rush. You might find a great atlas that will look good in your home, and teach the kids to locate various countries they hear about in the news.

4. SUNDAY. Buoyant. Your ideals and patriotism could get fired up if there is a political rally in your town. You will enjoy being part of the collective, waving the flag and chanting slogans. You could get carried away with the euphoria, and put your name down to help out or donate a sum of money. So just be careful that you do not overcommit yourself in the heat of the moment. If you feel like putting your thoughts on paper, you might have it published in a newspaper. Some of you may have had a lovers' quarrel, and now is a good time to make up.

5. MONDAY. Demanding. Conflict of interests could be the flavor of the day. A personal affair might demand that you take the day off work. But when you call in sick, the boss may not swallow your excuse. Do not allow your partner to push you to do something that you do not want to do. Pursue the most responsible course of action, and you cannot go wrong. A child's illness may be preying on your mind. Take the time to get them to a specialist and clear up the cause. An employer could be impressed with your work and offer you a promotion, which may mean longer hours away from home.

6. TUESDAY. Variable. Today could get off to a bad start if you have an argument with your lover before going to work. It will leave a bad taste in your mouth all day and put you in a temperamental mood. So choose your words wisely. Otherwise, you might allow your emotions to color your speech. Your popularity could be high, and you have a certain amount of influence over others now. So act responsibly, and you will maintain your ethics and feel pride in your position. An influential friend can help you obtain a promotion or a position in another company. You are determined to further your career.

7. WEDNESDAY. Exhilarating. Whatever you are planning to do today should be jam-packed full of excitement. Maybe you are arranging a vacation trip for two on an exotic island to surprise your partner. Or you could be off to a main event that will be the talk of the town. There are some pretty wild people out there on the streets, and you will want to be in the thick of it. So keep your eyes open, use your intuition, and rely on your own judgment of character. A new relationship could be about to bloom, with all the sensual and thrilling emotions that accompany falling in love.

8. THURSDAY. Disconcerting. Your employer could be making a loss and trying to pin the blame on your work. Stand up for yourself calmly. Point out what your job entails and all the good work that you do. Frank speech will put them back in their place without any untoward clashes. A partner's stories of their past may be part fantasy. But rather than trying to prove them wrong, extend your sympathy and look beneath the surface. It will give you a broader perspective on what makes them tick. Self-employed Taurus should check with your accountant to find out the correct tax payments so you can avoid a penalty.

9. FRIDAY. Quiet. A few close friends are all you need to have fun. Give the social circuit of the glitterati a miss, and instead have a small gathering at your place. You welcome a chance to show off your skills as a host, doubled with the opportunity for intimacy and sharing on a real level. The workload at this time of year is often very heavy, and you might prefer to catch up on your backlog at home alone. Whatever you arrange, peace and tranquility are your friends and will help to relax and rejuvenate your tired body. Have a soak in the tub to the strains of beautiful music.

10. SATURDAY. Invigorating. Philosophical topics are likely to spark your interest. A public talk could inspire you to start studying a special subject so that you can understand the bigger picture. If you are feeling stale and bored with your usual routine, escape into the great outdoors. Go hiking in a national park of exceptional beauty, or head for the coast to do some boating and fishing. The fresh air and natural sweetness of this great land will clear your mind and soul, as well as give you sanctuary from the stress of modern life. A friend may need your ear, so give them some time.

11. SUNDAY. Diverse. Being disillusioned with the world and your place in it can sometimes get you down. But instead of wallowing in self-pity, think of something you can do that will surprise and delight a friend or lover. You will be amazed at how different you will feel. A workshop may be held on making drums or masks or some other equally eccentric art form. Get on down and let loose! Besides having fun and meeting people, you might make something that you can use as a present and save yourself some money. Taurus singers and dancers, amateur or pro, will please attentive onlookers. Give it your all!

12. MONDAY. Mystical. Seeing the magic in everything transforms the mundane into the mystic. A visit from your parents can take away all your worries and doubts about being able to afford to have a good holiday. Their unconditional love for you will restore your faith in the power of love. A partner may have a function at work that they want you to accompany them to. If this conflicts with your schedule, bend the rules and make time. The fun you have together will more than compensate you. Romance is in the air for many of you Taurus singles. Dress up to the nines, and go out and be seen on the scene.

13. TUESDAY. Mixed. You could miss an important phone call or meeting if you get caught up in your own fantasies too much. A wise mentor may tell you a valuable secret or point you in the right direction to follow on your career path. A cultured foreigner might impress you so much that you will believe anything they tell you. Looks can be deceiving, so do not judge this book by its cover. Taurus students may receive some great news from their college or university. Exam results you have been dreading finally come through, to your surprise and delight. Now your eligibility for a special course is assured.

14. WEDNESDAY. Manageable. Good news may arrive if you are trying to set up a home-based business. This will give you the scope to follow your own ideas and work the hours that suit your lifestyle. A preferred course of study may be too expensive for you to pursue, and you now have to rethink your options for the future. Do not be disillusioned by this setback. Look into all your options and you may find a way around this problem, such as a scholarship or government subsidy. Buying the perfect gift for your partner can turn into a nightmare if you let it. Just relax and let it come to you.

15. THURSDAY. Misleading. A person in a position of power may try to intimidate you. Do not let this scare you into telling them too much, especially about your financial worth. Only give relevant information, and if it gets dicey pass the buck to your accountant. Your trust can be misplaced today. And your good intentions can be misconstrued, leaving you with egg on your face. To avoid this, make sure you express yourself clearly and ignore any urge to poke fun. A shopping spree could turn into a costly exercise, so leave your credit cards at home and only take the cash you can afford to spend.

16. FRIDAY. Surprising. Receiving a card from an old friend might get you cracking on your greeting card list. The sooner the cards are in the mail, the better, leaving you with one less task to do. A school celebration for you or your child could be full of surprises. Taurus parents and teachers may be honored with a prestigious award. A group meeting will give you a chance to have your say in its running. Get involved, instead of complaining about what others are doing. An acquaintance may delight you with an invitation to an evening of winning and dining. Put on your dancing shoes and have a ball.

17. SATURDAY. Exacting. Your thinking may not be quick enough to respond to snide remarks, so do not bother. Unless you can come up with an intelligent and humorous retort, it will do you no good to stoop to the other person's level. If you are attending a costume ball this evening, turn up in disguise as something out of the ordinary. You could feel used by some of your friends at the moment. If you do not want to do something, then do not. Be unafraid to go your own way. You are likely to have more fun than you have had in a while, and it will not cost you an arm and a leg.

18. SUNDAY. Spirited. The desire to be fashionable and appear cultured could lead you to overstep the mark. When shopping for home furnishings, browse around the flea markets and the stores that sell bric-a-brac and collectibles. You can find some fabulous items that could be revamped to suit your décor. You may decide it is time to decorate your house or apartment and hang on a tree your treasured decorations. All those personal touches are an expression of your individuality. A love affair may be moving to a deeply intimate level. Now you feel safe to express all your inner thoughts.

19. MONDAY. Hectic. Your hopes of getting all the million and one things on your list completed today could be wishful thinking. If you try to rush everything, nothing will be done to your satisfaction. Waiting on your parents to call back and confirm that they can baby-sit may have you on the edge of your seat. Do not panic, take one thing at a time, an everything will happen in its own good time. A property deal or contract could fall through due to an overblown evaluation. Do not let this worry you either, it is just par for the course.

20. TUESDAY. Transformative. If you have experienced a break-in and had some of your possessions burgled, then you may receive a payout from your insurance company, which will more than cover the cost of your loss. Some Taurus might be out looking for a new apartment that better suits your needs, and you should be lucky enough to find one that fits the bill and is moderately priced as well. If you are on a tight budget, you might think about recycling those old gifts that you have never opened. This is one way to cut down on holiday spending. Your partner may get a large bonus, which can be used to wipe out debts.

21. WEDNESDAY. Stimulating. A child may please and surprise you at the school concert. You might even find he or she has a natural artistic talent that can be developed. An office party could give you the chance to have some fun at work and together with a few cohorts carry out some sidesplitting practical jokes. Do not be surprised if you find yourself in the company of some real way-out folks who believe in some very odd philosophies or religious or rituals. It may make you nervous, but if you look at it as entertaining, you can have a good laugh.

22. THURSDAY. Pleasurable. The impending holiday break could have you cooking up all sorts of travel plans. You are sure to want to do something different with the few days off. See your local travel agent for some ideas. A new hobby may be opening doors into a world of influence and power. The types of people you are meeting through this interest could help you to change your life forever. You should be careful if you play contact sports, as there could be a chance of spraining a muscle in your leg. Try not to get too revved up over the game. If you throw caution to the wind trying to win, you may be sorry later.

23. FRIDAY. Smooth. Your normal routine should be the source of much comfort today. Stocking up on food and beverages, and thoroughly cleaning your living quarters, will put you in a happy mood. For Taurus at work, the conviviality is likely to weave its magic on your mood and make everything look good. The pressure of having everything finished up before the break often does wonders for the team spirit. If a theater production that was a box office hit when it first opened will be showing in your town, buy tickets for an evening of powerful entertainment.

24. SATURDAY. Cheerful. The anticipation that you will have everything perfect for entertaining guests could have you trying to run in different directions at the same time. Unforeseen obstacles may lie in your path. So to avoid too much confusion, make a list of must-dos and follow it meticulously. Some of you may have bought your child a pet, and now have the huge task of trying to hide it somewhere overnight. Ask a neighbor to do you a favor and mind it for you till tomorrow. Christmas Eve may see many Taurus hosting a gathering. Be careful not to overdo or overindulge.

25. SUNDAY. Merry Christmas! Taurus may want to honor some old world traditions as you observe Christmas and Hanukkah today. Young relatives will tune in and learn. You are not one to hide out in the kitchen at a party. But today you might find yourself doing a lot of the work cooking and serving. You will get a lot of pleasure out of being a gracious host. Some guests may not turn up, while others who were not on the guest list could arrive unannounced. Sit back and enjoy what may come. Harmonious vibes surround intimate relationships.

26. MONDAY. Relaxing. Do not worry about the housework, kick back and enjoy romance and partying with someone you love. You have done the hospitality thing. Now it is time to do your own thing. Family controversies that may have surfaced are best left forgotten for now. The gathering of the clan is never without its ups and downs. You would be wise to observe the interaction without becoming part of it. A whole new understanding of your roots could be a spark for your imagination. This may trigger a new way of expressing yourself artistically. Explore your creativity in writing, painting, music, or any medium that is natural for you.

27. TUESDAY. Upsetting. If a business agreement must be honored today, work will drag you away from your time off. You may need to leave your lover to attend to a family member who was too ill to visit you over the holidays. Such obligations upset all your leisure plans, but it is something you know intuitively that you must do. Your lover will understand, and may surprise you with plans for a romantic interlude at a prestigious restaurant. Some Taurus will be setting out on a journey later today, possibly a flight to the destination of your dreams.

28. WEDNESDAY. Opportune. You might get the chance to make extra money through teaching. Some of you are already studying to earn the credentials that are needed to obtain a teaching position. A subject that has been a hobby of yours for some time may suddenly become of popular interest, and you can write or speak about it. Membership fees for a social club may come due and shock you because they have risen so much. It could be a result of the exorbitant cost of insurance, now that litigation over large compensation payouts has blown out of all proportion. Call a general meeting to discuss other options.

29. THURSDAY. Chancy. A legal matter might be costing you more than you want to pay. If you decide to let go now, you will walk away with some money left in the bank. Then you might find out later that you chose the best option although it was painful at the time. If you enjoy some moderate gambling on the slot machines or at the racetrack, you might win a few extra dollars. But do not wager more than you can afford to lose. A brother or sister is likely to call on you for a serious discussion. They could be in a panic over a large debt, and you have no recourse but to help them out with a loan.

30. FRIDAY. Expansive. Your in-laws are likely to be full of wisdom. Talk over a desire to follow your dreams rather than be stuck in a rut. Your partner is sure to be very supportive. So stand back and look at what is your best option, then have a go. Some of you could be in the throes of packing for a vacation trip to a winter wonderland. Other Taurus might head to the tropical beaches for surfing and swimming. If you cannot afford such a break, start saving so you can go next year. Tonight's end-of-the-month New Moon puts the focus on travel and learning in the weeks to come.

31. SATURDAY. Low-key. With the excitement of New Year's Eve upon you, Taurus might spend the morning in quiet reflection of where you are heading. It is time to make another resolution for the year ahead. If you made one last year, it would be instructive to look at how well you held to it. Friends may be away or visiting relatives, and you feel at loose ends. Spend the day watching television, then plan your night's activities so you can be in all the right places. Or you might decide it is safer to stay at home with your lover and see in the new year cradled in each other's arms.

SONYA FITZPATRICK
THE PET PSYCHIC

She can talk to the animals.
Read their minds.
Diagnose their problems.
Heal their illnesses.
Find them when they're lost.
And offer comfort from
beyond the grave.
This is her story—and the remarkable
success stories of her "clients."

Includes Sonya's 7 simple steps to
communicating with pets
Plus—practical information on care and
feeding, emergency preparedness, illness, moving,
and introducing new pets into the household.

0-425-19414-0

Cell Phone Psychics

Horoscopes to Your Cell Phone

Send a text message with your date of birth and get your personalized daily horoscope via text message to your cell phone every day for only $1.99 for a week!

Just Text SUPER and your birthdate to 82020

If your birthdate is Feb. 15 1968
your message should look like this

SUPER02.15.68 and be sent to **82020**

Text YOUR Message to a LIVE PSYCHIC

Send a Text message to one of our LIVE Psychics from your cell phone any time, anywhere Just text the word ISEE to 82020 and get the answer to that important question!

Dating - Just Text DATE to 82020

to find that "Special Someone" right on your cell phone!

Chat - Just Text CHAT to 82020

Make new friends, have fun stay connected!

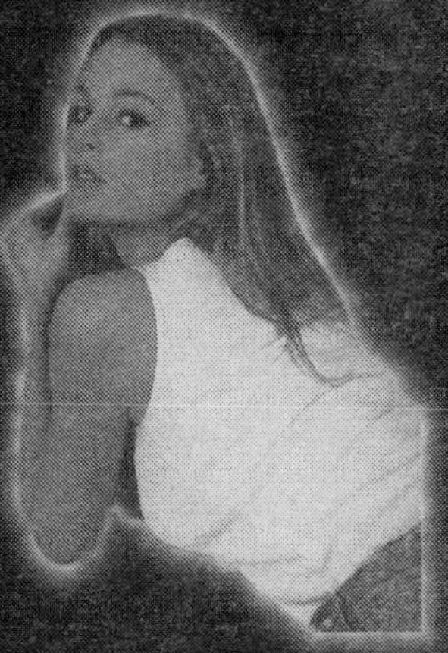

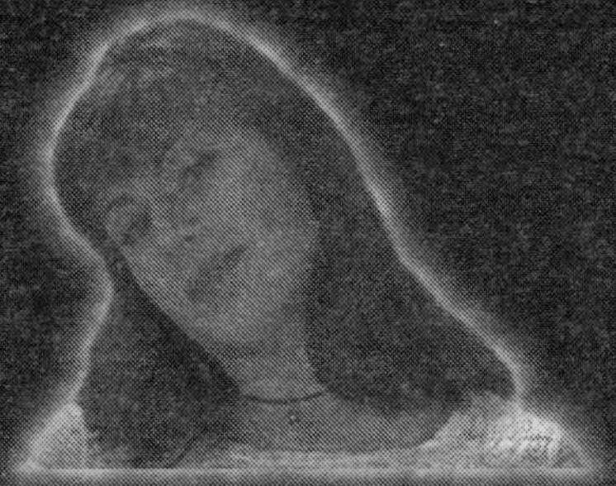

WHAT DOES YOUR
FUTURE HOLD?

DISCOVER IT IN *ASTROANALYSIS*—

**COMPLETELY REVISED THROUGH THE YEAR 2015,
THESE GUIDES INCLUDE COLOR-CODED CHARTS FOR
TOTAL ASTROLOGICAL EVALUATION,
PLANET TABLES AND CUSP CHARTS,
AND STREAMLINED INFORMATION.**